PARTNERS IN CONFLICT

ABRAHAM F. LOWENTHAL

PARTNERS IN CONFLICT
The United States and Latin America

The Johns Hopkins University Press • Baltimore and London

© 1987 The Johns Hopkins University Press
All rights reserved
Printed in the United States of America

Originally published, 1987
Second printing, 1987
Johns Hopkins Paperbacks edition and third printing hardcover, 1988 (updated)

The Johns Hopkins University Press, 701 West 40th Street, Baltimore, Maryland 21211
The Johns Hopkins Press Ltd., London

The paper used in this publication meets the minimum requirements of American National
Standard for Information Sciences—Permanence of Paper for Printed Library Materials,
ANSI Z39.48-1984.

Library of Congress Cataloging-in-Publication Data

Lowenthal, Abraham F.
  Partners in conflict

  Bibliography: p.
  Includes index.
    1. Latin America—Foreign relations—United States. 2. United States—Foreign
relations—Latin America. 3. United States—Foreign relations—1945–
I. Title.
F1418.L69   1987   327.7308   85-46291
ISBN 0-8018-3397-3
ISBN 0-8018-3398-1 (pbk.)

In memory of my father, Rabbi Eric I. Lowenthal,
who taught me, among many other things, that
"study is greater than action, for study leads to action."

Contents

Preface and Acknowledgments

Latin America is in the news. Almost every week, the region demands our attention: the war in Nicaragua; the economic crisis that has gripped all of Latin America during the 1980s; burgeoning immigration from Mexico and the Caribbean and increasingly from Central and even South America; the drug traffic from Bolivia, Colombia, Ecuador, Mexico, and Peru; and, on the brighter side, the strong turn toward democracy throughout the Americas.

Not since nearly thirty years ago, when Fidel Castro took power in Havana and continent-wide revolution seemed imminent, has Latin America excited such concern in the United States. But much of the attention being lavished on Latin America today is misplaced. Many of the policies the United States pursues in the Western Hemisphere are flawed. Latin American realities have shifted in the past generation much faster than U.S. concepts and perceptions. The images of Latin America that prevail in the United States are often both out of date and out of focus.

Latin America's economic, social, and political transformation during the past thirty years has not been adequately appreciated in the United States. We have not taken sufficient account of the implications for our country of the many positive changes that have occurred in Latin America: economic growth, industrialization, the turns toward democratic politics and pragmatic policy making. Nor have we considered seriously enough the deepening problems of the region: the enervating debt trap, sharpening social inequities, and, for many countries and people still, grinding poverty.

Instead, the United States has been preoccupied by Central America. For several years, Washington has been mainly concerned with what many U.S. leaders see as a Marxist-Leninist challenge in Central Amer-

ica. U.S. involvement in Central America's turmoil—especially in Nicaragua's bloody civil war—has expanded and intensified, provoking bitter debate.

This book argues against the self-defeating obsession with Central
America. It stresses that U.S. interests in Latin America and the Carib-
bean today are quite different from what they have been historically.
Traditional concepts and concerns have shaped the U.S. response to
Central America, but they are largely outmoded. Because the Hemi-
sphere has changed so much, the substantial interests of the United
States are now much more fully engaged in Mexico, in Brazil, and in the
islands of the Caribbean than in the isthmus of Central America. Central
America may be America, but it is not necessarily central.

This book proposes a new U.S. approach toward Latin America and
the Caribbean. It advocates moving away from a preoccupation with
U.S. national security, narrowly understood, and from policies that are
grounded in habitual attitudes of dominance. The United States should
instead aim to build cooperative relations, based on *confianza*—on self-
confidence and trust—with our neighbors in the Hemisphere.

Cooperation may not come easily in the next few years, to be sure.
Signs abound that our country, Latin America, and the world are troubled. Recession, repression, terrorism, crime, and hunger are all continuing dangers. Increased protectionism, struggles over immigration, territorial conflicts, destabilization efforts, even direct military
interventions—all are now occurring or seem likely. So are expropria-
tions, debt defaults and repudiations, and financial and commercial reprisals and counter-reprisals. The climate of inter-American relations
could well deteriorate in the coming period.

Yet my bias is positive. Like all optimists, I think the future is still in
doubt, and that we can affect it. Although increasing conflict is possible
in U.S.–Latin American relations, I believe the basis also exists for
enhanced cooperation in the Hemisphere, provided that new policies are
adopted.

To acknowledge all those who have helped me prepare this book would
be impossible. During the twenty-five years since I first began studying
inter-American relations, I have visited twenty-two countries of Latin
America and the Caribbean and have learned from hundreds of people in
those countries and in the United States.

I must single out several individuals for special mention, however.
Albert O. Hirschman stimulated my interest in Latin America through
his writings long before I met him, and my outlook toward the region
continues to be deeply influenced by his insights. Albert Fishlow encouraged me more than anyone to start this project and provided tren-

chant criticism of my first draft. Ambassador Sol M. Linowitz has given me exceptional opportunities to learn about Latin American policy issues, particularly in connection with the Inter-American Dialogue, a group of prominent citizens from throughout the Hemisphere who meet periodically to discuss regional problems. Peter Hakim, the Dialogue's staff director, commented skillfully on successive draft chapters. Jorge Dominguez, John Odell, and John Sheahan also kindly commented on the entire draft; William LeoGrande, Guillermo O'Donnell, Laurence Whitehead, and Peter Winn each commented on several chapters. Colleagues who commented on individual chapters are gratefully acknowledged in the notes on each chapter.

Sallie Mitchell Townsend and Karen Pokraka provided indispensable logistical support. Marjory Appel, David Ayon, Charles Becker, Katrina Burgess, Robertico Croes, Gaileen Fitch, Melissa Hyams, Linda Lowenthal, Dario Moreno, Phillip Pearson, Fred Samuel, Michael Shifter, Richard Stahler-Sholk, and Pamela Starr furnished valuable research assistance. Jackie Wehmueller was a meticulous editor; Nancy Hoepli and the staff at the Foreign Policy Association provided editorial help on chapter 5. Most important, Jane S. Jaquette has inspired and advised me, and helped me to finish.

Finally, this book has been made possible because of the help of a number of institutions. The Twentieth Century Fund supported part of the research on which this book is based. The Woodrow Wilson International Center for Scholars, where I worked from 1977 to 1983, provided an ideal place to learn about U.S.–Latin American relations. I also appreciate assistance from the Brookings Institution; the Rockefeller Foundation and its Villa Serbelloni; the University of California at Los Angeles and also at San Diego; St. Antony's College, Oxford; the Hebrew University of Jerusalem; CEBRAP in São Paulo, Brazil; El Colegio de Mexico; the Institute of the Americas; and the University of Southern California.

PARTNERS IN CONFLICT

CHAPTER ONE

LATIN AMERICA'S TRANSFORMATION

L atin America has changed fundamentally during the past generation. The countries of the region have had their ups and downs, and many of them face severe problems in the 1980s. Their experiences have varied greatly; they are not simply at different points on a continuum, for they have turned in different directions. Very few nations of Latin America and the Caribbean have been stagnant during the last thirty years, however; their accumulated movements amount to a basic transformation that alters the content of U.S.–Latin American relations.

LOOKING BACKWARD: LATIN AMERICA'S PROSPECTS IN THE
EARLY 1960S

A generation ago, Latin America was widely expected to undergo major change in the 1960s and 1970s, either through peaceful reform or through violence.

Knowledgeable observers in the United States generally viewed the Cuban Revolution as a challenge to the Hemisphere's stability, one that took the whole region to the brink of upheaval. As President John F. Kennedy put it, "Those who make peaceful revolution impossible will make violent revolution inevitable." It was up to Washington to help make Latin America and the Caribbean safe for profound reform. The response of the United States, announced by Kennedy in 1961, was the Alliance for Progress, a multi-billion-dollar U.S. aid program to help Latin America develop.

Those who sought reform, including the architects of the Alliance for Progress, stressed the importance of Latin America's middle class or

1

"middle sectors" (*class* was a term U.S. social scientists preferred to avoid) in spearheading reform. With the exception of Argentina, the few nations with substantial middle classes seemed the most democratic in their politics and the most successful economically. U.S. observers usually saw them, therefore, as the model for Latin America's future. Economic growth would lead to social change, an expanding middle class, and institutional development—all of which, it was thought, would lead to political democracy.

In contrast, both those who most admired Fidel Castro and those who most feared him believed that Cuba represented the wave of the future. The Andes, Castro predicted, would become the *Sierra Maestra* of South America, the equivalent of the hills where Castro's guerrilla forces hid in their successful struggle. In this view, it was not bourgeois liberal democracy but rather revolutionary socialism that would emerge from Latin America. While the United States government was sending foreign aid missions, Peace Corps volunteers, political development specialists, and counterinsurgency teams to Latin America in order to build middle-class capitalist reform, Castro and Ché Guevara were sending out guerrilla bands to "make revolutions"; they believed that rural unrest would favor the revolutionary cause.

A third view, advanced primarily by the small, Moscow-oriented orthodox Communist parties of Latin America, contended that objective conditions conducive to socialism were maturing in the more industrialized Latin American countries. Latin America's internal socioeconomic evolution would eventually improve the prospects for leftist gains through nonviolent means. Castro's enthusiasm for guerrilla war was regarded from this perspective as counterproductive and even "infantile."

All three versions of Latin America's future agreed that the region was entering a period of basic change. The late 1950s had been the "twilight of the tyrants." By 1960, old-fashioned despotism was coming to an end in many South American and Caribbean countries. Both advocates of reform and proponents of revolution believed that their time had finally come.

This consensus was based largely on prevailing views about the potential roles of key sectors in Latin American society. The traditional conservative triumvirate of Oligarchy, Church, and Army was understood to be weakening in most of the region, and thus was unlikely further to retard reform or revolution. The expected sources of dynamism were the middle class (the prospective interlocutors for those designing the Alliance for Progress, but also the heart of Castro's movement in Cuba), the peasants, trade union members, and the urban poor. Both the designers of the Alliance and the apostles of revolution believed that channeling support to leading elements of these sectors would help transform Latin America in the direction they desired.

Mainstream analysts singled out Chile, Uruguay, and Costa Rica as the best bets for democratic reform. These countries had entrenched constitutional systems, moderate politics, and pluralist ideologies. Democratic, reformist politics seemed much more fragile in Venezuela. A return to an old-style personalist dictatorship (which had occurred there in the 1950s) seemed entirely possible, and leftist insurgence was also growing. Proponents of democracy were similarly cautious about Colombia, then still feeling the effects of prolonged internal violence. They feared revolutionary outbreaks in the Caribbean, especially in the Dominican Republic, where praetorian politics prevailed after the fall of longtime dictator Rafael Trujillo, and in Haiti, where opposition to strongman "Papa Doc" Duvalier was intense. Brazil—with its militant peasant leagues and urban unrest—was thought to have considerable revolutionary potential, but also a history of unrealized promise. Peru was seen as one of the most volatile countries in Latin America. There the army, the "watchdog of the oligarchy," preserved the privileges of the entrenched elite, but violent peasant revolt remained a possibility.

Mexico, on the other hand, was then regarded as successfully evolutionary, solving its problems through a uniquely effective postrevolutionary party. Most Central American nations (except for democratic Costa Rica and for Guatemala, where chronic violence persisted) were portrayed as nearly impervious to change. The Commonwealth Caribbean territories, still British colonies at the time, were usually overlooked entirely. Cuba, because of its new revolutionary leadership, was viewed as the Latin American country most apt to be transformed radically. Argentina was the puzzler: instability seemed endemic in this country whose immense resources gave it the potential for democratic progress.

Those who pushed for violent change did not see Latin America very differently. They regarded Chile and Costa Rica as infertile ground. They mainly overlooked Central America, except for Guatemala, and did not think about the Commonwealth Caribbean. Prospects for revolution seemed best in Venezuela, Brazil, Peru, Bolivia, and in the Latin Caribbean; these were the countries targeted by Cuba in the early 1960s. Soviet analysts, in turn, concentrated on Chile, Brazil, and Argentina as nations open to evolutionary advances toward socialism.

As it turned out, neither democracy, nor revolution, nor evolutionary socialism flourished in Latin America during the 1960s and 1970s.

From the early 1960s through the mid-1970s, democratic institutions were snuffed out in country after country, until by 1975 Colombia and Venezuela were the only South American nations with competitive electoral politics. Democratic systems broke down in 1973 even in Chile and Uruguay, the two countries where they had long been most solidly entrenched. In many countries, civilian and military technocrats combined to install new, more harshly repressive, regimes that brooked little or no dissent and institutionalized themselves for long-term rule. These "bureaucratic authoritarian" dictatorships became the hallmark of Latin American politics during the 1970s.

Although the 1960s and 1970s did not bring democratic progress to Latin America, leftist revolution was no more successful. Cuban-supported guerrilla movements were decisively defeated in Venezuela, Bolivia, Peru, Colombia, and elsewhere. Salvador Allende, a Marxist, was elected president in Chile in 1970 and entered office peacefully, but he was toppled just three years later by a military coup that installed a brutal military regime under General Augusto Pinochet.

The main revolutionary triumph during these two decades occurred in Nicaragua, which in the early 1960s had seemed one of the most stagnant countries of the region. In 1979, a national upheaval against the Somoza dynasty brought to power a left-nationalist regime closer to the Cuban model than any other in twenty years. But both Cuba and the Soviet Union seemed surprised at this development.

Indeed, the past thirty years have been full of surprises. Chile and Uruguay, the most politically developed and democratic of Latin American nations in the 1960s, turned out in the 1970s to suffer the harshest authoritarian regimes. Parties were made illegal, elections were banned, constitutional guarantees were suspended, and torture was institutionalized. The Pinochet dictatorship in Chile, where constitutional government had been interrupted only rarely and briefly from 1830 to 1973, has lasted longer than any regime in that nation's history. Uruguay, ranked as Latin America's most democratic country in 1960, had more political prisoners per capita by the late 1970s than any other nation in the world.

Venezuela and Colombia, where democracy seemed so fragile in the early 1960s, have both survived the past twenty-five years without military coups. Scheduled elections have been held without disruptions, and power has been transferred peacefully several times from one party to another. Democratic political institutions have consequently been reinforced in each country, although not without some challenges, different in each case, from those outside the dominant centrist consensus. Both countries, too, have experienced massive social and economic changes, urbanization and industrialization foremost among them.

Brazil did not have a revolution after 1964, although the military takeover that year appropriated the term, but neither did it drift. Rather, Brazil experienced extended authoritarian rule coupled, for most of the period, with sustained economic dynamism. Annual rates of economic growth averaged over 6 percent per capita in Brazil between 1968 and 1980. Economic success in the 1960s and 1970s, in turn, was accompanied by some political advance. By the late 1960s, Brazil had more or less solved the problem of presidential succession by working out an institutional process, uncertain but stable, within the inner circle of the military hierarchy. Repression, torture, and censorship declined after 1974, as did left-wing insurgency.

The Brazilian model of economic development, however, suffered from serious inherent flaws. Brazil's extraordinary growth in the late 1960s and 1970s depended in part on temporarily favorable conditions—both internal and external—that could not be sustained indefinitely; by the 1980s, Brazil faced severe economic troubles.

Peru experienced some of the most profound changes in South America after 1969. These changes were brought about not by violent revolution, however, but under military auspices. The Peruvian armed forces launched innovative structural reforms affecting land tenure, industrial organization, property, and education. It was, as Castro put it pungently, "as if a fire had started at the fire house." The military regime mismanaged the country's economy and eventually turned away from some of its own reforms, until in 1980 Peru restored to office the very same civilian president whom the armed forces had ousted in 1968. But by then the locus and distribution of political power, the structure of the economy, and the role of the state had all been altered, along with national attitudes and expectations. The severe Hemisphere-wide economic depression of the past few years, particularly devastating in Peru, has limited but not reversed these shifts.

Mexico, generally considered successful in the early 1960s, was by the mid-1970s widely perceived as a country in trouble. Then the sudden discovery of massive oil and gas deposits calmed fears and for a time obscured the country's underlying socioeconomic and political problems. But by the early 1980s, Mexico, heavily in debt, was again in difficulty. For several years, Mexico had fueled rapid growth by borrowing against oil reserves. Then, in 1982, an unanticipated drop in oil prices—coupled with massive capital flight, higher interest rates on the external debt, and a drying up of foreign loans—forced it to suspend debt service payments. Painful austerity measures produced some recovery in 1984, but the recovery could not be sustained; with the drop in oil revenues in the mid-1980s, Mexico's debt worsened. Dark talk began about a severe crisis in Mexico, even of "another Iran" on the frontier of the United States.

The Latin Caribbean, believed in the early 1960s to be especially volatile and radical, seemed by the late 1970s to be relatively quiescent.

The Dominican Republic is the most dramatic case. In the early 1960s, it lived the "politics of chaos." Since then, however, the Dominican Republic has had six consecutive, regularly scheduled, contested presidential elections. At no previous time in the nation's history had even two such elections been held without a coup intervening. The Dominican Republic's record has not been matched in neighboring Haiti, but even there predictions of rampant instability proved false. "Papa Doc" Duvalier died in 1971, but his son, Jean Claude ("Baby Doc"), managed the transition without difficulty and clung to power for fifteen years. Only with the severe economic crisis of the 1980s did the Duvalier dynasty finally crumble.

The Commonwealth Caribbean has proved on the whole more volatile and open to radical change than the Latin Caribbean. In the mid-1970s, Jamaica, under Michael Manley, and Guyana, under Forbes Burnham, both announced plans to build socialism. Manley's efforts failed badly, leading to the election in 1980 of Edward Seaga, a figure from the center-right who promoted foreign investment, free enterprise, and close relations with the United States. By the late 1980s, however, Seaga, too, was floundering, and Manley's political star began to rise again. Guyana's experience was equally if not more unsuccessful. The leftist New Jewel Movement (NJM) in Grenada under Maurice Bishop overthrew the eccentric Eric Gairy in 1979, pulling off the first coup in the Commonwealth Caribbean and quickly unveiling a "revolutionary" program self-consciously modeled after Cuba's. Factional rivalries within the NJM led to a second coup in October 1983, the murder of Bishop, and then to U.S. military intervention and the staging of democratic elections.

Argentina, Latin America's most economically advanced country a quarter-century ago, is certainly no longer that. Beset by economic difficulties and political turmoil, torn by bitter violence between the insurrectionary Left and the military, unable to escape prolonged stagnation, Argentina seemed to reach its national nadir in 1982 when its invasion of the Malvinas-Falkland Islands led to military defeat at the hands of Great Britain. But Argentina has moved quickly since then toward restoring democratic rule. The election of Raúl Alfonsín in October 1983 brought to power a social democratic reformer deeply committed to civilian politics and trying to confront extremely difficult economic problems.

Central America, considered static in the 1960s and still thought safely stable by U.S. policy makers until the mid-1970s, erupted in violence in the late 1970s that was fueled and intensified by external interventions but rooted primarily within the region. Almost one hundred and fifty thousand people have been killed and at least a million and a half displaced by the civil strife that has shattered old power relationships.

In Nicaragua, the Sandinistas consolidated their control after the breakup of the broad-based coalition that overthrew the Somoza regime, but they have been challenged by U.S.-supported armed opposition. In El Salvador, the traditional hold of a few landowning families has given way to a bloody struggle among various military, civilian, and revolutionary factions. Guatemala has teetered frequently over the past twenty-five years on the brink of another such contest, during the preliminary rounds of which most centrist political leaders have been killed, exiled, or intimidated; the election in 1985 of Vinicio Cerezo, a democratic reformer, reduced but did not eliminate the likelihood of civil war. In Honduras, the civilian government elected in 1980 has seen its authority threatened by the military, whose power has been reinforced by the massive U.S. military build-up there. Costa Rica has struggled hard to maintain neutrality in the face of border operations by anti-Sandinista Nicaraguans, a severe financial crisis, and U.S. blandishments. Turbulent Central America, in short, bears little resemblance to the region it was a generation ago.

Cuba, meanwhile, has also changed considerably. Almost thirty years of socialist experimentation and education, reinforced by the reduction of dissidence through repression and periodic waves of emigration, have made Cuba unlike any other Latin American country. Its dominant values and its modes of social, economic, and political organization are unique in the region. Health care, education, and social services have been provided to Cuba's population on a more equitable basis than in any other country of the Hemisphere. Perhaps as striking, however, are some fundamental continuities with Cuba's past. Cuba retains a mono-cultural dependence on sugar, intense trade concentration, broad dependence on a single nation, and a long-term personal dictatorship.

Very few Latin American countries have evolved as expected during the past generation. Equally surprising, the sectors once thought likely to bring about major changes have rarely been significant or reliable allies, either for reform or for revolution. The impetus for transformation came instead, to a truly remarkable degree, from unexpected quarters.

Broad elements of Latin America's middle class turned out, in the 1960s and 1970s, to support moves to restrict participation, repress labor, and block changes that might threaten their own interests. Latin America's peasants, in most cases, were relatively passive; they did not back guerrilla movements or exert much pressure on reformist governments, especially after land reforms were enacted. Latin America's ur-

ban masses were equally far from revolutionary; they eagerly sought
housing and improved access to basic services but did not challenge the
prevailing system. Except in Nicaragua—where landless peasants,
marginalized city-dwellers, and middle-class groups radicalized under
intense repression—Latin American peasants and urban poor have not
been at the forefront of movements for social and economic change.

Pressure and leadership for fundamental reforms have emerged instead, in several countries, from within the Roman Catholic Church and,
in some cases, from the professional armed forces.

Twenty-five years ago, the Church was widely (although already
somewhat inaccurately) regarded as a bastion of the established order.
Since then, rifts in the Latin American Church have become evident. Its
leadership has become divided in several countries, while others have
experienced a deep split between the hierarchy and a grass-roots "popular Church." The Church has evolved differently from country to country, but it has generally leaned toward more equitable distribution of
power and wealth and an emphasis on protecting human rights. This
orientation was registered in the Conferences of Latin American Bish-
ops in Medellín in 1968 and Puebla in 1979, and has been confirmed
even under the relatively conservative reign of Pope John Paul II. In
several countries—particularly in Brazil, Chile, and in parts of Central
America—the Church has become a focus for resistance to authoritarian
rule and even an advocate of structural change. Protestant evangelical
sects have also gained a foothold, particularly in Central America and in
the Andean region, and have joined the drive for socioeconomic reform.

In a few countries, the armed forces have also favored progressive
change. Peru's experiment is the clearest case, for there a comprehensive program of economic and social transformation was launched under
military auspices. Similar tendencies emerged, at least for a time, in
Ecuador, Bolivia, Honduras, Panama, and in a faction of the Brazilian
military. A reformist military movement also surfaced in El Salvador in
1979, although it was quickly stifled.

In sum, Latin America did not evolve during the 1960s and 1970s
according to earlier predictions. Latin America on the whole chose
neither reform nor revolution. It found its own way: eclectic, experi-
mental, sometimes repressive, and certainly not always in the direction of progress.

LATIN AMERICA'S TRANSFORMATION

Although Latin America did not evolve as anticipated, it has changed
dramatically. The region has experienced major alterations of its population, economy, social conditions, politics, institutions, and international

relations. These shifts have not been uniform across the region, nor have they affected all sectors of any one country with equal force. Taken together, however, they have transformed the region. Latin America's future, as well as its relationship with the United States, will be fundamentally conditioned by what has happened since 1960.

Population

Perhaps the most striking changes in Latin America during the last generation are demographic. In 1960, Latin America's total population of less than 200 million was barely larger than that of the United States. Except for Argentina, Cuba, and Uruguay, Latin America was overwhelmingly rural; fewer than one-third of the region's people lived in cities of 20 thousand inhabitants or more.

By the late 1980s, however, Latin America's population of more than 400 million people is almost 65 percent larger than that of the United States; by the end of the century, Latin America's population will be nearly double this country's. Although the birth rate in most of Latin America has been decreasing steadily, the number of children already born insures a rapid increase in the economically active population for the next generation.

All over the continent, rapid urbanization continues apace. Whereas there were seven Latin American cities with a population of over 1 million in 1950 and still only ten cities that size in 1960, by 1980 Latin America had twenty-five cities with more than 1 million inhabitants, nine of them in Brazil alone. By the year 2000, there are expected to be about forty-eight such cities, ten with a population of over 5 million. More than half of all Latin Americans today live in cities of over 20 thousand inhabitants.

Dramatic improvements in public health have helped reshape Latin America. Infant mortality dropped rapidly in every country from 1960 to 1980. The average life expectancy at birth lengthened from fifty-one to sixty-four years between 1950 and 1980. More than two-thirds of all Latin Americans alive today have been born since Castro took power; more than 40 percent of Latin Americans are fifteen years old or younger. As a consequence, regional demands for education, jobs, and social services continue to grow.

Economy

A second major trend in Latin America, sometimes overlooked today because of the region's severe financial crisis, has been its economic expansion and restructuring. Latin America's economies grew steadily and often rapidly for a generation until 1981.

The scope and intensity of Latin America's economic growth have varied across the continent. The greatest surge has occurred in Brazil, but economic expansion has also taken place in other nations, particularly Mexico, Colombia, the Dominican Republic, Venezuela (thanks to the dramatic rise in the price of oil during the 1970s), and, until the late 1970s, most of the Central American countries.

From 1950 to 1960, the economies of Latin America and the United States grew at about the same annual rate. From 1960 to 1980, however, the rate of growth in Latin America overall was almost twice that of the United States; it was also consistently higher than that of most of the industrialized countries and than the average rate of growth for all developing nations.

Industry has been Latin America's most dynamic sector. A few figures speak volumes. From 1950 to 1978, Latin America's production of steel multiplied almost seventeen times. Its output of electric energy, metal, and machinery each multiplied ten times, and production continued to accelerate until the 1980s. Latin America's automobile production multiplied ten times; cement production increased eightfold. Although these statistics obviously reflect a low starting point, Latin America's industrialization during the 1960s and 1970s was rapid by any standard; the rate of growth is remarkably comparable to that the United States experienced from 1890 to 1914, during this country's industrial transformation.

Latin America's economic structure shifted as the region's largest countries turned increasingly from resource extraction to import substitution and the export of manufactured goods. The share of Latin American exports accounted for by manufactured goods increased from 3.6 percent in 1960 to more than 17 percent in 1979, while the combined share of agriculture and mining fell from 65 percent to less than 47 percent in the same period. The share of Brazil's exports accounted for by manufactured goods jumped remarkably, from about 2 percent in 1960 to more than 25 percent in 1977 and to more than 65 percent by the mid-1980s. During the 1970s, exports of manufactured goods in Brazil, Mexico, Argentina, and Colombia increased at an average annual rate of more than 30 percent. An estimated 55 percent of Latin America's economically active population toiled in agriculture in 1950; by the late 1980s, the estimated figure is less than 35 percent.

By and large, Latin America's economies adjusted better than the economies of most other countries to the first energy shocks of the 1970s, but this success was illusory. By relying on recycled "petrodollars" to pay for their oil imports and for their expanded productive capacity, most Latin American countries sustained high growth rates during the mid-1970s. They attracted additional loans during those years, in part because of their impressive economic performance. This strategy was risky, however, for it increased Latin America's vulnerability to a world recession.

Even before the severe international economic downturn that began in 1979, it was clear that Latin America, despite its growth, had serious economic problems. Huge segments of even the most dynamic countries—northeastern Brazil and southern Mexico—remained desperately poor, as did Bolivia, Haiti, Honduras, the highland regions of several Andean nations, and some of the Caribbean ministates. Two out of five Latin American households in the 1970s had incomes that placed them in the United Nations classification of "extreme poverty." The absolute number of extremely poor persons in the region continued to increase. Nutritional levels in many parts of Latin America remained inadequate. Income distribution worsened in many countries, including some of the fastest-growing ones.

All these underlying problems were heightened by the worldwide economic downturn of the early 1980s. Latin America's difficulties derive both from the wider international economic problems and from the responses individual Latin American countries made to these problems. During the mid-1970s, increases in oil prices drastically worsened the terms of trade for most Latin American nations, while sluggish growth in the industrialized countries simultaneously limited the market for Latin American exports. Many Latin American countries sought to sustain their own growth rates by borrowing abroad to finance needed imports, build infrastructure, and permit continuing consumption. Bank loans were preferred to direct foreign investment, partly on political grounds and partly because banks were so eager to lend. The banks recycled billions of petrodollars to finance Latin America's continued expansion.

Between 1970 and the early 1980s, accordingly, Latin America multiplied its external debt more than ten times, from $27 billion in 1970 to almost $370 billion by the end of 1984. Commercial bank loans and credits accounted for most of this increase, overtaking foreign aid, loans from international financial institutions, and direct foreign investment as the major external source of capital for Latin America.

The shift to commercial bank lending shortened the average maturity of Latin America's debt and made the region more dependent on changing market interest rates, thus further heightening Latin America's vulnerability to a worsening international economic environment. Latin American nations wagered, as did the lenders, on a prompt and sustained international recovery that would enable the borrowing countries to service their mounting debts, in part by expanding their exports to the recovered industrial nations. They also counted on continuing world inflation and declining real interest rates.

As the world recession deepened, these expectations proved to be misplaced. By the beginning of the 1980s, much of Latin America was facing a liquidity crisis. Nominal and real interest rates were rising, export markets stopped expanding, and debt service requirements became more burdensome. Latin America's weaker economies were quickly hurt by the "scissors effect" that resulted from higher interest rates and reduced foreign exchange earnings due to declining trade.

Commodity prices fell, while the prices of industrial exports and capital goods from the industrial countries continued to rise. The terms of trade index for the non-oil-exporting countries fell to its lowest level in more than fifty years. Export markets for Latin American goods stagnated and even contracted. The real interest rates on foreign loans began to rise, in part because of the U.S. government's inflation-fighting measures.

A few countries initially seemed immune to this decline: Brazil, because of strong and diverse exports; Colombia, because of coffee and drug booms and a low level of borrowing; Chile, because of high copper prices; Mexico, Ecuador, and Venezuela, because of major oil resources. By 1981, however, Brazil was in severe trouble, in large part because its trading partners in Latin America, Africa, and Eastern Europe had to cut back their imports. Chile's economy collapsed in 1982 as copper prices fell and interest rates rose. And by 1982, falling oil exports and prices, together with rising interest rates, had brought the crisis to Mexico with a vengeance.

The commercial banks responded to Latin America's crisis first by shortening maturities and eventually by curtailing lending. Latin American borrowers shopped frantically for any available credit, even on unsustainable terms. Argentina's mounting difficulties, similar to those of most Latin American nations, were compounded by the costly Malvinas affair. This desperate gambit shook international confidence not only in Argentina, but, by extension, in all of Latin America.

By mid-1982, the severity of the financial bind was recognized throughout Latin America. In August, Mexico announced that it could not meet its interest payments. The Mexican moratorium brought the problem dramatically to the attention not only of Wall Street but also of Washington, which urgently focused on immediate measures to relieve Mexico's plight.

Alarmed by Mexico's severe liquidity crisis and the worsening condition of most other Latin American economies, the commercial banks restricted loan commitments in Latin America. The "regional" banks—local banks throughout the United States which had been attracted for the first time into the foreign loan business by the unusually high rates of return—virtually ceased making loans. European and Japanese banks without much previous experience in Latin America also became skittish. The commercial banks' early exuberance and sudden reversal reinforced the underlying ups and downs of the economy, exacerbating the problem. Whereas Latin American countries had received about $55 billion in new private credits in 1981, the flow declined sharply to about $24 billion in 1982 and then to less than $1 billion in 1983. These sums, in fact, were significantly smaller than the remittances paid to foreign investors plus interest payments, so that Latin America was, in effect, financing other regions for the first time in fifty years. From 1982 through 1986, Latin America transferred more than $130 billion to the industrial countries, almost 5 percent of the region's gross product. The flight of private capital—particularly evident in Mexico, Venezuela, and Argentina—augmented this unsustainable outflow.

Emergency measures taken in 1982 and 1983 by the Latin American nations themselves, the United States, the International Monetary Fund (IMF), the International Bank for Reconstruction and Development (the World Bank), and the Inter-American Development Bank eased the financial pressure in most Latin American nations by 1984. Austerity programs, including drastic reductions in imports, were instituted in most countries of the region. A surge in Latin American exports to the United States, spurred by this country's recovery and by the strong dollar, alleviated balance-of-payments difficulties somewhat. Finally, debt reschedulings by the commercial banks relieved the immediate sense of crisis.

Latin America as a region, and most of the individual nations, achieved positive economic growth in 1984 for the first time since 1980. This recovery could not be sustained in 1985, however, except in Brazil; the rest of Latin America registered overall growth of less than 1 percent, or negative growth per capita for that year. Although 1986 and 1987 were somewhat better years for many countries in Latin America, overall growth for the region was only about 3 percent, barely positive per capita.

Latin America is still facing its most severe economic and social problems since the Great Depression. Indeed, the current crisis is in some ways worse than that faced fifty years ago. In the 1930s, many Latin American countries could turn to inward-oriented economic strategies that are not viable for most of them in the highly interdependent world economy of the 1980s. Latin America's debt service requirements create an enormous drain that was not present in the 1930s. Latin America's economies today are extremely vulnerable; they are hurt by low commodity prices, sluggish growth and protectionism in the industrial countries, and continuing high real rates of interest on Latin American debts. And the urban masses of Latin America have a much more difficult time reverting to a subsistence mode during a period of economic downturn than did their rural forebearers.

Latin America's economic difficulties, both structural and conjunctural, should by no means be underestimated; they are, in fact, a major concern of this book. But neither should these painful setbacks obscure Latin America's overall economic achievements of the past twenty-five years. On many indicators, Latin America's expansion during the 1960s and 1970s was indeed impressive. The real gross domestic product (GDP) of Latin America and the Caribbean grew more than 200 percent from 1960 to 1980. Even in per capita terms, the growth was almost 100 percent. Per capita GDP grew for every country in the Americas (except possibly Cuba) in the 1960s, and for every country but Jamaica, Haiti, and Peru in the 1970s. Nine Latin American nations, with a combined population of 280 million in 1980, experienced a growth in per capita GDP between 1960 and 1979 that exceeded the growth rate of the U.S. economy.

For all their troubles, Latin America's economies have come of age during the past generation. The issues Latin America poses for the United States, and the potential for conflict or cooperation in the Hemisphere, flow directly from this economic transformation.

Social Conditions

Demographic shifts, economic growth, and deliberate national policies have combined during the past thirty years to reshape Latin American societies.

Education, a key agent and indicator of change, has been vastly expanded. Levels of educational expenditure have risen sharply, with dramatic results. From 1950 to 1985, enrollment in Latin America's primary and secondary schools multiplied almost seven times; the share of the relevant age group enrolled in school rose from 28 percent to 76 percent in the same years. At the university and postgraduate levels, the growth of Latin America's educational infrastructure has been perhaps even more noteworthy. Major cadres of professionals in fields ranging from agriculture, economics, and astrophysics to sociology and veterinary medicine have been trained. Latin America's capacity to generate and diffuse knowledge has grown almost exponentially.

Communications, too, have exploded. Radios, televisions, telephones, and telexes have proliferated at an enormous rate, changing the nature of national and international linkages. For example, an estimated 91 percent of households in Lima, Peru, had television sets in 1982, and some 71 percent had them even in Peru's main provincial cities; these figures reflect a tenfold increase within a decade.

Other aspects of modern urban life also spread quickly through Latin America. The number of Latin American homes with access to potable water and to sewage facilities shot up. Thousands of miles of roads were paved, binding together heretofore isolated regions. The rates of adult literacy rose significantly, from an estimated 58 percent to more than 70 percent across the whole continent. The percentage of Latin Americans participating in the cash economy has risen steadily, as well.

Another important social change in Latin America is the new role of women. Only a generation ago, Latin American women were mainly absent from higher education, from professional achievement, and, in some cases, even from suffrage. In recent years, however, the movement toward full participation has rapidly accelerated, at least in the urban middle class. Within the past generation, although not equally rapidly in all countries, Latin American women have entered the paid work force, the university, and the polity. In Colombia, for example, where women were denied the right to vote until 1957, an estimated 30 percent of the paid labor force and almost 50 percent of the country's university students now are women.

All these changes have helped to promote the fuller integration of Latin American societies. To be sure, national integration has been incomplete and uneven. The highland regions of Peru, Bolivia, and Guatemala remain conspicuously isolated, as do Paraguay and parts of the Caribbean. More generally, the pattern of economic growth prevailing in Latin America has accelerated income concentration and left large groups impoverished. The fairly stable portion of the region's population which comprises an "informal sector" outside the tax system has received a declining relative share of income.

Yet, in one Latin American country after another, a number of previously marginal groups have been drawn into the mainstream of national life during the past thirty years. Modern nations are emerging, even in several countries where that possibility seemed remote just a generation ago.

Politics

Demographic explosion, economic expansion, and social change have in turn contributed to the diffusion of political power.

Power in Latin America was probably never lodged as neatly and exclusively in the triumvirate of Oligarchy, Church, and Armed Forces as the conventional wisdom supposed a generation ago, but the concentration of power has in any case diminished sharply since then.

Each of the old sources of authority—traditional families, large land-holders, military caudillos, and foreign (especially U.S.) corporations and diplomats—has lost influence.

Power has spread to many new groups. Industrial and commercial associations have institutionalized and consolidated their influence. Technocrats and bureaucrats have become major actors in many countries. Labor unions have grown and become more militant. Peasant cooperatives and urban community associations have become important. Local religious groups, so-called "base communities," have achieved considerable strength in many countries, as have evangelical Protestant movements in some. The armed forces in several nations have become more professional, more institutional, and more broadly and consistently influential.

Political participation has expanded throughout Latin America, except in cases of outright suppression, and even in those cases, repression highlights the intensified demands for participation. The reality in most countries sharply contradicts the image of Latin American political participation as being limited to small sectors. The voting population has risen steadily throughout most of Latin America, and the numbers of people active in parties and other mobilizing institutions have grown. Political participation has even increased in authoritarian Cuba, through "Poder Popular" and local organizations; within Mexico's system of one-party dominance; and amidst Central America's turmoil, through mass organizations, insurgent movements, and elections.

Latin American politics have become much more socially and institutionally complex. The region has been emerging slowly, by fits and starts, from authoritarian repression. Central America's turbulence, occurring in societies that are still dynastic and oligarchical, may yet produce new authoritarian regimes; elections there from which large sectors feel themselves excluded cannot produce instant democracy. But throughout much of South America, democratic political processes are becoming attractive once again.

In Argentina, the new civilian government has restored a sense of the possibility and promise of electoral politics. In Brazil, national elections for state governors and for the National Congress in November 1982 stimulated a massive voter turnout and revealed strong support for the main opposition parties, especially in the most modern and populous states. In 1984, Brazilians staged massive demonstrations in favor of direct presidential elections, and in 1986 the new civilian regime indicated that Brazil would soon hold such elections, for the first time since 1962.

In Peru, where the armed forces had ruled since 1968, former President Fernando Belaúnde Terry regained office in 1980 in an election in which all the main candidates had opposed the military regime. Despite subsequent difficulties—severe economic setbacks and the onset of a major terrorist movement—Peru held its presidential elections in 1985 without disruption. Ecuador's course has paralleled that of Peru. Bolivia's, though much rockier, has been similar. In Uruguay's 1982 party elections, more than 80 percent of the voters favored candidates who opposed the military regime, and in November 1984 the country elected a civilian president for the first time in thirteen years.

Chile is still suffering the Pinochet dictatorship, but a broadening civic coalition—including the Church hierarchy, trade unions, most political parties, and many entrepreneurs, technocrats, and professionals—are insistently demanding a return to democracy. Throughout the Hemisphere, and particularly in South America, the tide of democratic renewal is gaining strength.

Institutions and the State

Latin America has seen many kinds of institutional development during the past generation, but the most striking has been the almost universal growth of the state. Contemporary Latin American governments of all political tendencies tax, regulate, and invest much more than they did thirty years ago.

Peru, for example, had a state so weak in the 1950s that private banks collected taxes and charged the government interest on the use of its own revenues. National planning was anathema, and the state was no match for major foreign corporations. By the end of the 1970s, however, Peru's state apparatus had become large (if not always efficient), economic planning had become an established part of the government's function, and foreign corporations were accustomed to state regulation. In Brazil, government expenditures account for more than 40 percent of the national product; nine of the country's top ten firms are state-owned enterprises, and state regulation of foreign investment is pervasive. In Venezuela, the state has nationalized the petroleum and iron industries, the country's two largest revenue producers. In Mexico, federal government expenditures rose from less than 8 percent of gross domestic product in 1960 to more than 20 percent in 1980, almost at the level of expenditures in the United States.

Cuba's outright socialist regime, where only minor residual sectors of the economy have been left to private initiative, represents the extreme, but the state has vastly expanded throughout Latin America. In Chile, where state intervention peaked under the Allende regime before being drastically reduced by Pinochet, the state has in recent years retaken control of many bankrupt industries and financial institutions; the ultimate legacy of the past twenty-five years is a strong government bureaucracy staffed by modern technocrats. In almost every Latin American country, public sector employment has climbed steadily during the past twenty-five years. The power of public employees—technocrats, bureaucrats, and workers—has grown accordingly.

The expansion and strengthening of the Latin American state, sought by Latin American reformers in the 1950s and 1960s, has been far from an unmixed blessing. Bloated bureaucracies and inefficient public enterprises are a serious problem in many countries. The need to strengthen the institutions of civil society and to decentralize various kinds of decision making is recognized throughout the Hemisphere. But Latin America today is powerfully shaped by the existence of modern state structures, absent just a generation ago.

International Relations

Latin America's larger nations, and many of its smaller ones, have in the last generation become much more involved in international affairs, both within and beyond the region. Latin American nations are active in world trade and financial markets and in various international political forums. The nature of the region's role in the international system has been changing.

Economically, Latin America has become more externally oriented. The inward-oriented development strategies of the postwar period required imports of intermediate and capital goods for industrialization, imports that were financed by extensive borrowing. The confluence of favorable commodity prices and cheap loans in the 1970s boosted the region's participation not only in financial markets but also in world commerce. Trade as a percentage of GDP rose impressively throughout most of Latin America. Some of this increased trade was intraregional, taking advantage of various economic integration arrangements which effectively expanded markets. A good deal of it was also with other Third World countries, as "South-South" links began to develop.

Politically, too, Latin American and Caribbean nations have in the last generation become much more active and influential in a number of international organizations: the United Nations, the UN Conference on Trade and Development (UNCTAD), the "Group of 77" organization of developing countries, and the Non-Aligned Movement. They figure prominently in negotiations on issues ranging from the Law of the Sea to various commodity agreements. No longer do major diplomatic initiatives from Latin America tend to pass through Washington.

What holds true of the region as a whole is even more striking for particular countries.

Brazil, possessing the world's tenth-largest economy (likely to become the sixth-largest by 1995), is the developing world's largest borrower (owing over $110 billion) and its second-largest exporter of manufactured goods. Brazil has diversified its political and commercial relationships to include substantial intercourse with Iran, Iraq, Libya, China, the Soviet Union, several African nations, and many countries in eastern Europe. And although it does not usually seek visible leadership, Brazil plays an influential role in international forums on a wide variety of issues.

Mexico also significantly expanded its international role during the past generation. Indeed, Mexico's current plight in part results from and reflects that country's heightened international activity. Mexico in the 1970s aggressively entered world finance, developed new markets for its export products, and involved itself actively in various diplomatic efforts. Mexico has cut back its international presence somewhat since the debt crisis began, especially under President Miguel de la Madrid; but, even so, Mexico is much more active in the world arena than it used to be. It has taken the leading role, for instance, in the Contadora Group (which also includes Colombia, Panama, and Venezuela), a forum organized to seek a peaceful settlement in Central America.

Other Latin American nations, too, are more prominent in the world arena than they have ever been before. Colombia, once called the "Tibet of Latin America" because of its self-imposed isolation, pursued a vigorous foreign policy in the early 1980s. Peru was very active internationally under its military rulers of the late 1960s and early 1970s, and it now aspires again to an increased international presence. The extent of Cuba's international activity, undertaken in close alliance with the Soviet Union, is unprecedented for a Latin American country of its size.

PROSPECTS FOR DEMOCRATIC REFORM

These trends—economic expansion and restructuring, social change, national integration and diffusion of power, the strengthening of institutions and the state, the broadening and reorientation of international involvements—are fragile. They are subject to slowdown and setbacks, especially in times of severe international economic difficulties. And they have taken place at an unequal pace among the various countries of the Western Hemisphere. Latin America's nations have less in common than they did a generation ago. Brazil's dynamic growth has outpaced that of any other nation, for instance; its share of the region's total production grew from about 27.5 percent in 1960 to about 36 percent by 1985. The degree of economic and political diversification among the countries of Latin America has varied considerably; the Caribbean nations and Mexico, for example, are becoming more economically integrated with the United States, while the countries of South America have become less so.

But the overall pattern in the Hemisphere is clear. Latin American nations are much more populous, urban, literate, industrialized, mobilized, and organized now than in 1960. They are more integrated, prosperous (even in a period of worldwide economic downturn), and complex than they were a generation ago. Their states are more autonomous and powerful. These countries are considerably more involved internationally, in both economic and political terms. Latin American countries have emerged forcefully into the world arena. The economic and social difficulties now facing Latin America are real and painful, but they cannot negate a generation of regional transformation.

These shared elements of today's Latin America will decisively affect the region's future. So, too, will the wide variety of approaches to political and economic development Latin America has experienced during the past twenty-five years.

In the early 1960s, when the "modernization" paradigm and theories about the "stages of economic growth" still had great influence, many scholars and practitioners assumed that economic growth, social equity, expanded popular participation, and political stability all went hand in hand. Countries were assumed to be moving together, at different times and paces, through a series of phases. Economic development brought with it a series of other positive trends: the erosion of oligarchical social and political structures, the expansion of the middle class and its influence, an increase in political involvement, and the strengthening of institutions.

Argentina, with its perpetually stormy politics, was then the one exception. It was a relatively prosperous country, and had been for decades, but it could not seem to keep its political act together. It was a largely middle-class nation, yet it was torn by class strife. Political participation in Argentina always seemed to threaten institutions rather than to strengthen them.

In 1973, Guillermo O'Donnell, an Argentine social scientist, suggested that his country's experience might not be exceptional, but, rather, an advanced case of a new paradigm. Drawing mainly on the cases of Argentina and Brazil, O'Donnell argued that relatively high levels of modernization and the limits of import-substitution industrialization together place severe strains on democratic institutions. These pressures facilitate authoritarian rule by technocrats, allied with the military, as a way of protecting middle-class privileges against rising popular demands.

O'Donnell's analysis of intensified social conflict, stalemate, and an eventual move to institutional "bureaucratic authoritarian" rule aptly described not only developments in Argentina and Brazil but also subsequent events in Chile and Uruguay. His thesis helps explain the cruel paradox that those countries with the highest level of social mobilization were precisely the ones that became the most brutally repressive during the 1970s. In fact, the most salient approach to political and social organization in Latin America during those years was neither constitutional democracy nor leftist revolution, but authoritarian rule by military and civilian technocrats of the Right.

Most of these authoritarian regimes were characterized not only by exclusionary political demobilization but also by a monetarist approach to economic policy. To varying degrees, they enshrined market capitalism in its relatively pristine version, revising the public policies of previous decades in order to integrate national economies more fully into the international capitalist system. Import and exchange controls were dropped or made substantially less restrictive, prices were decontrolled, and unemployment was allowed to rise to help bring inflation levels down.

Neither the political nor the economic approach of "bureaucratic authoritarianism" succeeded, however. Not even in Brazil, by far the least doctrinaire and the most dynamic of these countries, did the authoritarian approach wear well; its appeal eroded steadily for a decade, fueling the pressures for *abertura*. The coalition of social and political forces which helped bring authoritarian governments to power in Argentina, Chile, and Uruguay also disintegrated in each case, albeit in different ways and to different degrees. The military has already left office in Argentina, Brazil, and Uruguay. Chile's Pinochet regime has scant support outside the military.

Despite initially positive indications, it has also become clear that the monetarist "free-market" approach has failed, perhaps in direct proportion to the purity and inflexibility with which it was administered. Nowhere was its failure more dramatic than in Chile. National production fell 14 percent in 1982, urban unemployment rose to more than 20 percent, and workers receiving only a twenty-dollar monthly minimum wage accounted for another 13 percent of the population. The situation in 1983 was even worse, and recovery in Chile since then has been slow and incomplete. Chile's foreign debt has swelled from $5.5 billion in 1979 to about $20 billion in the mid-1980s, almost 300 percent of export earnings.

In sum, enthusiastic talk of the Brazilian and Chilean "miracles"—unjustified early tributes to the apparent early economic success of the authoritarian regimes—has long since ended. The bureaucratic authoritarian path turned out to be a dead end.

A second approach to development has been the military populism epitomized by Peru's experiment, tried briefly also in Bolivia, and proposed by military officers and civilian ideologues in several other countries. These regimes paralleled the "bureaucratic authoritarian" ones in their reliance on military leadership and technocratic expertise and in their deep distrust of political parties. They differed, however, because they tended to empower previously disenfranchised or less powerful groups. They were more open to socialist or quasi-socialist forms of organization, less repressive in their means of social control, and less closely tied to the United States and to multinational corporations.

None of these military populist regimes survived into the 1980s. On the whole, they left behind them disappointment, political rejection, and economic disaster. The military governments were unable either to mobilize popular support for their programs or to manage the economy successfully, and none gained lasting legitimacy. For the foreseeable future, the reformist military path in Latin America has been discredited.

A third generally unsuccessful approach in Latin America has been the socialist path. This course has been followed since 1960 in Cuba, in Chile under Allende from 1970 to 1973, since 1979 (with interesting variations) in Nicaragua, and in Grenada from 1979 to 1983. St. Lucia also flirted briefly with socialism, and Jamaica, Guyana, and Suriname experimented with it to a very limited extent.

The Allende period in Chile, cut short by the Pinochet coup, underlined the difficulties of implementing a socialist approach in precisely the highly mobilized and relatively modern settings that Soviet strategists previously had thought most conducive to socialism. Polarization, internal sabotage, and international pressures combined to reveal the narrow constraints within which an elected socialist regime must work in Latin America.

In Cuba, a highly personal autocracy has gradually been institutionalized as the roles of the party and the government bureaucracy have expanded. Means have been developed over the years to allow for some public involvement in decision making, at least on local issues. Economic organization slowly evolved in the 1970s to provide for private incentives and rewards, largely as a response to admitted failures in various sectors, but these experiments are apparently being abandoned in the late 1980s, as they, too, have proved disappointing.

Heavily subsidized for a quarter-century by the Soviet Union, Cuba has been a poor showcase for socialism. The Mariel incident of 1980 (in which more than 125 thousand Cubans emigrated within a few weeks) revealed the high level of dissatisfaction that persists there after a generation. Although Cuba still has some influence in Central America and the Caribbean, it is not as appealing a model in any country of South

America as it was in 1960. A few student activists and other would-be revolutionaries still advocate following the Cuban path, and Fidel Castro's personal stature remains high in some quarters (in part, perhaps, because of the David and Goliath relationship between Cuba and the United States), but the Cuban approach is widely regarded as unpromising.

The Sandinistas in Nicaragua and, until 1983, the New Jewel Movement in Grenada have made efforts—apparently heeding Cuba's advice—to keep political leadership collective and allow scope for private sector economic activity, if not for much autonomous political expression. Neither country has prospered, however, in any case. Jamaica experienced seven successive years of negative growth and gathering social unrest under Manley, though the subsequent experience of the Seaga regime has made it clear that there is no easy path to growth in Jamaica. Guyana and Suriname, too, have had negative experiences with socialism. St. Lucia abandoned its socialist program almost before it began. In short, socialism has been consistently unsuccessful in Latin America. Persistent and sometimes intense U.S. opposition may be one of the reasons for this record, but it is not the only or the main one.

Mexico's system of one-party dominance is the fourth approach tried in Latin America during the past twenty-five years. A generation of import substitution, followed by the discovery and rapid development of major petroleum and natural gas deposits, enabled Mexico to grow, with some setbacks, until 1982. Then a number of simultaneous reverses forced the country into a severe liquidity crisis. But even before Mexico's financial difficulties emerged, the country was facing serious problems: widening income disparities, incipient inflation, and political violence. Mexico was able partially to address these problems during the 1970s with a series of political reforms which broadened the scope for opposition, and the bonanza of oil wealth temporarily obscured the nation's economic difficulties. In the 1980s, however, Mexico has been facing severe economic problems, and opposition to the dominant party is growing. The Mexican path has proved far from satisfactory.

The most successful Latin American experience during the past quarter-century has been with reformist democracy, which was practiced throughout the entire period in Colombia, Venezuela, and Costa Rica, and since 1966 in the Dominican Republic. All these nations have placed some limits on the democratic contest for power, whether through a strong two-party system or by reaching agreement, explicit or tacit, on the rules of politics. These four countries have gone at least a generation in each case without a coup, and they have maintained generally favorable records on human rights in recent years. The Venezuelan and Colombian economies have been stimulated, and to some extent distorted, by massive injections of capital—from petrodollars in Venezuela and the profits of the massive drug trade and periodic coffee booms in Colombia. All four countries have felt increased strains: economic and financial problems, some political violence, and incipient military restlessness in Venezuela and Colombia; side effects of the Central American turmoil and the impact of recession in Costa Rica; and the social effects of prolonged and painful austerity in the Dominican Republic. In all these nations, the centrist consensus underlying institutional stability is still fragile. But by continental standards, all have done well in managing internal tensions and sustaining some economic advance.

The past generation's experience in Latin America has renewed the appeal of formal democracy, mixed economies, and evolutionary reform, and it has at the same time discredited alternative pathways to progress. On the whole, those nations that have maintained reformist democracy and mixed economies have fared best. The countries that turned to authoritarian political solutions have ultimately found these wanting and have moved back toward participatory politics. The regimes that have been most ideological in their economic policy have also met with failure. A new pragmatism has been gaining strength in Latin America.

In several countries, the painful years of authoritarian rule convinced groups across the political spectrum of the need to moderate their demands and expectations in the interests of restoring and strengthening viable civilian politics. Elites, in turn, have recognized that long-term stability depends on the enhanced legitimacy and reduced polarization provided by popular participation. A good deal of political learning has taken place in Latin America during the past generation.

Social mobilization, national integration, and political experience, taken together, have improved the prospects for democracy in Latin America. And they have made it more likely that democratic politics in Latin America will last, especially in the complex, modern, and industrial countries of South America. The social and political bases for democratic politics that were lacking in South America in the 1960s have since then been laid.

The strength of South America's new democracies should not be overstated. All these countries face fierce pressures in these difficult years of economic trauma. But what has happened during the past thirty years makes democratic reform a real possibility in much of Latin America. This central goal of the Alliance for Progress is now within much closer reach than it was in the 1960s. Whether effective inter-American cooperation will now occur depends on policies adopted in Washington and in Latin American capitals, but the foundations for it now exist throughout the Hemisphere.

CHAPTER TWO

The United States and Latin America Since 1960

Latin America has evolved remarkably during the last quarter-century, economically, socially, and politically. Latin America's transformation, together with developments in the United States and on the broader international scene, has fundamentally reshaped inter-American relations. The severe economic difficulties troubling the Western Hemisphere since 1981 have slowed these shifts, and even temporarily obscured some of them, but the underlying tendency has not been reversed.

During the 1960s and the 1970s, Latin American nations increased their strength and diversified their international links. The United States, meanwhile, faced growing economic and political competition that weakened its world position. The economic presence of the United States in Latin America, although still extensive, became increasingly subject to competition and challenge. Asymmetry between the United States and Latin America has persisted, and it has been reinforced since the onset of Latin America's current economic and financial crisis, but it was substantially reduced during the 1960s and the 1970s.

By 1980, the United States exerted less dominance in the Western Hemisphere than at any time since World War II. Neither Latin America's economic woes nor the intense efforts of the Reagan administration to reassert a strong U.S. role has restored U.S. hegemony in the 1980s. This chapter analyzes how and why inter-American relations have changed during the preceding generation.

THE UNITED STATES AND LATIN AMERICA IN THE 1950S AND 1960S

In 1950, the international stature of the United States was at its height, while much of the rest of the world was in shambles. In the aftermath of World War II, before the recoveries of Europe and Japan, the United States was virtually unchallenged in the world; only the Soviet Union, China, and the occupied countries of Eastern Europe were beyond its sway. The United States accounted then for one-third of the world's production, one-third of global defense expenditures, and approximately one-third of international trade. At that time, the United States still had a nuclear monopoly. Washington retained the diplomatic and political initiative. Global trade and monetary regimes had been established and institutionalized under U.S. leadership. The dollar had replaced gold as the major form of international reserves. Numerous military alliances radiated outward from Washington.

By the end of the 1950s, the immediate consequences of World War II had begun to recede, and with them some of the more extraordinary aspects of U.S. predominance. Yet the United States was still by far the world's strongest nation. It faced some unexpected challenges—for example, the Soviet Union's 1957 launch of Sputnik, the world's first space satellite—but it responded to these with confidence, usually by channeling additional resources to meet the test.

The predominance of the United States in the late 1950s was especially evident in the Western Hemisphere, where U.S. influence had climbed to unprecedented levels. Overwhelming U.S. influence in the immediate border region of the United States (Mexico, Central America, and the insular Caribbean) was extended in the postwar years to virtually the entire Hemisphere.

Economically, almost all of Latin America moved into the U.S. orbit. The share of Latin American exports destined for the United States reached a high of 45 percent in 1958 after a steady rise from about 12 percent in 1910. The share of Latin American imports coming from the United States reached 50 percent in 1950, and remained at about 40 percent in 1960. The share of U.S. imports coming from Latin America reached 37 percent in 1950, a 50 percent increase over the pre–World War II level.

U.S. investment in Latin America quintupled in the twenty years after World War II. U.S. investors sought out opportunities in manufacturing and services to complement earlier involvements in natural resource extraction and public utilities. In country after country, U.S. investors crowded out European competitors. In many cases, U.S. firms came to control the "commanding heights" of national economies.

U.S. political influence also expanded enormously in the years immediately following World War II. An "Inter-American System" was created, institutionalizing U.S. dominance. The Rio treaty of 1947 (the Inter-American Treaty of Reciprocal Assistance) formalized close political and security cooperation between the United States and the other countries of the Americas. The Organization of American States (OAS), established in 1948, was headquartered in Washington primarily to facilitate regional political leadership by the United States. A host of other mechanisms—schools and other training programs, defense councils, joint exercises, and the like—were designed to ensure continuing U.S. influence on security matters. Programs to sell or grant arms to Latin America spread until, by the end of the 1950s, almost all weapons in Latin America had been manufactured in this country. Through various programs of economic and technical assistance, the United States influenced Latin America's educational, agricultural, and industrial development, as well.

The countries of Latin America and the Caribbean followed the U.S. lead in their relations with the rest of the world. With their own motives reinforced by U.S. pressures, Latin American governments almost uniformly supported Washington's foreign policy initiatives. The United States obtained widespread Latin American support in the establishment and organization of the United Nations, in opposing Soviet expansionism, in backing Israel's creation, in "uniting for peace" to thwart North Korea's invasion of South Korea in 1950, and in opposing international recognition of the People's Republic of China.

U.S. preoccupation with the Cold War during the 1950s and 1960s was adopted as their own by most of the governments of Latin America and the Caribbean. An OAS resolution adopted at Caracas in April 1954 barred international communism from the Hemisphere, for instance. This resolution provided a semblance of legitimacy for the invasion, covertly organized by Washington, which overthrew the left-leaning government of Guatemala's Jacobo Arbenz two months later. During this period, under U.S. pressure, several Latin American countries broke diplomatic relations with the Soviet Union, which had but three ambassadors in the region in 1960. No Latin American country had any international relationship even remotely comparable in significance to its ties with Washington, except for those Caribbean islands that retained their links with European colonial powers.

United States dominance in the Western hemisphere after World War II inevitably produced strong negative reactions. Latin American attitudes toward the United States had long been ambivalent. The United States had inspired most Latin American constitutions and served as the model for economic development and technological ingenuity. But many Latin Americans saw the United States as materialistic, culturally impoverished, domineering, and even imperial; the record of U.S. interventionism in the Caribbean Basin countries during the first three decades of the century had left a legacy of anti-U.S. sentiment. These resentments and fears were strongly reinforced by the increasing U.S. presence in Latin America in the late 1940s and the 1950s. Latin Americans disliked, too, the postwar U.S. tendency to take the Hemisphere for granted and to concentrate U.S. energies, attention, and resources elsewhere. These feelings were exacerbated during and after the Korean War, when U.S. economic policies were seen as detrimental to Latin American development prospects.

Latin American countries had contributed cheap strategic minerals, diplomatic support, and in some cases even troops to the United States during both World War II and the Korean War. The United States expected similar support for its global strategy of "containment" during the Cold War. Latin America's own priorities, however, were low on Washington's agenda. After the 1954 hemispheric declaration against communism, Latin American countries pressed the United States to return the favor by considering a "Marshall Plan" for the region. But Secretary of State John Foster Dulles did not even stay at the Caracas conference to hear these proposals once the United States had secured the anticommunist declaration he sought.

When Raúl Prebisch, director of the UN Economic Commission for Latin America (ECLA), presented Latin American pleas for expanded aid, credits, commodity price stabilization, and the creation of an Inter-American Development Bank at a 1954 meeting of the Inter-American Economic and Social Council of the OAS, these ideas were summarily rejected. In 1958, a similar fate befell a plan by President Juscelino Kubitscheck of Brazil for a hemispheric development program he proposed to call "Operacão Panamericana."

The growing opposition to the United States, first evident in intellectual and political circles, became more widely obvious with Vice-president Nixon's traumatic visits to Lima and Caracas in 1958, when angry crowds nearly crushed Mr. Nixon's limousine. That the United States faced increasing hostility from its neighbors was strongly corroborated by President Dwight Eisenhower's brother Milton on his extensive tour of the region that same year.

The most dramatic challenge to the position held by the United States came with Fidel Castro's revolution in Cuba. U.S. policy toward Castro's insurrectionary movement had been ambivalent, even positive in some quarters. Within a few months of his triumph in January 1959, however, it became clear that Castro wanted to escape U.S. control.

Opinions still differ sharply about whether the deepening hostility between Havana and Washington could have been avoided, but there is little doubt that Castro himself aimed from the start to end U.S. hegemony in Cuba. Within two years, he had achieved remarkable success. United States firms, until then overwhelmingly important in Cuba's economy, were nationalized. Barred by a coercive U.S. government decision from selling sugar to the United States, Castro turned to the Soviet Union. Diplomatic relations with Washington cooled, and then became intensely and mutually hostile. With the decisive defeat of a U.S.-supported invasion force at the Bay of Pigs in April 1961, it became clear that a nation once described as "no more independent than Long Island" had fundamentally revised its relationship with the United States.

Washington responded to Castro's challenge, first under President Dwight Eisenhower, and then much more forcefully under President John F. Kennedy, not only by attempting to reverse Cuba's course but also by intensifying U.S. involvement in Western Hemisphere affairs generally. The Inter-American Development Bank, long sought by Latin Americans, was finally established in 1960, as the U.S. government dropped its previous opposition to the idea. Bilateral U.S. aid programs, especially in the Caribbean Basin, were expanded; the other side of the coin was the training of an invasion force intended to topple Castro.

The Kennedy administration came to office determined to reestablish U.S. dominance in the Western Hemisphere. Drawing on the advice of Latin American political figures and U.S. scholars and specialists on Latin America, the Kennedy team quickly designed a comprehensive plan for the region. On March 13, 1961, less than two months after his inauguration, the new president unveiled the Alliance for Progress to the assembled ambassadors from Latin America and the Caribbean. The Alliance—which combined political, economic, and security measures—was the most ambitious U.S. approach to Latin America ever designed.

The Alliance for Progress represented a creative attempt to reassert U.S. influence in Latin America, one based on a new understanding of the nature of the challenge. The Arbenz regime in Guatemala, the riots sparked by Nixon's 1958 trip, and above all the Cuban Revolution prompted U.S. policy makers to recast the danger of Communist expansion in terms of internal rather than external security threats. The architects of the Alliance recognized the revolutionary potential of extreme poverty and inequality. Accordingly, the United States undertook to promote economic development and social reform in Latin America as an antidote to revolution. As chapter 1 emphasizes, it was believed that economic development, the expansion of the middle sectors, social reform, democratic politics, and enhanced stability all went hand in hand, and that these processes could be aided from outside.

As initially conceived, the Alliance called for an infusion of $20 billion in public and private funds over a ten-year period. Alliance planners hoped to raise the per capita income in Latin America by 2.5 percent annually. Income distribution was to be improved, illiteracy eliminated, and infant mortality halved. U.S. economic assistance and political leverage would reinforce democratic reform, while U.S. military aid and training programs would be expanded and reoriented toward counterinsurgency.

Although in practice the Alliance turned out rather differently from its design, it did temporarily push Latin America toward the forefront of U.S. policy attention. During the next several years, in implementing the Alliance, the United States substantially expanded its presence and involvement throughout the Americas. The number of U.S. government personnel assigned to Latin America jumped, crowding the suburbs of various Latin American capitals with embassy officers, technicians, and cultural and military advisers, and dotting the countryside with Peace Corps volunteers and military special forces.

The U.S. government immersed itself in the domestic affairs of virtually all countries of the Americas. U.S. pressure often forced elections to be held and sometimes determined the results. U.S. influence caused Latin American armies to start civic action programs, prompted the creation of national planning boards, and forced the devaluation of currencies. The United States powerfully affected Latin American countries by offering or withholding diplomatic recognition and economic aid, by training and supplying military and police units, and by manipulating the media.

A few examples convey the flavor of inter-American relations during the period.
—In Chile, the United States covertly spent at least $3 million on behalf of Eduardo Frei's 1964 Christian Democratic campaign, more money per capita than had previously been spent in any U.S. election.
—During the 1950s and 1960s, the United States retained several Bolivian cabinet officers on the CIA payroll, supported over one-third of the national government's budget, and flooded the country with advisers.
—In Guyana (British Guiana) in the early 1960s, the U.S. government used its infiltration of the trade union movement as well as other instruments of covert intervention to thwart Cheddi Jagan's Left-Nationalist party.
—In Brazil, U.S. enthusiasm for the 1964 overthrow of nationalist João Goulart by the Brazilian military was so palpable that Washington sent its congratulations even before the new regime could be installed.

A U.S. naval force was apparently available to support the coup, if needed.

—Most dramatically, more than 22 thousand U.S. Marines and paratroopers landed in Santo Domingo in 1965 to forestall what President Lyndon B. Johnson perceived as a possible Communist takeover. The Dominican "request" for U.S. forces, drafted in English with the help of a U.S. defense attaché, came from a hastily assembled military junta that had itself been set up with frantic American encouragement. What is more, the United States was able (within two days of landing its forces) to obtain an OAS vote to create an Inter-American Peace Force in Santo Domingo, into which the U.S. contingent could be incorporated. The fact that the crucial vote to reach the required two-thirds was provided by the delegate from the Dominican government, the very existence of which was at issue, did not prevent the OAS from providing the required fig leaf.

The Dominican invasion ended this country's prolonged adherence to Franklin D. Roosevelt's 1934 pledge to end unilateral U.S. military intervention in Latin America. Instead, the Johnson administration reinforced and extended the hegemonic presumption—the belief that Latin America is a rightful sphere of U.S. influence. That belief led U.S. officials to regard as unacceptable the emergence to power in any Latin American country of a political group that based its appeal largely on opposition to the United States and that cultivated close ties with the Soviet Union.

The United States did not confine its influence to the political realm during this period. It went to extraordinary lengths to aid U.S. corporations when they clashed with Latin American states. The United States pressed for specific social and economic reforms, and sought predominant cultural influence, as well. Washington determined what military equipment Latin American nations could purchase. Because its grants and loans represented such a significant share of Latin America's external financing for development, Washington also shaped many of Latin America's economic choices.

The United States, in sum, considered it normal during the 1960s to have a major voice in the internal affairs of Latin American and Caribbean countries and a virtual veto on their foreign policies. Overwhelming U.S. power made it feasible for the United States to involve itself so deeply in regional affairs that no movement that might challenge U.S. domination could easily come to power or last long. Cuba, protected by its alliance with the Soviet Union, was the one exception that continued to provoke Washington's anxiety.

THE UNITED STATES AND LATIN AMERICA SINCE 1970

Like a streak of lightning, the 1975 report on Chile of the U.S. Senate's Select Committee on Intelligence illuminated the contours of U.S.–Latin American relations even as the landscape was changing.

The Senate's report documented that the United States had covertly engaged for a decade in a massive and sustained campaign against Salvador Allende and the Left in Chile. The report recorded U.S. efforts (major in 1964, less active in 1970) to prevent Allende's popular election. It revealed, as well, that Washington first promoted an abortive military coup and then considered and apparently attempted bribery to prevent Allende's formal selection by the Chilean congress, acting as an electoral college.

After Allende was finally elected, the United States hampered his government in countless ways until he was overthrown at last in 1973. From 1970 to 1973, the United States spent some $8 million on clandestine intervention in Chile: financing political activities among workers, students, women, professional organizations, business associations, and other civic groups; stimulating "news" stories and editorials in the Chilean press; and inspiring and diffusing in the world press articles on Chile by CIA-subsidized "journalists" from other countries. The United States government also weakened Allende's regime by cutting off Chile's access to international loans and credits and by encouraging local capital flight. The United States spread misinformation to Chilean military officers to foster fear of supposed Cuban subversive activities. It also financed various opposition efforts—even, to a small extent, the terrorist Right. The Allende government faced a great deal of domestic opposition, to be sure, but U.S. efforts were significant in preparing the way for the 1973 coup.

The U.S. government's actions in Chile during the 1960s and early 1970s were not unique in U.S.–Latin American relations. That intervention, however, was more extensive and sustained than any other, presumably because the circumstances were unique; no other socialist movement had come close to achieving power in South America, much less by free election.

The exceptional U.S. covert intervention against Allende was, in any event, anachronistic, for the objective bases of U.S. hegemony in the Western Hemisphere had begun to erode. By the time Allende was toppled in 1973, U.S. preponderance in the Americas was already substantially diminished. Washington could weaken Allende and contribute to his fall, but it could not effectively shape Chile's future after Allende was ousted.

Several other examples highlight the diminished capacity of the

United States to impose its will in Latin America. In June 1979, the foreign ministers of the Organization of American States met to consider the crisis in Nicaragua. Secretary of State Cyrus Vance presented the U.S. position. He called not only for collective repudiation of the Somoza regime, but also for an OAS mission to negotiate a political transition in Managua and for a multilateral "peacekeeping force" to restore order in the beleaguered country. In contrast to the success of the U.S. proposal in the 1965 Dominican case, however, the U.S. suggestion for Nicaragua got nowhere. Washington was forced to accept an alternative plan, put forward by the Andean nations, that left the Sandinistas free to take power in Nicaragua. Rumors that U.S. forces were being readied for possible use in Nicaragua died quickly in the face of overwhelming Latin American resistance even to the idea of collective military action.

In 1980, Washington promoted an international boycott of the Olympic games, held that year in Moscow, as a means of protesting the Soviet invasion of Afghanistan. Fifteen Latin American nations defied the boycott. Argentina's refusal in the same year to cooperate with the U.S grain embargo of the Soviet Union made that measure ineffective.

In 1982, the United States government found itself powerless to dissuade Argentina from launching its invasion of the Malvinas-Falkland Islands, despite a personal appeal by President Ronald Reagan to Argentine President Leopoldo Galtieri. After the invasion, the United States could not persuade Argentina to accept any compromise solution for ending the conflict, notwithstanding the strenuous efforts of Secretary of State Alexander Haig. Worse yet, Washington was also unable to convince many other Latin American countries to oppose Argentina's adventure. Even Colombia, which had initially appeared to support the U.S. stance, soon found it convenient to join the Non-Aligned Movement, partly in order to demonstrate the country's distance from Washington.

The decline of U.S. preponderance in the Western Hemisphere has been pervasive and fundamental.
—The share of Latin American exports going to the United States decreased from 45 percent in 1958 to 34 percent by the end of the 1970s. The decline from most of South America was considerably greater, as Mexican, Venezuelan, and Caribbean exports to the United States grew substantially. Although the U.S. share of Latin America's exports has shot back up to nearly 50 percent since 1983, this sudden rise is almost certainly a temporary consequence of the region's financial crisis. Latin America's renewed dependence on the U.S. market has resulted in large part from this country's deficit-financed recovery

and its overvalued dollar. It has also reflected the contraction of imports by all Latin American countries, which reduced nonfuel trade among them by half. Finally, it results from the economic reverses suffered by most of Latin America's other trading partners, which cut imports and increased protectionism. Eventually, with a global economic recovery, Latin America's trade diversification should resume.

—The composition of Latin American exports to the United States has changed considerably. Exports of oil, manufactured goods, and new agricultural crops have all sharply increased. With the diversification of its exports, Latin America's vulnerability to sudden shortfalls of export revenues diminished somewhat during the 1970s, and the bargaining power of Latin American nations was correspondingly enhanced. The region's susceptibility to the effects of an international recession remains high, and massive foreign debts have produced a critical new vulnerability, but Latin America's diversification of exports is still significant.

—The U.S. share of foreign investment in Latin America has also declined. In 1965, for example, the United States accounted for more than 50 percent of Brazil's foreign direct investment; by 1979, the U.S. share of foreign investment in Brazil had dropped to 30 percent, even though U.S. investment was growing faster in Brazil than in any other Latin American country. Similar figures exist for most countries of the Americas, except the Caribbean, where the U.S. share of foreign investment has grown. Throughout South America, European and Japanese investment rose during the 1970s and is still expanding, although at a slower pace, during the 1980s.

—Latin American nations have also considerably increased their bargaining power vis-à-vis multinational corporations. In the late 1960s and 1970s, they were able to impose performance, export, and remittance requirements on foreign companies. They were also able to secure more favorable terms for the transfer of technology and services, and to win other concessions, as well. Although many countries are now once again eager to attract foreign investment, they are able to negotiate with multinational firms from a much stronger position.

—The U.S. government's level of activity in the Western Hemisphere has been drastically reduced from its peak in the mid-1960s. U.S. foreign aid and diplomatic personnel in Latin America were cut back sharply during the 1970s. U.S. economic assistance amounted to only 30 percent of bilateral aid to Latin America in 1980, down from 77 percent in 1970. Most of this country's assistance in the 1980s is concentrated in the Caribbean Basin, with much less than previously going to South America. The number of U.S. military advisers in

Latin America dropped from more than eight hundred in 1968 to fewer than one hundred in 1980 (before additional advisers were sent to El Salvador and Honduras); the renewed build-up of U.S. military advisers since 1980 has been strictly limited to the Caribbean Basin.

—The Latin American dependence on U.S. arms during the period from World War II until 1965 has given way to a remarkable diversification of weapons sources. Beginning in the late 1970s, arms sales to Latin America from each of several suppliers—the Soviet Union, France, Italy, the United Kingdom, Israel, and even Brazil—have been equal to or, often, greater than those from the United States, and several Latin American nations besides Brazil are producing their own weapons.

—The Soviet Union has increased its diplomatic representation in the Western Hemisphere from three countries in 1960 to nineteen today. It has expanded its trading relationships to twenty countries from four in 1964. Moscow has established itself as Argentina's principal trading partner and a significant partner of Brazil. It has sent technical assistance missions to numerous countries, and it has trained many thousands of Latin American students. Most notably, the Soviet Union has furnished substantial military equipment and training to Cuba, Nicaragua, and Peru, and it has built close political and economic relations with Cuba, Nicaragua, and (from 1979 to 1983) Grenada.

—The Soviet presence in the Americas, however, has in many ways been overshadowed by the rapidly expanding involvement of Japan, West Germany, France, and Spain. Japan's trade with Latin America multiplied seventeen times from 1960 to 1980, reaching a level in 1980 of $10.6 billion, ten times the amount of Soviet–Latin American trade. West Germany has increased its investments in Latin America, especially in Brazil, as well as its political and cultural links with many Latin American countries. France has reasserted an economic, political, and cultural presence in Latin America. Spain's investment in Latin America has also been growing rapidly, and its political involvement in the region has expanded under Prime Minister Felip Gonzalez. Other significant foreign influences in Latin America include the European Social Democrats and Christian Democrats, Israel and many Arab nations (as well as the Palestine Liberation Organization), Canada, the Scandinavian countries, the European Economic Community, and the Eastern European COMECON. None of these actors challenges the United States as the primary foreign influence in Latin America, but, taken together, they substantially dilute Washington's previously overwhelming predominance.

All these trends reflect and reinforce the growing tendency of Latin American and Caribbean nations to pursue their own interests, even in opposition to Washington's preferences. That determination has often been illustrated: by Brazil's early recognition of the Soviet-backed Popular Movement for the Liberation of Angola (MPLA), its interest in obtaining advanced nuclear technology from West Germany, and its Middle Eastern links; by Mexico's initiative in promoting the 1974 UN Charter of Economic Rights and Duties of States and the 1981 Cancún Summit, as well as by its activist stance in the 1980s against the posture of the United States in Central America; by Venezuela's leadership role in OPEC and its opposition to the U.S. position on Puerto Rico; and by Latin American support for Nicaragua's election in 1982 to the UN Security Council. It is also clear in the increasingly frequent Latin American cooperative efforts that exclude the United States, such as the Latin American Economic System (SELA), the Contadora initiative to seek a diplomatic settlement in Central America, the Cartegena group on finance and trade, and the "Rio Group" formed in December 1986.

The emerging pattern of inter-American relations resembles that which prevailed in the 1920s and 1930s. During the two decades before World War II, the United States was a significant but not a domineering power in Latin America. Its influence was substantial but not exclusive. The United Kingdom, Germany, France, and Italy also had important commercial, financial, cultural, and military involvements in this Hemisphere. Argentina, Brazil, and Mexico participated in international affairs as middle powers. The United States recognized the stature of these nations and their diverse links. It confined its intense involvement in domestic affairs to the countries in its immediate border region.

Many aspects of the contemporary period are entirely new: the influence of Japan and the Soviet Union in Latin America; the emergence of several Latin American nations as major industrial exporters; the beginning of significant arms manufacture in South America; the dramatic rise in the relative power of Brazil; and, especially, Latin America's transformed political economy and the correspondingly altered nature of U.S. economic involvement in the region. But the relative influence of the United States in the Western Hemisphere today is probably closer to what it was in the 1920s and early 1930s than to what it was in the period from 1945 to 1965.

The years immediately following World War II were, in fact, highly unusual. Concepts, policies, and institutions forged during that period are no longer valid today, when power is much more diffuse and the asymmetries between the United States and the countries of Latin America have been reduced. The capacity of the United States to control events in the Western Hemisphere has diminished. Adjusting to this decline has been the underlying challenge for U.S. policy toward Latin America during the past generation.

FROM KENNEDY TO REAGAN: CYCLES OF CONCERN AND NEGLECT

The U.S. government has responded in fits and starts to Latin America's transformation during the last thirty years. Periodic bursts of official concern with the Western Hemisphere have given way time after time to relative neglect. Continuity of policies and personnel has been lacking. U.S.–Latin American relations were allowed to drift for a generation, until the outbreak of revolutions in Central America and the Hemispheric debt crisis of the 1980s made it impossible for Washington to continue to ignore the region.

John F. Kennedy's Alliance for Progress—proclaimed unilaterally, like most U.S. initiatives before and since—responded to Latin America's internal changes. It did so, however, mainly by attempting to reassert and extend U.S. domination in the name of development and democratic reform. The early Kennedy approach presented a comprehensive program for Latin America: substantial support for broad social and political reforms designed to preempt leftist gains; declaratory backing for constitutional government to help end Latin America's debilitating cycle of military coups; infusions of military training, advice, and equipment to counter internal security threats; and major transfers of public resources to spur Latin American economic development.

In practice, however, the Kennedy administration backed away from many of its early commitments. Security assistance was unstintingly provided, even when it conflicted with the aim of curbing military intervention in politics, but other aspects of the Alliance atrophied. Economic assistance fell far short of original projections. Much of the aid that was provided turned out to be mainly a device to secure immediate advantages for a variety of U.S. private interests. The Kennedy administration's commitment to constitutional democracy also proved to be short-lived; by the time President Kennedy was assassinated in 1963, that objective had been shelved in the wake of the Honduran and Dominican coups.

A number of inherent limits and contradictions worked against the Alliance. The notion that the United States could selectively promote reform in Latin America while undercutting revolutionary movements there implied an unrealistic assessment of this country's capacity to fine-tune Latin American developments. Extensive U.S. involvement in Latin America's domestic affairs sometimes had the effect of reinforcing nationalist reactions. Reforms crucial to development conflicted with U.S. business and financial interests. Short-range political objectives clashed with long-term development goals in the administration of aid programs. By strengthening military establishments, security assistance and counterinsurgency programs at times undermined democracies. Both U.S. military advisers and the local armed forces balked at the political instability often associated with major social reform.

The elevation of Lyndon B. Johnson to the presidency accelerated the decline of the Alliance. The Johnson administration's stance toward Latin America was punctuated by bursts of attention after the Panama Canal Zone riots of 1964, during the Dominican uprising of 1965, and at the time of the Punta del Este meeting of presidents in 1967. But its concern always focused on the immediate crisis and did not take fully into account the underlying changes taking place in Latin America. The Johnson administration's attention was, in any case, soon absorbed by the growing U.S. involvement in Vietnam.

As the Cuban shock wore off and U.S. attention shifted to Vietnam, it became politically difficult in this country to sustain the massive commitment of resources required by the Alliance for Progress. Moreover, the Johnson administration chose not to rely on the scholars and other outsiders who had served as Kennedy's advisers and had influenced the temporary shift of U.S. priorities away from business interests. Johnson reorganized the Latin American policy-making channels and centralized control over them by combining the posts of assistant secretary of state for inter-American affairs and U.S. coordinator for the Alliance for Progress. His appointee to the top Latin American policy position, Thomas C. Mann, promptly announced the "Mann Doctrine," which altered the cast of the Alliance. Reversing the Kennedy commitment, Mann announced that the United States would take a neutral stand on domestic social and political reforms in the region and would "deal with governments as they are" rather than favor democracy or constitutionalism. Under the new policy, the United States would promote private investment, not the transfer of public resources, to foster economic growth in Latin America. Washington soon began to intervene on behalf of U.S investors throughout Latin America. At the same time, it built friendly relations with the new military regime in Brazil and stepped up covert operations in Chile.

The Republican administration of Richard M. Nixon and Gerald R. Ford responded in two distinct phases to the changing facts of hemispheric life. In the first phase, from 1969 until late 1973, the Nixon administration sought to lower the profile of the United States in Latin America. Except for its efforts to undo Allende's electoral triumph in Chile in 1970 (considered by the White House to pose an intolerable threat to U.S. security), the Nixon administration responded to Latin American assertiveness by cutting back U.S. programs, toning down U.S. rhetoric, and generally reducing the U.S. presence.

In adopting its "Mature Partnership" policy of diminished U.S. involvement, the Nixon team rejected the advice of Nelson Rockefeller, who had undertaken a series of trips to Latin America on behalf of the new administration. Rockefeller recommended ambitious new economic, political, and security initiatives that would have institutionalized a "special relationship" between the United States and Latin America.

The Rockefeller report called for a special cabinet-level secretary of Western Hemisphere affairs, who would report directly to the secretary of state and the president. The report also recommended tax breaks and other incentives for foreign investors; expanded tariff preferences and trade credits for Latin America; fewer restrictions on U.S. aid; a U.S.-funded Western Hemisphere Institute for Education, Science, and Culture; and increased aid and training for Latin American military and police forces. The Rockefeller report also lauded the potentially progressive role of Latin America's modernizing military institutions.

Rockefeller proposed, in short, a major new commitment of U.S. attention and resources to the Western Hemisphere. Unlike that of the Alliance for Progress, however, his focus was mainly on promoting immediate private investment and U.S. security interests. Instead of emphasizing social reform, the Rockefeller report stressed economic growth and political solidarity. This program would rely as much on military governments as on democratic regimes.

The Rockefeller report was quickly shelved, however. The Nixon administration's tendency, on the contrary, was to minimize the differences between Latin American and Caribbean nations and other Third World countries. Latin America's needs, the administration felt, did not merit special regional approach. The global strategy devised by President Nixon's national security adviser, Dr. Henry A. Kissinger, centered on the world's five main powers: the United States, the Soviet Union, Western Europe, China, and Japan. This strategy was more or less equally indifferent toward almost all other countries, except insofar as Soviet involvement was perceived. Latin America and, in fact, the whole Third World, were paid little positive heed. The Nixon administration's disregard for Latin America was epitomized in August 1971, when the United States overnight, and without consultation with other nations, imposed an import surcharge despite its very adverse effects on the Hemisphere.

In the second phase of the Republican period, the 1973 Arab oil embargo and OPEC's price hike triggered a rediscovery of the Third World. The realization that the United States was now more vulnerable to pressures from developing countries, together with the knowledge that relatively secure sources of energy and other new materials could be found in Latin America, led naturally to a desire to shore up regional ties. Rockefeller's long-espoused concept of preferential arrangements based on underlying Western Hemisphere harmony came belatedly to influence the rhetoric adopted by Dr. Kissinger in his new role as secretary of state.

When the foreign ministers of the Hemisphere met in Tlatelolco, Mexico, in February 1974, Kissinger spoke of a U.S. commitment to a "New Dialogue" with Latin America based on hemispheric "community." Many of Latin America's assembled foreign ministers were skeptical, however. Colombia's representative, for instance, pointedly noted that "Latin America's community is the Third World." But Kissinger remained undaunted when all references to "community" were eliminated from the draft conference communiqué. He simply reverted to the familiar phrase, "special relationship," which he employed frequently in an address in Caracas in 1976.

Rhetoric aside, however, top officials of the U.S. government paid little sustained attention to Latin America. Secretary Kissinger found it necessary to cancel three planned visits to Latin America to go to the Middle East. In 1976 Brazil was formally accorded a special status under an agreement signed by Kissinger and Brazilian Foreign Minister Antonio F. Azaredo da Silveira, but U.S. policy did not change on any significant matter in dispute between the two countries, and frictions therefore continued. Kissinger signaled his interest in the Hemisphere by trying to negotiate a new status for the Panama Canal Zone and beginning secret discussions with Cuban representatives regarding the possible reestablishment of bilateral relations, but these initiatives were shelved as soon as domestic political constraints emerged.

The Nixon-Ford-Kissinger response to Latin America's economic concerns was also slow and insufficient. Just before its end, the Ford administration did adopt a more forthcoming rhetoric toward the Third World, unveiled by Kissinger in addresses prepared for the 7th Special Session of the United Nations General Assembly in 1975 and the 1976 UNCTAD conference in Nairobi. But the administration did little, in its brief remaining time, to make its new posture meaningful. Compared with its much more forceful shift of policy toward southern Africa, for instance, the Ford administration's new approach to Latin America remained largely symbolic. Like that of the Kennedy and Johnson administrations before it, the policy for the Hemisphere employed by Nixon and Ford was essentially a rear-guard attempt to prevent Latin America from escaping U.S. control.

The Carter administration came to office in 1977 intent on shaping a new approach to inter-American relations as part of a general reformulation of U.S. foreign policy. In its initial posture, the Carter administration was influenced by the recommendations of the Commission on United States–Latin American Relations, a private, bipartisan undertaking of prominent citizens chaired by former Ambassador Sol M. Linowitz.

In contrast to the Rockefeller report of 1969, the Linowitz reports of 1974 and 1976 urged that the United States deal with Latin American issues in their North-South and global contexts. The reports recognized the new diversity of Latin America's international links and consequently did not propose a hemispheric consensus under U.S. leadership. The Linowitz commission recommended renegotiating the Panama Canal treaties, calling this "the most urgent issue the new administration will face in the Western Hemisphere." It called for a new attempt to explore the possibility of improved relations with Cuba, and it recommended that the United States pay more attention to the economic concerns expressed by Latin American and Caribbean nations. The Linowitz reports also decried a "plague of repression" in Latin America and proposed stronger U.S. support for democracy and human rights there.

From the start, the Carter administration concentrated on what it regarded as the key issues in the Hemisphere, issues deriving from the changed international context: the diffusion of power, "detente" with the Soviet Union, and the increasing importance of North-South issues. The new president criticized earlier policies that, he stated, reflected an "inordinate fear of communism." He urged focusing instead on what he considered more fundamental matters: economic development, conservation of energy and other resources, eliminating hunger, defending human rights, limiting nuclear proliferation and arms races, and keeping the peace.

The Carter approach explicitly took into account changes in Latin America and in inter-American relations. The United States promised to respond to Latin American concerns on North-South economic issues: trade, aid, finance, and technology transfer. It recognized the increasing international significance of the middle powers emerging in Latin America and elsewhere in the Third World. As one important element of its policy, the Carter team proposed new policies and procedures to improve U.S. relations with Mexico and the Caribbean.

The Carter policy also began to respond to Latin America's social and political evolution by loosening ties between the United States and unpopular authoritarian regimes. Spurred by congressional initiatives that had begun in response to Secretary Kissinger's perceived indifference to the subject, the Carter administration introduced a strong emphasis on human rights. This policy immediately created ties between Washington and opposition movements in Latin American countries, even as it strained U.S. relations with repressive governments.

The Carter administration also tried to adapt to declining U.S. influence by changing the style of U.S. policy. It invested the political capital necessary to get the Panama Canal treaties negotiated and ratified. It explored the possibility of gradually renewing U.S. relations with Cuba. Washington proclaimed U.S. tolerance for "ideological pluralism," even in the Caribbean and Central America. And the Carter administration reformed the rhetoric of U.S. policy by purging from official pronouncements any mention of a "special relationship," a concept that in the past had so often masked paternalistic, discriminatory, or interventionist treatment. Instead, the new administration announced that it would deal with Latin America in a broad, global context.

Although the Carter administration responded verbally to changing hemispheric realities, notable gaps soon emerged between its rhetoric and its actions. Winning Latin American cooperation turned out to be important only insofar as doing so affected the issues most urgent to the United States: energy, narcotics, and nuclear nonproliferation. The U.S. government continued to pay little attention to the main aims of Latin American countries: improved access for middle-income countries to the markets, capital, and technology of advanced industrial countries; more automatic and generous aid to the least advantaged countries; more stable and favorable commodity trade arrangements; and more responsiveness by multinational corporations to the host countries. Foreign aid from the United States (and other industrial nations) to support economic growth in Latin America failed to expand. Specific U.S. decisions on tariffs, taxes, and other matters continued to hurt individual Latin American countries.

Most important, Carter took few concrete steps to accommodate the economic needs of the increasingly important newly industrialized countries, many of them in Latin America. Measures to improve access by the developing countries to the markets, capital, and technology of the industrial world made little headway during the Carter period. Such steps would inevitably have hurt marginal industries, sectors, and regions in the United States and in other industrial nations, and would therefore have required making some painful domestic adjustments. The Carter administration, not ready to face these costs, did not seriously address a basic issue in contemporary inter-American relations. On matters of dollars and cents, the Carter administration produced, in sum, small change.

On other issues, too, the Carter administration moved away from its original position. The declared interest in improving relations with Mexico was largely undercut by unilateral and even peremptory U.S. decisions on immigration and natural gas, compounded by maladroit presidential diplomacy. Relations with Havana returned to frostiness in the wake of Cuba's involvement in Ethiopia. The administration's initial relative openness to leftist experiments in the Caribbean Basin gave way to distrust and hostility toward Nicaragua and Grenada. Even the emphasis on human rights was eventually soft-pedaled.

By the time the Carter administration left office in January 1981, it had reverted considerably toward earlier U.S. policies. The outgoing president's decision on January 15 (just five days before he left office) to provide military assistance to El Salvador's beleaguered government, despite its unsatisfactory record on human rights, highlighted this retreat. The trend had been unmistakable before that, however. Over time, the Carter administration's policies toward Latin America turned out to be much less different from previous U.S. approaches than had been proclaimed or anticipated.

Ronald Reagan and his key advisers on Latin America did not criticize the Carter regime for abandoning its initially innovative approach to Western Hemisphere affairs. On the contrary, the new administration's main policy makers on Latin America made it clear, both in what they wrote before the election and in what they said and did soon after taking office, that they fundamentally rejected the original Carter approach. On issue after issue—Cuba, Central America, human rights, Law of the Sea, the relative priority of East-West versus North-South questions, and others—the Reagan administration introduced new policies that reasserted an earlier U.S. stance.

The Reagan administration's Latin American policy was influenced by the 1980 report of the Committee of Santa Fe and by the writings of academic specialists, particularly those of Dr. Jeane Kirkpatrick, whose article "Dictatorships and Double Standards" had attracted Mr. Reagan's personal attention. In contrast to the Linowitz reports, these studies argued that the decline in U.S. control over events in the hemisphere was fundamentally caused by past U.S. policy and was therefore reversible. The Santa Fe committee's preeminent concern about Latin America was the growth of Soviet influence in the region. To combat this danger, the report called on the United States to reestablish its influence in Latin America through both increased private investment and the exercise of military power.

Professor Kirkpatrick attributed the deterioration of this country's position to misguided U.S. policies derived from the Linowitz reports and other products of the "foreign policy establishment." She argued that the Carter team's intellectual and political errors had brought down the Somoza regime in Nicaragua and had "positively contributed to . . . the alienation of major nations, the growth of neutralism, the destabilization of friendly governments, the spread of Cuban influence, and the decline of U.S. power in the region." Kirkpatrick called for a reversal of the Carter approach and a vigorous restoration of activist U.S. policies in the Hemisphere.

From its first days, the Reagan administration set out boldly to reduce perceived Cuban and Soviet inroads, build more solid alliances with like-minded forces, increase the military presence and capacity of the United States in the region, strengthen traditional inter-American institutions, and restore ideological harmony in the Hemisphere.

Rather than accommodate or adjust to international and regional tendencies it found undesirable, the new administration proposed energetic measures to reverse the unwelcome trends. It proclaimed its intent to combat Cuban subversion "at the source" and "draw the line" against leftist gains in El Salvador. It sought to intimidate, harass, and, if possible, overthrow the fledgling revolutionary regimes in Nicaragua and Grenada. The Reagan team explored the possibility of establishing a South Atlantic Treaty Organization with Argentina, Brazil, and South Africa. It aimed to remove restrictions on military aid and arms sales to various Latin American countries that previously had been barred on human rights grounds from receiving U.S. weapons.

The new administration sought to restore U.S. dominance in the Western Hemisphere through declarations and demonstrations of force, overt and covert assistance to pro-U.S. regimes and counterrevolutionary movements, and clandestine action against unfriendly regimes. During its first sixteen months in office, the Reagan team focused sharply on two main goals in the Hemisphere: to counter Cuba in Central America and the whole Caribbean Basin, and to improve relations between the United States and Mexico. To a large extent, it ignored South America and paid little heed to economic issues.

The Malvinas-Falklands imbroglio in April–May 1982 starkly revealed that the Reagan administration's approach had not significantly enhanced Washington's influence in South America. On the contrary, the war illustrated the fissures in the Hemisphere and the limits on U.S. power. Concern about the tattered state of inter-American relations grew in Washington and in U.S. foreign policy circles.

Then came the Mexican liquidity crisis of August 1982. Mexico's inability to meet interest payments on its foreign debt forced the U.S. Treasury Department to spend a frantic weekend mobilizing an emergency package of assistance. Washington finally focused on Latin

America's financial straits. The administration's preoccupation with Central America had distracted attention from Latin America's mounting economic problems. It became obvious that the region's economic plight could substantially reduce U.S. influence in the Americas.

Although the Reagan administration continued to be concerned by the crisis in Central America, it also devoted increased attention to Latin American economic problems. It was not eager, however, to adopt any major new policies to cope with them; it preferred, by and large, to rely on the workings of the market to restore economic health in the Hemisphere. Only in 1985, after a further economic downturn in Latin America, did the administration shift ground somewhat through the "Baker Plan"—a set of proposals advanced by Secretary of the Treasury James Baker III which called for Washington to respond more directly to the worsening problem of Third World (principally Latin American) debt. But even this initiative was modest in concept, scope, and impact. It proposed leaving most of the response up to the commercial banks, expecting them to increase voluntary lending at a level that would not have been sufficient even had it been obtained—and it was not.

The Reagan administration's experience suggests that the decline of U.S. influence in Latin America cannot easily be reversed. Some of the administration's early measures turned out to be counterproductive. Its rush to embrace authoritarian regimes cost the U.S. government credibility with influential opposition groups in Latin America and yet gave Washington little leverage with the military regimes themselves; by the mid-1980s, the U.S. government moved steadily back to a policy of clear preference for democratic regimes. The administration's confrontational stance in Central America and the Caribbean disturbed several major Latin American nations. The joint declaration issued in May 1983 by the presidents of Mexico and Brazil opposing U.S. intervention in Central America reflected gathering Latin American sentiment against the Reagan administration's resurrection of the "big stick." That sentiment grew stronger during the mid-1980s, particularly after Latin Americans perceived that the United States was undercutting the Contadora diplomatic initiative in Central America. It was further reinforced as the countries of Latin America began to work more closely together to find solutions for the regional economic crisis and as the United States stepped up its campaign against Nicaragua.

The 1983 military operation in Grenada illustrated the Reagan administration's aspiration to reestablish U.S. predominance in the Hemisphere. Seven thousand U.S. troops invaded the tiny Caribbean island and successfully ousted its Marxist leaders in the midst of an internal power struggle among leftist factions. Within a year, democratic elections were organized, a successor regime was installed, and U.S. troops departed. Invading a tiny Caribbean ministate and reorganizing its politics, however, was far simpler than restoring U.S. influence elsewhere.

Extensive U.S. efforts, including large-scale covert military intervention, have failed to remove the Sandinistas from power in Nicaragua, or even to alter their course significantly. Large-scale U.S. assistance to the government of El Salvador has thus far been inadequate to defeat a guerrilla challenge. Serious exploration of what could be done to reverse the Cuban Revolution revealed, more than anything else, the limits on U.S. power. Strong U.S. pressures on Mexico to modify its posture toward Central America have provoked repeated reassertions of Mexico's independence. Neither "silent diplomacy" at first nor increasingly vocal U.S. representations more recently have induced the Pinochet regime in Chile to reopen the political process. Latin America's nearly unanimous opposition to the U.S. war against Nicaragua illustrates how far the United States is from being able to reimpose inter-American harmony.

The Reagan administration's experience has shown that U.S. fiat no longer works in the Americas. Long gone are the days when the United States was "practically sovereign" in the Western Hemisphere, as Secretary of State Richard Olney put it in 1895. Gone, too, are the more recent days of the Alliance for Progress, when the United States could almost unilaterally define the agenda and the modes of inter-American discourse. The Reagan administration demonstrated its willingness to apply substantial pressure, even military force, to restore U.S. control in the Western Hemisphere. It went a long way toward renewing an interventionist U.S. stance toward Latin America and the Caribbean.

The Reagan administration's approach to the Western Hemisphere is decidedly out of date, however. The United States is still by far the strongest nation of the Americas, but its predominance has declined during the past generation for reasons that go beyond the specific policies of particular administrations. Underlying economic, social, political, technological, and military trends have contributed to a fundamental realignment of power.

The capacity of the United States to control events in the Western Hemisphere has been undercut during the last thirty years primarily by Latin America's major domestic transformations. The overwhelming influence of the United States in the world arena, especially in the Americas, has been radically diminished since its peak in the immediate postwar era. Latin America's internal changes make it unlikely that overwhelming U.S. dominance in the Hemisphere will ever be restored.

The period of U.S. hegemony is over both because Latin American nations are able and determined to forge their own policies and because the objective bases of U.S. predominance have eroded. This has not happened because the United Sates lacks political will. Even if reassertionist U.S. policies could partially restore U.S. dominance during a period of severe Latin American economic reversal, this restoration would likely be short-lived, because the underlying distribution of power has changed.

The Reagan administration's attempt to reimpose U.S. preponderance in the Hemisphere has begun to backfire, indeed. Interventionist U.S. policies antagonize major Latin American nations that do not see themselves as unconditional followers of the United States. What Washington may gain in subservience from Honduras or Costa Rica is being lost in terms of cooperation from Brazil, Mexico, Colombia, Peru, and Argentina. If the United States is to protect its interests in the Western Hemisphere on an enduring basis, it must accept the end of U.S. hegemony. The United States must move from a stance of dominance to one of cooperation.

CHAPTER THREE

Rethinking U.S. Interests in the Western Hemisphere

The countries of Latin America and the Caribbean, and consequently their relations with the United States, have changed considerably during the past thirty years. Latin American and Caribbean nations are more populous, urban, industrialized, organized, and assertive than they were a generation ago. Even in a period of extensive economic difficulty, Latin America's nations are today more prosperous than in 1960. Most are better integrated into the world economy and are much more involved in international politics.

Latin American nations today are far less closely tied to the United States than they used to be. Few, if any, Latin American nations today are "banana republics," meekly following the lead of the United States. Many Latin American nations actively pursue their own interests in the world arena, often in opposition to U.S. policies. Although the countries of Latin America have been badly hurt in the 1980s by economic and financial reverses, they have not returned to the previous pattern of subordination to the United States. Instead, they have retained many of their diversified international involvements.

United States policies toward Latin America and the Caribbean have not kept pace with all these changes. Often they have been based on outdated assumptions rather than on current assessments of Latin America's evolving capabilities and needs. Particularly during Ronald Reagan's administration, the United States has reverted to traditional approaches that fail to take into account how much Latin America has evolved.

This chapter considers the implications for the United States of Latin America's transformation, as well as of its economic problems in the 1980s. It seeks to clarify U.S. interests in the Western Hemisphere today, and to explain how U.S. interests have altered over time.

U.S. INTERESTS: THE TRADITIONAL VIEW

Traditional discussions of U.S. policy toward Latin America take up a familiar litany of security, political, and economic concerns. Formulations have differed, but most discussions have given primacy to security: protecting the United States against direct military threats to itself or to its military assets in the region; protecting vital maritime routes, including the Panama Canal; and assuring access to strategic raw materials. Political interests have included winning Latin America's diplomatic support in various international forums; enhancing neighborly harmony; or, more vaguely (and more frequently implied than stated), preserving ideological harmony in the Western Hemisphere. Finally, U.S. economic interests have historically meant assuring adequate scope and favorable treatment for U.S. trade and private investment.

Washington's security concerns, the main organizing focus of policy in the Western Hemisphere for over a century, have evolved with shifting international power relationships and changes in technology. Keeping Caribbean coaling stations out of potentially hostile control was a chief preoccupation in the late nineteenth and early twentieth centuries. Assuring sources of rubber, balsa wood, quinine, copper, tin, and other strategic materials was important in the first half of the twentieth century, especially during World War II. So was the need during World War II to control landing strips, to prevent Nazi interference with Allied shipping, and to guard against a possible German invasion of the Western Hemisphere from West Africa. More recently, the focus has been on keeping Soviet missile launching sites and hostile nuclear submarine bases or tenders out of the region, excluding hostile combat forces, protecting the Panama Canal and the sea lanes, retaining Caribbean and Central American military facilities, and maintaining secure access to critical raw materials.

The political strand of the traditional U.S. concern for Latin America and the Caribbean has long been based on Washington's assumption that the nations of the Western Hemisphere are natural allies of the United States. A combination of similar struggles for independence, compatible values, geographical proximity, economic complementarity, and long-unchallenged U.S. dominance tended to reinforce the notion of regional solidarity. As is emphasized in chapter 2, hemispheric unity was manifest during World War II, then in the founding of the United Nations, and later during the early Cold War. U.S. policy makers have believed that a "special relationship" binds the countries of the Americas, that this close cooperation helps the United States internationally, and that it should therefore be preserved.

Historically, U.S. economic policy in the Western Hemisphere has sought to improve the general climate for U.S. investment, to assist U.S. corporations operating in the region and broadly to facilitate inter-American commerce. Financial and technical assistance missions, public loans and guarantees, insurance schemes, persuasion and less subtle pressures—all have been used to promote U.S. trade and investment and to back particular firms. In periods of international tranquility, when other overriding concerns are absent, U.S. policy has often been identified with particular private interests.

The major concepts underlying historic U.S. policies toward the Western Hemisphere derive largely from the late nineteenth and early twentieth centuries. In that era, direct military threats to the United States were sometimes posed in or through Latin America and the Caribbean; disruption of U.S. shipping, for example, was a major concern. Pan American unity was still central to this country's diplomacy. The "Western Hemisphere idea"—that the United States and Latin America stood together and apart from the rest of the world—was a cornerstone of U.S. foreign policy. Latin America was the main arena for U.S. foreign investment and accounted for a large share of U.S. commerce.

CHANGING REALITIES

Traditional security, political, and economic concerns undoubtedly retain some validity. Their legacy must in any case be taken into account in the political world, where memories count and where interests and power are partly in the eye of the beholder. But whereas our historic interests in Latin America are no longer so important today, Latin America matters for the United States in new ways.

In the security realm, for instance, the nature and degree of the possible risks have changed considerably in recent years. The threat to U.S. military security posed by realistically imaginable events in the Western Hemisphere is much less serious than it used to be. No direct military attack on the territory of the United States is likely to be mounted in the foreseeable future from locations in the Western Hemisphere. Because the probability of attack from the south has declined since 1962—intercontinental missiles launched from bases or submarines are much more threatening—the air defenses of the United States in the southern part of the country have, in fact, been considerably reduced. U.S. bases and other facilities in the Caribbean and Central America have declined in importance. By the late 1970s, the Pentagon had scheduled the closing of half these bases during the mid-1980s and had also begun to cut back U.S. forces in the southeastern United States. Although the trend toward reducing U.S. forces in the Caribbean area has been reversed in the 1980s, and new radar and other facilities have been built or are now planned, the motives for the recent U.S. build-up are more political than defensive. The United States wishes to reverse leftist gains in the Caribbean Basin; it does not fear a military threat.

The essentially symbolic (3,000-man) Soviet presence in Cuba, which cannot have much more than a trip-wire or harassment function, poses no danger to the security of the United States. Nor is any significant military challenge presented by Cuba's armed forces, which have been trained, deployed, and equipped—according to the U.S. Defense Intelligence Agency—primarily for that island's defense, not for invasion of the United States or of any other country. Cuba has built up a substantial military capability in recent years, but it does not have the capacity to project force effectively against hostile countries larger than ministates. The Cuban military build-up since 1980 (which may well be a defensive reaction to the perceived threat from the Reagan administration) would no doubt make it harder for the United States to neutralize Cuba in the event of general war. Some U.S. forces would have to be committed to deal with Cuba in that contingency, and U.S. military planners must take this possibility into account. It is hard to concoct a credible scenario, however, in which Cuba would risk devastation by using its force against the United States or any of its allies.

Should Cuba ever directly attack another Western Hemisphere nation, the United States would be more than capable of repelling the Cuban thrust with conventional forces deployable from bases in the United States. Only in the event of a prolonged conventional general war could Cuba's armed forces seriously affect U.S. force deployment. Logic suggests, and Pentagon war games reportedly confirm, that under those circumstances Cuba would probably disassociate itself from the Soviet Union rather than risk devastation.

Unrestricted access to the Panama Canal remains an important U.S. interest, but it is no longer as "vital" as it used to be. The share of U.S. foreign commerce passing through the canal has declined considerably, to less than one-sixth of this country's ocean-bound trade. Neither today's supertankers nor U.S. aircraft carriers, around which U.S. naval forces are organized, can enter the canal; they are simply too big.

Continued unhampered shipping through the Caribbean's Sea Lanes of Communication (SLOCs) is a vital interest of the United States, for both economic and strategic reasons. Nearly half of the crude oil imported by the United States and a similarly substantial share of this country's foreign commerce pass through Caribbean waters, and these routes would be crucial for resupplying NATO forces in the event of a general war. However, it is difficult to imagine a threat to the sea lanes short of a worldwide military confrontation, in which case interference with U.S. shipping would be much more likely to occur in the North Atlantic than in or near the Caribbean, where overall U.S. predominance remains likely.

The existence in Cuba and in Nicaragua of regimes hostile to the United States and aligned with the Soviet Union undoubtedly complicates U.S. defense planning. In the event of war, certain U.S. antisubmarine warfare facilities might be stretched thin, for example, if they had to deal simultaneously with Soviet forces in the Atlantic and with Cuban (or Nicaraguan)–supported Soviet submarines in the Caribbean. It is time to recognize, however, that absolute U.S. hegemony in the Western Hemisphere—total exclusion of unfriendly vessels from Caribbean waters, for instance—simply can no longer be assured. Unchallenged U.S. dominance of the Caribbean Basin ended with the failed invasion at the Bay of Pigs in 1961, and it is unlikely ever to be restored. That fact needs to be fully incorporated into our thinking about hemispheric security; it cannot be blinked or blustered away.

Every U.S. administration since John F. Kennedy's, including that of Ronald Reagan, has concluded that eliminating the Castro regime in Cuba is not an important enough objective to warrant the enormous cost of achieving it. What *is* achievable at a bearable cost is not the elimination of Soviet influence in the Hemisphere but, rather, the exclusion of Soviet military bases, strategic facilities, and combat forces.

The possibility of a new strategic threat being introduced into the Hemisphere, as occurred in 1962 with the introduction of Soviet missiles into Cuba, cannot be entirely discounted, but it is noteworthy that the Soviet Union's periodic probes to increase its military presence in Cuba since the withdrawal of its missiles in 1962 have always led to a narrower definition of the agreed constraint on their presence. Preventing the introduction of a strategic threat into the Hemisphere rightly remains a primary U.S. objective, one that should be pursued both by military deterrence and by multilateral diplomacy.

Latin America's importance as a source of strategic materials has declined with the expansion of U.S. trade and the increased use of synthetics. Though Latin American and Caribbean countries are still a principal foreign source of many products—iron, copper, tin, bauxite, petroleum, coffee, cocoa, sugar, and bananas—the United States no longer depends on Latin America for any single commodity in the way it depends on South Africa for chrome and on the Soviet Union for platinum. Mexico has become one of our largest sources of imported petroleum, but Mexican oil accounts for less than 5 percent of U.S. consumption, and the oil trade is far more important for Mexico than for the United States.

In sum, although the U.S. retains tangible security concerns in the

Western Hemisphere, these are not as central to inter-American relations as they were decades ago. The possibility that the United States
will someday have to protect itself against a direct military threat in the
Americas cannot be entirely excluded. The aim of preventing Soviet
forces from gaining a foothold in the Hemisphere, therefore, remains
important. But the United States is much more likely to face a critical
challenge to its security interests in the Middle East or Western Europe
than in Latin America or the Caribbean.

Latin America is also less significant for the United States in political
terms. The region's presumed international solidarity with the United
States is both less assured and less important than it used to be.
   It is less assured because many of the central issues in world affairs
place the United States and the countries of Latin America on different
sides. On various "North-South" issues, Latin American nations have
acted like other developing countries, uniting more often against Washington than with it. Although their rhetoric and presumed Third World
solidarity often mask genuine differences of interest and perspective
among themselves, Latin American leaders now take more of their cues
from one another than from Washington.
   Latin American and Caribbean nations are going their own way on
many international questions. Brazil's dependence on Middle Eastern
petroleum has caused it to distance itself from the United States on the
Arab-Israeli conflict and to develop ties with various Arab countries,
including adversaries of the United States. Other Latin American countries have found an intermediate ground on Middle Eastern issues, but
they no longer automatically support the international position of the
United States. In the 1985 session of the United Nations General Assembly, for instance, tiny Grenada was the only country in Latin America and the Caribbean to vote with the United States on more than 50
percent of the issues. Apart from Cuba and Nicaragua, which concurred
with the United States on less than 10 percent of the issues that were
voted on, the three Latin American countries that voted with the United
States least frequently (agreeing with the United States less than 16
percent of the time) were Mexico, Brazil, and Argentina, the region's
three largest nations.
   Even on hemispheric issues, regional solidarity has broken down.
Divisions among Western Hemisphere nations have become even more
pronounced since 1980, despite the Reagan administration's efforts to
reassert inter-American harmony. As chapter 2 points out, the South
Atlantic War of 1982 between Argentina and Great Britain revealed and
reinforced these fissures. Profound disagreements have emerged as
well on Nicaragua and, more generally, on approaches to Central Amer-

ica and the Caribbean, on commercial and financial issues, and even on
Puerto Rico, a matter Washington considers strictly internal.

A Latin American bloc united in support of U.S. foreign policy is no
longer attainable. Even if it were, its importance would now be limited.
In a UN General Assembly swollen to 159 members, a potential bloc of
33 votes means much less than the 20 Latin American votes Washington
could virtually command in the 60-member General Assembly of the
1950s. On key contemporary issues, Washington must expect most
Latin American nations to vote according to their individual interests.
Each vote must be lobbied for; none can be taken for granted on the
basis of presumed regional harmony.

Of the traditional reasons for U.S. concern with Latin America, only
economic interests have expanded in recent years, but these interests,
too, have changed a great deal. The relative significance of direct U.S.
investment in Latin America has declined, while the financial stake this
country has in the region has increased. At the same time, a smaller
share of U.S. imports have come from Latin America, but the region has
become a more important market for U.S. exports.

Latin America's share of total U.S. foreign investment has declined
from 38 percent in 1950 to less than 13 percent in 1985. United States
firms now have almost twice as much invested in Canada than in all of
Latin America and the Caribbean; they have as much invested in the
United Kingdom and Ireland as in all of South America; and more
invested in Denmark than in all of Central America.

The nature of direct U.S. investment has also altered. It used to be
concentrated in natural resource extraction and utilities, sectors that
were directly responsive to state policy and thus were readily affected,
in the days of overwhelming U.S. dominance, by pressures from the
U.S. government. Now U.S. investments are mainly in manufacturing
and services, sectors where international economic competition prevails
and where the United States would have a harder time protecting specific firms even if U.S. influence had not declined.

United States investments in Latin America's manufacturing sector
have created a U.S. interest in the prosperity and the markets of the
region. This was not true of traditional U.S. investments, which were
mostly in export enclaves. Latin America's importance as a market for
U.S. capital goods creates a strong U.S. interest in Latin America's
general economic health, as does the huge financial stake of U.S. banks
in Latin America. This is especially true in the larger countries—Brazil,
Mexico, Argentina, Colombia, and Venezuela—where U.S. investments,
loans, and exports are concentrated.

Much of the established rationale for U.S. concern with the Western Hemisphere, thus, has eroded. From the standpoint of military security, traditional international political support, equity investment, and imports, Latin America is not as important to the United States as it used to be.

That does not mean, of course, that traditional interests have completely disappeared, or that claims about their significance will end soon. On the contrary, the aim to reconstruct a hemispheric policy along classic lines has epitomized the Reagan administration's approach to Latin America. But the familiar case for Washington's concern with the Western Hemisphere is no longer compelling.

TOWARD A REVISED CONCEPT OF U.S. INTERESTS

Although the old reasons for paying attention to Latin America and the Caribbean have been undermined, the countries of the Western Hemisphere could become more important to the United States in the next few years.

Latin America's likely increased significance to the United States derives from a different calculus. U.S. military security is no longer seriously threatened by direct attack from the Western Hemisphere. But U.S. security in a broader sense—the capacity to protect the individual and collective welfare of this country's citizens—could be importantly influenced by events in Latin America and the Caribbean.

Four trends have increased Latin America's potential impact on the United States.

First, Latin America has a growing influence on the economy of the United States and on the world economy. It is an important market for U.S. exports and a major locus of the international activity of U.S. banks. The major Latin American nations (together with advanced developing countries in other regions) could help expand international flows of finance, trade, and technology—or they could contribute to deepening world recession.

Second, massive migration from a few Western Hemisphere nations—particularly Mexico, the Caribbean islands, and some countries in Central America—will directly affect life in the United States.

Third, the larger Latin American countries are well situated either to help resolve or to aggravate some of the most urgent international problems, including narcotics, terrorism, environmental degradation, and nuclear proliferation.

Fourth, circumstances in Latin America and the Caribbean will affect the prospects for preserving values fundamental to the society of the United States, especially respect for individual human rights.

These four factors, not hoary axioms, should orient U.S. policy toward Latin America and the Caribbean. They furnish a framework for determining which issues, countries, and regions are of greatest significance for the United States. And they suggest why substantially increased cooperation with the nations of the Western Hemisphere, rather than an attempt to restore U.S. dominance, would be advisable. Although the countries of Latin America and the Caribbean are no longer docile clients or automatic allies of the U.S., they are potential partners.

Latin America's Economic Significance

Latin America's nations—especially Brazil, Mexico, Argentina, Colombia, and Venezuela—have expanded their role in the world economy and consequently their impact upon the United States. Latin America's general economic conditions, not just the specific interests of U.S. firms, are now important for this country as a whole.

Latin America's increased economic significance for the United States derives from the basic changes in Latin America and this country discussed in chapters 1 and 2. Both the United States and Latin America are increasingly involved in the world economy. Latin America is now far more industrialized than previously, and is thus more important to the United States both as a source of manufactured products and as a market for capital goods. Latin America's massive borrowing from U.S. banks and international institutions significantly affects the U.S. financial system. The United States, in turn, is much more dependent on its international economic relationships than it used to be. Renewed U.S. prosperity depends to a considerable degree on global recovery, including that of the developing countries, and particularly of the advanced developing countries clustered in Latin America.

A few figures help drive this point home.
—Until 1981, Latin America's increasingly industrialized economies constituted a major growth market for U.S. exports of capital goods, including heavy machinery and farm equipment, as well as of agricultural commodities and other items. Eighteen percent of U.S. exports went to Latin America in 1980. From 1976 to 1981, Latin American markets accounted for 25 percent of the growth of U.S. exports. From 1981 through 1983, however, U.S. exports to Latin America fell from $39 billion to $22.6 billion, accounting for about one-half of the worldwide decline in U.S. exports in those years. The drop in U.S. exports to Latin America is estimated to have cost the United States at least

half a million jobs, and perhaps twice that figure. The estimated potential Latin American contribution to reviving U.S. exports is substantial, probably as much as 20 percent of the current U.S. trade deficit.

—Almost one-third of all U.S. corporate profits today derive from the overseas activities of U.S. firms. In 1985, Latin America accounted for some 20 percent of earnings abroad by U.S. firms.

—Despite a nearly 40 percent decline in the claims-to-capital ratio since the height of the debt crisis in 1982, the nine largest U.S. banks had, on average, over 140 percent of their primary capital exposed in Latin America at the end of 1986. Nearly 100 percent of the primary capital of all U.S. banks, on average, was exposed in Latin America as of that date. A significant share of these banks' profits still derives from their Latin American activities.

Latin America is important in the world economy of the 1980s. If Latin America can resume expanding its imports of industrial products, capital goods, and services and also increase its exports of manufactured goods, agricultural products, raw materials (including energy), and labor, this could help restore dynamism to the international economy. Latin America's exports could also help the world cope with the specter of inflation, both by reducing the risk of shortages and by keeping down the price of those goods on which Latin American producers have a comparative advantage. Orderly service of Latin America's massive debts, even though on the basis of some relief, would also make a substantial contribution to world recovery.

By the same token, however, prolonged economic decline in Latin America could have severe international consequences. If Brazil were unable to surmount its economic problems—whether because of heavy debt servicing, rising costs for many of its imports, increased Northern protectionism against its exports, falling demand for its products, or as yet unforeseen factors—the impact would reverberate in the international system. If Mexico could not resolve its present difficulties (for the same reasons, compounded by the reduced world price of oil), the international effects would be serious and the impact on the United States, so closely tied to Mexico, would be immediate and direct. Simultaneous default by several major Latin American countries could severely hurt individual U.S. banks and could harm the U.S. banking system and even the international financial order. Prolonged Latin American economic reversal would be felt most strongly in the United States—the source of so much of Latin America's capital, technology, industrial goods, and other imports, and the destination of most of Latin America's products and surplus labor.

A major challenge for U.S. policy is to help shape procedures and institutions that will facilitate expanded exchange in a world in which political power and productive capacity are much more widely dispersed than previously. New rules and modes of exchange are needed to help produce a new opening of global trade—a freer flow of capital, technology, and labor.

Following World War II, the United States took the lead in organizing international trade and monetary arrangements. It promoted the establishment of such institutions as the International Monetary Fund, the International Bank for Reconstruction and Development, and the General Agreement on Tariffs and Trade (GATT). These institutions worked effectively, and international economic transactions multiplied. Sustained economic growth occurred at unprecedented rates in both the industrial and the developing countries.

As U.S. dominance has receded since the 1960s, many of the established arrangements have suffered crises. This country's sudden devaluation of the dollar in 1971, along with subsequent U.S. monetary policies, helped to undermine the Bretton Woods financial structures; the dollar was no longer "as good as gold." Liberal trade policies increasingly have given way to protectionist restrictions.

On many issues, both technical and political, international economic structures are now facing a severe challenge. The next few years may see an intensifying struggle, such as that which characterized the 1930s, with nations each pursuing "beggar-thy-neighbor" policies to the eventual detriment of all concerned: monetary policies geared toward immediate advantage, protectionist trading practices, and generally neomercantilist approaches.

Latin American countries, particularly the larger ones, complain that some established international practices discriminate against them. They want to restructure existing debts so as to lengthen maturities, lower interest rates, reduce fees and spreads, and keep debt service obligations to a reasonable share of export earnings. They seek to improve the terms of trade, to gain better access to capital and technology, and to take a greater role in decision making within international organizations. But they share with the United States the overriding aim of expanding international economic exchange. If policies of cooperation are pursued, Latin America and the United States could help each other strengthen the world economy.

A more effective and stable international economic order is more likely to emerge if the advanced developing countries of Latin America and elsewhere in the Third World participate fully in its design. These nations will not be defenseless if the international system fails to address their interests. If exports from Latin American and other newly industrial countries encounter worsening Northern protectionism, these nations might eventually attempt restrictive reprisals: increased protectionism of their own, debt delays or defaults, perhaps even a debtors' cartel. If international monetary institutions do not take into account the need of Latin America's economies, then Brazil, Mexico, Argentina, and other countries will have a greater incentive to push for inflationary growth of the world money supply. If international commerce in commodities does not become more predictable and profitable for developing countries, renewed efforts to build other cartels on the OPEC model can be anticipated. Even if no cartel is likely to be as successful as OPEC was in the 1970s, the resulting friction would hamper efficient international trade. If multinational corporations and their home governments are not sensitive to the needs of host governments, a new surge of nationalist and populist policies may emerge. Restrictions on profit remittances, discriminatory taxes, more stringent requirements regarding the proportion of local materials and local personnel used in the manufacturing process, higher export level requirements, and even outright nationalizations in some cases—all are possible.

If international institutions do not provide adequately for the expanded participation of key Latin American and other Third World countries, Southern ties might solidify along radical lines. This could affect not only economic issues but also the Law of the Sea, nuclear proliferation, the Middle East, environmental protection, and other issues. The chances of shaping an effective and expansive international order will depend to a considerable degree on whether Latin American nations feel their economic, political, and status-psychological interests have been fairly taken into account.

Migration

Immigration from Mexico—legal and illegal, seasonal and long-term—is increasingly visible in the United States today. Estimates of the number of persons of Mexican descent living in this country range from eight million to fifteen million. Taking into account those who work in the United States for a significant part of each year, a reasonable guess, including illegal immigrants, would be at least ten million. Persons of Mexican descent comprise the majority in some regions of the United States. And the flow of Mexicans into this country has stepped up dramatically in the 1980s in the face of Mexico's major economic setback.

Latino students now outnumber non-Hispanic whites in the public schools of Los Angeles; by the end of the 1980s, the majority of public school students in four southwestern states are expected to be of Mexican descent. Even without additional immigration, the percentage of Latinos in the U.S. population would grow, because their birthrate is considerably higher than the U.S. mean. Early in the next century, Hispanic-Americans will probably become a majority in the work force of California. The Spanish-speaking community in the United States is already the world's fifth largest; by the end of the century, it is expected to become larger than Spain's and second only to that of Mexico.

The highly visible Mexican immigration, primarily but not exclusively to the "Sun Belt" states, is paralleled by a significant influx from the Caribbean and from Central America. These waves are primarily directed toward the eastern states, especially southern Florida, New York, New Jersey, New England, and the District of Columbia, although there is also a substantial Central American flow to California.

One out of every eight living persons born in the Caribbean now resides outside that region, mostly in the continental United States. Close to five million Caribbean-born persons have entered the United States since World War II, from Puerto Rico, Cuba, the Dominican Republic, Haiti, Jamaica, Barbados, and numerous other islands. The highly publicized entry of Cubans has been paralleled by immigration from elsewhere in the Caribbean at a similar rate. What might have once seemed like a series of special cases is now understood to be a sustained, regionwide response to shared demographic pressures and to the U.S. labor market.

Since the late 1970s, the pace of immigration from Central America has also intensified; in the past ten years, at least half a million persons are estimated to have entered the United States from El Salvador alone, and the flow from both El Salvador and Nicaragua is increasing.

These massive migrations will affect the United States in such areas as education, employment, public health, business, politics, and culture. Local governments in regions with high concentrations of immigrants must devise special programs to service the immigrants' needs for education, public health, and other services. Substandard working conditions and depressed wage scales, often below the mandated minimum wage, sometimes adversely affect the existing pool of low-income native-born workers, including those of Hispanic descent. In a few regions, agricultural harvesting, labor in some industries, and certain services (for example, in restaurants and car wash establishments) have become dependent on illegal alien workers. Conversely, however, immigrant workers are estimated to contribute considerably more in taxes than the cost of the services they consume, and their presence has made it possible to keep open businesses, employing many other workers, that might otherwise fail. Whatever the ultimate balance, Latin American migration has a significant economic impact on the United States.

The presence of millions of recent immigrants of Latin American and Caribbean background, many of them illegal entrants, affects the assimilation process for the far larger number of persons of Hispanic descent and reinforces discrimination against them in some regions. The degree of residential segregation of U.S.-born Hispanics appears to be directly related to the percentage of recent immigrants of that background in the particular area. More generally, an ugly backlash has begun to emerge against immigration from Latin America and the Caribbean, illustrated by trends in several regions to bar bilingual education and to insist on English alone being used for official purposes. Efforts in recent years to stem the tide of immigration, particularly by concentrating on border enforcement, have not been successful, leading to frustrations, frictions, and a sense that control has been lost of an important element of national sovereignty.

Conditions in Latin America and the Caribbean that influence migration flows will directly affect the United States, therefore. The failure of Latin American economies to generate sufficient employment opportunities, combined with social dislocation due to upheaval or repression, creates powerful migratory drives. This pressure cannot be reduced without substantial changes in the underlying conditions of Latin America and the Caribbean.

The immigrant communities from Latin America and the Caribbean already in the United States are bound to influence how this country conceives its stake in the Hemisphere's social and economic conditions. In California, Texas, and Florida—increasingly important states in electoral terms—voters of Hispanic and Caribbean origin are already crucial. In these areas, Latin American issues are increasingly salient in the political debate. The nature of inter-American relations, in short, will be reshaped by the northward flow of millions from Latin America and the Caribbean.

International Problems

In addition to their potential importance in helping to shape the global economic order, Latin American countries will substantially influence how the world deals with other key international issues. Among the major challenges of the next few years will be:
—how to control and curb the burgeoning narcotics traffic, with its corrosive impact on individuals and societies;
—how to combat terrorism, increasingly a transnational phenomenon;
—how to limit the proliferation of nuclear weapons technology;

—how to avoid aggravating the problems of industrial pollution and environmental degradation;
—how to expand the production, marketing, and distribution of food so that hunger and its sociopolitical consequences are reduced;
—how to manage the production, conservation, marketing, and distribution of renewable and nonrenewable sources of energy to maintain supplies at reasonable and predictable prices; and
—how to manage the efficient development of other raw materials, including those of the seas.

On each of these issues, Latin American countries are crucial. The drug problem cannot be solved without effective narcotics control in Bolivia, Colombia, Ecuador, Mexico, and Peru—and in the United States; no one nation can deal effectively with the issue by itself. A number of Latin American countries, particularly Brazil and Mexico, are central to the issues of global resource management and environmental protection. Argentina and Brazil are among the most likely potential nuclear powers. Mexico and Venezuela (with its tar belts) have the resources to expand petroleum production, and Colombia is a key source of coal. Latin America is a prime area for expanded agricultural production.

On all these matters, securing the cooperation of Latin American countries, in the mutual interest of all, should be a central goal of U.S. foreign policy. That cooperation cannot be assumed or coerced; it will have to be achieved.

Fundamental Values and Foreign Policy

Less demonstrably but not less importantly, the climate for the preservation of values basic for North American society will also be affected by conditions in Latin America and the Caribbean.

The rise of bureaucratic-authoritarian regimes in Latin America during the 1960s and 1970s, some of them directly or indirectly supported by U.S. policies, raised troubling questions about whether the United States was contributing, inadvertently or perhaps even consciously, to the institutionalization of injustice. As a nation committed to freedom, equity, and respect for the individual, this country cannot comfortably appear to induce or even condone poverty or repression anywhere, especially in a region where U.S. influence is important. Explicit or even tacit alliances between the United States and repressive regimes inevitably produce a tension between this nation's domestic consensus and its foreign policy. Failure by the U.S. government to concern itself with dire poverty and grossly inequitable income distribution, especially in neighboring countries tied to the United States by shared traditions and continuing interpenetration, would evoke a similar strain. Systematic contradictions of this sort, if continued over time, could erode the credibility of our national values and the commitment of our citizens. Those who take seriously our nation's heritage and proclaimed values will necessarily object to U.S. cooperation with repressive regimes in Latin America.

What is more, the prospects for good relations with the countries of the Hemisphere are enhanced when Latin America's governments base themselves on public support rather than on brute force. Political order based on repression is ultimately fragile and volatile—Iran, Nicaragua, South Africa, Haiti, and the Philippines are only the most recent and obvious examples. The transformation of Latin America discussed in chapter 1 reinforces this point. Only participatory processes can bring lasting stability to the increasingly modern, mobilized, and complex societies of Latin America.

It is fundamentally in the interest of the United States, therefore, to support Latin American efforts to base development on individual autonomy, social equity, and civic participation rather than on repression and inequality. The United States has a legitimate reason for helping to show the viability of the open and democratic way.

IMPLICATIONS FOR U.S. POLICY

Latin American and Caribbean nations, thus, will matter increasingly to the United States for four reasons: (1) their economic and political weight; (2) their demographic links with the United States; (3) their capacity to affect global problems; and (4) their effect on the climate for preserving basic U.S. values. Focusing sharply on these interests would help the United States define more clearly which countries, regions, and issues will be of greatest consequence. Understanding how and why Latin America will affect the United States in the future should help this country design more effective policies.

Brazil and Mexico (and to a lesser degree Argentina, Venezuela, and Colombia) will be most significant in the areas of international influence and problem-solving capacity; their cooperation will be increasingly vital for the United States. Mexico and the Caribbean islands (and to a lesser extent Central America) will be important because of migration. All the countries of the Hemisphere will affect the climate for protecting U.S. values, but this will be true especially of Mexico on our border, the Caribbean islands most fully in our country's orbit, and all the nations struggling to assure respect for fundamental rights.

Taking all four criteria together, U.S. interests are most fully engaged in the relationships with Mexico, Brazil, and the Caribbean islands. Mexico is a large nation so intertwined with the United States that domestic choices there inevitably affect the United States. Brazil is a country of such scope that it has a major impact upon the rest of Latin America and upon the United States. The islands of the Caribbean have an effect upon this country—derived from proximity, compounded by migration—that greatly exceeds their size.

Conversely, this analysis implies that the United States does not have a major stake in Central America's turmoil. The countries of Central America are small and weak. Their capacity to resolve international problems is limited. U.S. investment, financial, and commercial interests are meager. The region's persistent failure to achieve lasting democracy or sustained respect for human rights has never had a profound impact upon the United States, because Central America's economic and demographic connections with this country have been much less significant than those of the Caribbean and Mexico. And Central America's economy—primarily dependent on the export of bananas, coffee, cotton, cocoa, and sugar—is likely to remain integrated into the international capitalist system on more or less the same terms, regardless of the region's internal politics, unless (as in the case of Nicaragua) the United States imposes economic sanctions.

The U.S. interest in Central America, therefore, is sharply circumscribed. The current U.S. response to Central America's turmoil—the impulse toward ever-deeper U.S. involvement—has more to do with inherited attitudes than with objective realities.

The issues on which U.S. policy should focus in the future are those highlighted in this chapter: trade, finance, and investment; migration; resource management; narcotics control; and democracy and human rights. These are the questions of the future. Concern about who governs in Central America responds primarily to a yearning for the past, for a recovery of hegemony lost.

President Reagan and many others talk about the Central American crisis in terms of U.S. "national security" interests. That terminology obscures the main point. What is at stake for Washington in Central America is not so much national security but, rather, "national *in*security": the discomfort of coping with loss of control, of something we are used to controlling, even when control may not be worth as much as it once was, and even when it is very costly to retain or restore. Fashioning a policy to deal with this problem, and with the attendant issues of self-esteem and international prestige, will not be simple. But it may be easier for the United States to forge a sensible approach if we understand clearly that a main concern in Central America is psychopolitical— and if we put that concern into proper perspective.

The central argument of this book can now be advanced. It would be best for the United States if Washington looked beyond the current (and partly self-imposed) crisis of credibility in Central America. The security and stability of the Americas are more deeply threatened by Latin America's economic problems than by the internal conflicts in Central America. Latin America's transformation during the past generation creates significant opportunities for inter-American cooperation, but these opportunities are being overlooked because of the obsession of the United States with Central America. The countries of Latin America and the United States are potential partners, but they are increasingly at odds.

The United States should adopt policies that respond to Latin America's needs. New approaches are required to resolve the hemispheric crisis of debt and growth and to reinforce the regionwide turn toward democracy. The United States should focus much more on trade, finance, and migration—and less on MIGs and guerrillas. It is high time for the United States to design more effective policies toward Mexico, Brazil, and the islands of the Caribbean—and to become less absorbed in Central America.

CHAPTER FOUR

The United States and Mexico

Uneasy Neighbors

No country in the Western Hemisphere, and very few anywhere, affects the United States more than Mexico. No other country (not even Canada) is more pervasively influenced by the United States than our neighbor to the south. Probably no bilateral relationship in the world is more complex.

On each side of the nearly two-thousand-mile border, millions of persons—employers and workers, tourists and thieves, migrants and millionaires—engage in an intricate web of transactions, most of them legal but many not. Countless problems arise between the two countries every year. They include not only classic questions of international affairs, but also many domestic choices in each country which significantly affect the other: choices on budgets, taxes, welfare, labor, and immigration.

It has long been obvious that what happens in the United States significantly influences Mexico. The general health of the U.S. economy, especially interest and employment rates, evidently has a major impact on our southern neighbor. What has become much more clear in the past few years is that what happens in Mexico can also substantially affect the United States.

Mexico's recent economic difficulties—its downturn in 1976 and especially the more serious and prolonged crisis since 1982, Mexico's worst recession in fifty years—have underscored the country's importance to the United States. Eight of the ten largest U.S. banks have more than one-third of their primary capital at risk in Mexico, so that Mexico's ability to service its foreign debt is important to the U.S. financial system: The reduction in U.S. exports to the troubled Mexican economy has cost nearly three hundred thousand jobs (actual and potential) in the United States. Repeated sharp devaluations of the peso have severely hurt business in a number of U.S. border cities. Illegal migration into the United States has swelled in the 1980s. So has the flow from Mexico to the United States of dangerous drugs.

The people and the government of the United States have long taken Mexico for granted, however: it has been considered a good place to visit, even to retire, a sure (if sometimes touchy) friend of the United States in case of a grave international crisis, but not a major cause for enduring concern. Episodic bursts of attention to Mexico have never been sustained. According to one poll, 98 percent of U.S. leaders and some 75 percent of the U.S. public would say that Mexico is of "vital interest" to the United States, but very few in this country know much about what Alan Riding has called our "distant neighbor." Press coverage of Mexico in the United States has generally been minimal and stereotyped.

In the mid-1970s, Mexico's announcement of its major deposits of oil and gas quickly produced an outcropping of studies and seminars in the United States. Mexico's financial crunch in 1982 brought this border country, in turn, to the business sections and then to the front pages of U.S. newspapers. Mexico's even graver problems in the mid- and late 1980s—deepening economic and social problems, compounded by natural disasters—renewed U.S. concern. But public understanding in the United States of what is at stake in the relationship with Mexico is still lacking.

This country's incomprehension of Mexico was illustrated during the late 1970s by the discussion of a proposed "North American Common Market" or "North American Accord," which would have included Canada, Mexico, and the United States. Political leaders of such different tendencies as Jerry Brown of California, John Connally of Texas, and Ronald Reagan (the last during the 1980 presidential campaign) pushed the idea, despite highly negative reactions in both Canada and Mexico. Precisely what many Mexicans see as the greatest problem in bilateral relations—the threat of increased influence by the United States—was presented by proponents of the common market concept as if it were the solution. Even when U.S. indifference to Mexico gives way to concern, gross insensitivity often persists.

By the beginning of the 1980s, this combination of heightened importance and sustained insensitivity had brought U.S. relations with Mexico to a low point. Numerous incidents punctuated this decline. Mexican President Luis Echeverría's flamboyant Third World–oriented policies in the mid-1970s stimulated antagonistic responses in the United States, including from seventy-six members of Congress, who publicly warned

in 1976 of Mexico's drift toward "communism." Former President
Jimmy Carter's mishandling of his trip to Mexico in 1978 also contributed to the deterioration of relations. The erection by the United States
in 1978 of a barbed-wire fence along part of the Texas-Mexico frontier
provoked emotional reactions in Mexico. Frictions grew as well over
restrictive proposals by the Carter administration to amend U.S. immigration laws and procedures; Mexico's decisions not to allow the exiled
Shah of Iran to reside there and not to join the General Agreement on
Tariffs and Trade; and Mexico's refusal to provide compensation for the
extensive damages done to the Texas coastline by the massive Ixtoc I oil
spill in 1979. Differences regarding how to respond to revolutionary
movements in Central America compounded these tensions.

In 1980, Ronald Reagan's announcement that his only preinaugural
visit abroad would be to Mexico symbolized the new administration's
aim to reverse this deterioration. Within weeks, however, Mexico and
the United States resumed serious clashes. Mexico abrogated its fishing
agreement with the United States late in December 1980. Shortly thereafter, in separate disputes, Mexico announced that it would keep San
Diego's tuna and shrimp boats out of its territorial waters. President
José López Portillo warned that U.S. policies in Central America might
lead to another Vietnam, while at the same time he declared his admira-
tion for Fidel Castro.

Some of the frictions between the United States and Mexico were
soon worked out in cordial discussions between Reagan and López Portillo, but others remained. The Reagan administration's decision to undertake emergency measures to shore up Mexico's shaky finances in
August 1982 did not end bilateral tensions. Nor was the succession to
the Mexican presidency of Miguel de la Madrid, Harvard educated and
U.S. oriented, enough to stop U.S.-Mexico conflicts. On the contrary,
they have been increasing during the 1980s, even while intimate cooperation between the two governments on energy and finance has been
taking place.

Early in 1985, heavy-handed U.S. pressures on Mexico to step up its
drug enforcement efforts dramatized a new deterioration in bilateral
relations. Later in the year, on the very day that Mexico City was
shocked by the first of two massive earthquakes, the International Monetary Fund in Washington had announced new financial pressures on
Mexico and the U.S. Senate passed legislation to restrict Mexican migration.

Tensions in U.S.-Mexico relations continued to build in 1986. The
chairman of the U.S. Senate's Subcommittee on Western Hemisphere
Affairs, Jesse Helms, accused Mexican government officials of corruption and involvement in the narcotics trade, and he attributed the Mexi-

can governing party's electoral victories to fraud; some of his charges appeared to be corroborated by the testimony of administration officials. On the same day that Presidents Reagan and de la Madrid met to smooth things over, an official of the U.S. Drug Enforcement Administration complained that he had been arrested and tortured by Mexican police. The climate of U.S.-Mexico relations grew increasingly tense. "Mexico bashing" became part of the political discourse in the United States, and Mexican resentments continued to build.

MEXICO'S TRANSFORMATION: GROWTH AND CRISIS

Since the end of World War II, and especially during this past generation, Mexico has changed profoundly. It has grown, modernized, and been transformed: from overwhelmingly agricultural to increasingly industrial, from mainly rural to primarily urban, from strongly provincial to defiantly cosmopolitan, from a relatively tranquil neighbor of the United States to an ever more restless and troubled one.

A striking dimension of Mexico's transformation has been demographic. Mexico is the eleventh most populous nation in the world; its population has reached some 82 million, more than twice what it was in 1959 (three times what it was in 1950), and greater than West Germany's today. Infant mortality has dropped dramatically and average life expectancy has increased. Mexico's urban population rose from about one-third of the total in 1940 to one-half in 1960 and over two-thirds by 1980. About 18 million persons crowd Mexico City, almost as many people as live in all of Central America. Although fertility rates in Mexico have dropped remarkably since 1970, most experts believe Mexico's population will reach at least 110 million by the year 2000; even the most conservative government projections forecast 100 million.

A second major aspect of Mexico's change has been economic. Mexico's aggregate economic growth after 1940, and especially from 1960 through 1980, was striking. Its average annual real rate of economic growth for 1940 to 1960 was greater than 6 percent. Mexico's gross domestic product reached over $175 billion in 1987, making Mexico's the world's eleventh or twelfth-largest market economy. Per capita income has climbed to almost $2,200 a year.

The structure of Mexico's economy has also changed fundamentally. The share of Mexico's economically active population employed in agriculture has declined sharply, from 65 percent in 1940 to 55 percent in 1960 and about 30 percent in the 1980s. The share of Mexico's national product accounted for by manufacturing climbed from 17 percent in 1940 to 25 percent in 1979, before dropping back to about 22 percent in the mid-1980s. Although agriculture remains a major employer, its contribution to the Mexican economy had fallen below 10 percent of GDP by 1979.

Mexico's social structure has been transformed by the combined effects of urbanization, industrialization, and modernization. Mexico's middle class grew more (in absolute terms) from 1960 to 1980 than it did during the country's entire previous history. The number of Mexicans participating in the rapidly expanding modern economy increased sharply during these same years. Education boomed; the number of children finishing elementary school doubled during the 1970s, and the share of Mexicans of university age obtaining higher education jumped from 3 percent in 1960 to some 15 percent in 1980.

A fourth major change in Mexico during the past generation has been institutional. The Mexican state has grown enormously since 1950, and especially since 1970. The number of state-owned or state-controlled enterprises mushroomed to more than one thousand by the end of 1982. The number of public sector employees climbed, the degree and effect of state intervention in the economy grew, and Mexico's economy became increasingly centralized.

By the late 1960s, these demographic, economic, social, and institutional changes had begun to generate problems. The limits of easy import substitution had been reached, and new industrial growth became much harder to achieve. Mexico's work force was expanding much faster than employment opportunities. An increasingly educated and politicized generation of young people was frustrated by the lack of opportunity for effective political participation. The economic, social, and political repercussions of all these bottlenecks began to be evident in the late 1960s. Growing concern about them culminated in a series of protests on the eve of the 1968 Olympic Games in Mexico, protests that led to the massacre of scores (hundreds, by some estimates) of student demonstrators by army troops at Tlatelolco Square in October.

Political protest subsided after the Tlatelolco incident, particularly as a result of the co-optive approach of President Luis Echeverría in the early 1970s. Renewed economic difficulties arose by the mid-1970s, however, compounded by the increasing social and political polarization that arose in response both to the economic problems and to Echeverría's populist policies. By 1976, during the final months of Echeverría's term, class tensions were rife, land invasions by peasants were multiplying, capital flight soared, and a major devaluation of the peso was required. There were even hints that a military threat to Mexico's institutional stability might be contemplated. Mexico in the mid-1970s seemed to many a nation in crisis.

Then, in 1976, Mexico announced its major deposits of petroleum and natural gas. A new boom began. Oil production climbed from 575 thousand barrels a day in 1974 to more than 2.75 million in 1982. Mexico became the world's fourth-largest oil producer, the biggest in Latin America, and the main source of U.S. crude oil imports.

The petroleum bonanza, reinforced by the government's investment policy and by increased foreign investment and massive external loans, fueled a major expansion in many sectors. Electric generating capacity nearly tripled during the 1970s. Production of petrochemicals, steel, and cement exploded. Mexico rapidly built the infrastructure for a concerted drive to accelerate its industrialization. Mexican exports (mainly of oil but also of manufactured goods to some extent) grew rapidly, though imports jumped even faster.

Foreign investment flowed to Mexico during the late 1960s, and then again in the late 1970s, after oil was discovered. Direct foreign investment rose from $2.3 billion in 1968 to more than $10 billion in 1980. Mexico's total external public debt skyrocketed even more quickly, from $3.2 billion in 1970 to more than $50 billion in 1980. Mexico became the second-largest borrower from the World Bank, as well as the holder of the developing world's second-largest foreign private bank debt. Mexico's prospects for continuing growth seemed so promising that *Institutional Investor* identified it in 1981 as one of three Third World countries with the best credit ratings. Mexico's combined public and private foreign debt reached some $75 billion in 1981.

But the music slowed in 1981 and virtually stopped in 1982. The immediate causes were international; petrodollar revenues declined because of a world oil glut beginning in 1981, while world interest rates jumped in part because of U.S. policies to fight domestic inflation. But the root causes of Mexico's difficulties were primarily internal. A galloping public sector deficit (almost 18 percent of the gross domestic product in 1982)—arising largely from the combination of grandiose oil boom projects and the inefficiency and corruption of a bloated public sector—fed inflation. Diminishing agricultural productivity led to increased imports of grain and other food products. Expanded imports of food, capital goods, and consumer products contributed to a trade deficit of $3.2 billion in 1982. Sustained high real interest rates on Mexico's external debt aggravated these problems; Mexico's interest burden rose from $5.4 billion due in 1980 to $8.2 billion in 1981 and nearly $10 billion in 1982.

The economy declined sharply in 1982, registering no growth for the first time in memory. Unemployment and underemployment rose to unprecedented levels, affecting almost one-half of the work force. Inflation went over 100 percent. New foreign direct investment fell by about 50 percent. A cumulating sense of collapse contributed to massive capital flight.

By mid-1982, Mexico faced a national crisis of liquidity, if not of solvency. The gathering calamity came to a head in August, when Mexico's government acknowledged that it could not keep up its debt service payments. An emergency program of U.S. government assistance, devised in an intense weekend of frantic negotiations in Washington, provided Mexico the cash to meet its immediate obligations. In return, however, Washington extracted a substantial amount of Mexican oil at a preferential price, as well as Mexico's agreement to implement IMF-approved austerity recipes. Although President López Portillo soon sought to regain public esteem by nationalizing Mexico's private banks, he could not eliminate a widespread perception that Mexico had failed.

This image of utter failure was somewhat overdrawn. In part it was an artifact of Mexico's sexennial cycle; a Mexican president loses authority toward the end of his term, and tough issues are left to accumulate. To some degree, it reflected the extent to which the world was surprised by Mexico's plight. To some extent, in fact, Mexican policy makers may have consciously exaggerated their country's woes to attract sympathetic attention in Washington and New York. The sense of sudden crisis also revealed the biases of a few alarmist policy makers within the Reagan administration, some of whom had long predicted major problems in Mexico.

Mexico's difficulties are indeed severe, however. Mexico had another bad year in 1983—with gross domestic product down more than 5 percent, national investment down 25 percent, and open unemployment up to more than 12 percent. Some recovery began in 1984; by the end of that year, Mexico had cut annual inflation to about 59 percent, economic growth (albeit modest) had been resumed, and the federal deficit had been reduced to more or less manageable proportions (less than 8 percent of GDP). But this progress could not be sustained in 1985, due primarily to the falling price of oil, overwhelmingly Mexico's major export. Mexico's economic picture clouded again.

Then, in September 1985, Mexico City suffered two devastating earthquakes that took at least five thousand lives, caused billions of dollars in damage, and severely dampened tourism. Further sharp declines in the price of oil in 1986 brought Mexico's economy into severe trauma. Capital flight reached new levels, unemployment and underemployment climbed, new investment stopped, inflation rose again, and the value of the peso plummeted. 1987 brought some relief at first, but then another downturn, and the economic crisis continues.

Mexico's recurrent and deepening difficulties in the 1980s have resulted from and drawn attention to the country's underlying problems. Mexico's fundamental difficulties had begun to be evident in the late 1960s, were temporarily allayed during the early 1970s, flared anew in the mid-1970s, but were then camouflaged for several years by the oil-induced expansion. While Mexico's oil-fueled economy was booming in the late 1970s, the basic problems that had become evident earlier continued to worsen. Mexico's locally oriented agriculture, neglected by government policy for many years, had become less productive. Far from keeping up with population growth, food production was so stagnant by 1983 that Mexico had to import 50 percent of the country's grain needs, up from 10 percent in 1975. Much of Mexico's industry—protected from international competition by tariffs, subsidies, import licenses, and quotas—became inefficient and uncompetitive. The Mexican government and its state and parastatal enterprises grew too large.

Mexico's problems in the 1980s arise in part from the fact that from 1950 through the 1970s Mexico's growth was not only very rapid but also highly uneven. While modern Mexico has been growing, many of the country's citizens have been left out. Seventy-five years after the Revolution, and after forty years of industrial transformation, many Mexicans have yet to reap the benefits of these two processes.

The share of Mexico's income received by the lowest 20 percent of income earners has actually fallen since 1950, to less than 3 percent. Half of Mexico's population today earns only 17 percent of the country's income, while the top 10 percent appropriate over 40 percent. Nearly half of the dwellings surveyed in the 1980 census lacked sewage connections, 29 percent had no piped water, and 25 percent no electricity. More than 20 percent of Mexican adults are still functionally illiterate. At least forty million Mexicans, about half, are believed to suffer nutritional deficiencies. The entry of at least three-quarters of a million persons (perhaps closer to a million) into the labor force each year clouds employment prospects. The real wages of the working class have fallen more than 30 percent since 1982, down to the level of the mid-1960s. The recession threatens to wipe out a generation of gains.

Millions of Mexicans are severely alienated. Urban crime rates are up, as are the incidences of alcoholism and drug abuse. Despite the institutionalized political dominance of Mexico's government party (the Partido Revolucionario Institucional, PRI), opposition parties have been showing unprecedented electoral strength in recent years. As the political opposition grows, the PRI faces the prospect either of sharing power or of retaining its hold through fraud or intimidation; neither option is attractive. Public attitudes about the government and the political system in Mexico, cited a generation ago as a positive model of a "civic culture," now reflect deep resentment over corruption, repression, and privilege.

Unless Mexico can regain the momentum of economic dynamism, spread its benefits more widely and equitably, and renew widespread public confidence, pressures on Mexico's long-term stability will continue to increase. Mexico is by no means a tranquil neighbor. It is deeply troubled, and its troubles are increasingly affecting the United States.

THE CONTEXT OF U.S.-MEXICO RELATIONS

U.S. relations with Mexico will be shaped in the future not only by these serious problems but also by several other fundamental factors: by the two countries' extended contiguity and their resulting interconnection; by the major asymmetries between them; by the differences between their economic, social, cultural, and political traditions; and by the history the two peoples share but understand so differently.

The U.S.-Mexico border is the longest anywhere between an advanced industrial country and a developing one. Inevitably porous, the boundary assures that Mexico and the United States will be closely tied. The border is crossed, legally or illegally, more than 300 million times a year. Almost 10 million persons dwell in the towns on either side. They work in a more or less integrated transnational capital and labor market. The northern states of Mexico, long oriented toward economic and cultural exchange with the United States, are in many ways more closely tied to this country than to Mexico City.

Decisions taken on one side of the border quickly affect life on the other. Retail sales and employment in Chula Vista, San Ysidro, El Paso, and elsewhere along the frontier drop sharply after each Mexican devaluation. Diseases of plants, animals, and humans spread easily from one country to the other. Sewage disposal, copper smelting, smog, and oil spills on one side of the border produce pollution on the other. Strikes in one nation disrupt commerce in both. Ground water use in one country affects ground water quality in the other. Capital and labor flow easily back and forth, regardless of what the two governments decree. The difficulties Mexico had in implementing exchange controls in September 1982 provided a textbook illustration of this point; the problems the United States has faced in enforcing its immigration laws provide another. The reciprocal impact of the two countries is seen in the areas of health, education, social services, economic development, employment and trade unions, culture, and law enforcement.

Mexico has attempted in recent years to diversify its international relationships, but its ties with the United States have nevertheless become more extensive. Trade between the United States and Mexico nearly quadrupled (mainly because of oil) between 1976 and 1981, reaching $31 billion in 1981. Although bilateral commerce fell dramatically in 1982 and 1983, when Mexico had to constrict its imports very sharply, it was back to over $30 billion in 1984 and 1985. Mexico is the third-largest trading partner of the United States and the third-largest market for U.S. exports.

U.S. direct private investment in Mexico has grown to more than $8 billion. Although Mexico has tried to attract investment from Japan and Europe, U.S. sources still account for close to 65 percent of Mexico's foreign investment. More than 75 percent of U.S. investment in Mexico now is in industry, thus tying U.S. firms closely to Mexico's most dynamic sector, aside from energy.

The financial connections between the United States and Mexico have also multiplied dramatically. The approximately 27-billion-dollar exposure of U.S. commercial banks amounts to about one-fourth of Mexico's foreign debt and nearly one-half of its debt to private lenders. The U.S. share in Mexico's finance has grown during Mexico's crisis, as European lenders have become more cautious. Before 1982, moreover, pressures were growing to allow for an even more substantial flow of U.S. capital to Mexico, through measures to allow insurance companies to increase the share of their assets which can legally be invested in Mexico.

Links between Mexico and the United States go well beyond trade, investment, and finance. There are cultural ties, as well. Monday-night football and major league baseball games from the United States are telecast live to Mexico City. Many of the most popular television programs in Mexico are produced in the United States, and Mexican television provides considerable material for the burgeoning Spanish-language television market in the United States. One of Mexico's best-selling magazines is *Selecciones del Readers Digest*. Almost all of Mexico's advertising agencies are U.S. controlled. The fast-food cuisine of the United States has penetrated Mexico, just as tortilla chips and tacos have become part of the diet in the United States.

Tourism between the two countries is big business. More U.S. air passengers go to Mexico than to any other foreign destination, and Mexico is the second-largest single source of tourists for this country. The effect of Mexico's severe depression in 1982–83 on that country's middle class significantly decreased travel abroad during those two years, but by 1984 it was up again.

Perhaps the major tie between the two countries is the massive, sustained migration of Mexicans to work (and some to stay) in the United States. No comparably large movement of people back and forth across a national frontier has continued longer. Well over 1 million Mexican workers enter the United States each year; the numbers and the estimates fluctuate sharply, but they have been rising dramatically during the 1980s. Some come legally, but most enter without documentation. About 80 percent stay for six months or less, although many of these reenter the following year. Others stay for longer periods, causing a net addition each year of at least 150 thousand (sometimes more, depending on the year) to the permanent resident population in the United States. Large sections of the United States, particularly in the southwestern states that were once Mexico's territory, are now being re-"Mexicanized," at least in the sense that Spanish is becoming the main language. Adding these recent immigrants to those of Mexican descent already living here, there are at least 10 million persons of Mexican origin in the United States.

An estimated 20 percent of the total population of Mexico depends to some degree on income earned by a family member in the United States. At least $1 billion a year of these earnings, more likely at least $1.5 billion (and perhaps more), is remitted back to Mexico. The contribution of Mexican workers to the U.S. economy accounts for a significant part of the boom in the "Sun Belt" of this country. By one estimate, more than 10 percent of the growth in the labor market of the southwestern part of the United States since 1960 has been due to Mexican workers.

Interpenetration between the United States and Mexico is evident. "Interdependence"—in the sense of roughly equivalent interconnection—is not, at least not in Mexican perceptions. Despite Mexico's growth, the United States continues to be overwhelming.

The United States is more than three times as large as Mexico by population, and almost five times as large by area. Its economic production is twenty-three times greater, and its per capita income is more than six times higher. The United States uses about twenty times as much energy as does Mexico. Its public spent seventeen times as much on jewelry and watches in 1980 as Mexico devoted to national defense. The United States has seventeen times as many people in its armed forces as does Mexico. This country produces about as many automobiles each day as Mexico does in a month. Mexico's total national product is approximately equal to that produced within a sixty-mile radius of downtown Los Angeles.

As important as Mexico has become to the United States, the United States is still far more important to Mexico. About 60 percent each of Mexico's exports and imports in the 1980s are to and from the United States; the reverse figures are less than 7 percent and less than 5 percent, respectively. U.S. investment in Mexico, so crucial there, amounts to less than 3 percent of all U.S. investment abroad. Fully 85 percent of Mexico's tourists come from the United States, but just 15 percent of foreign visitors to this country are from Mexico. U.S. culture pervades Mexico at all levels and classes; in comparison, Mexico's cultural impact on the United States, outside of the Southwest, is scant.

These imbalances, and others like them, make Mexicans consider themselves vulnerable. The more linkages Mexico develops with the United States, the more susceptible Mexicans think their country is to U.S. exploitation. Mexico's tourist bonanza, for instance, has made the country subject to the effects of periodic scare stories about crime or other unpleasantness, and even to possible boycotts such as the one Jewish-Americans organized in 1976 to protest Mexico's vote on the United Nations resolution equating Zionism and racism. By integrating its feedlot cattle industry with the sources of grain in the United States, Mexico put itself at the mercy of sudden contractions in the U.S. meat market. By exporting tomatoes and other fruit and vegetables to the United States during this country's winter season, Mexico has expanded its revenue from foreign exchange, but some critics argue that the emphasis on export agriculture has reduced the country's autonomy by increasing its dependence on imported food.

Even Mexico's reserves of oil and gas have been a mixed blessing. Energy resources have brought Mexico added revenue and power, but they also have contributed to inflation and social dislocation, and they clearly added to the country's woes when oil prices fell. The sense of vulnerability Mexicans feel has been strongly reinforced by the debt crisis of the 1980s.

Proximity, interpenetration, and asymmetry fundamentally structure U.S. relations with Mexico. No policy on either side can ever fully remove these dimensions, which help determine what issues will arise between the two countries and how they will be approached. The relationship is also shaped by the fact that the two nations are so different from each other: in cultural traditions, social and demographic composition, economic levels and structures, and political values and institutions.

The Mexican intellectual Octavio Paz has brilliantly analyzed the cultural abyss between Mexicans and North Americans. As Paz observes, Mexicans and North Americans treat life and death very differently, in ways that flow directly from their very distinct relations to Europe's Reformation and to America's aboriginal peoples, and from their sharply divergent visions of both the future and the past. Communication between Mexicans and North Americans is difficult, Paz points out, because North Americans tend not to listen and Mexicans not to talk.

The relevant differences between Mexico and the United States go well beyond culture. Mexico is a society of youth, where almost 50 percent of the population are under sixteen, more than 70 percent are under thirty, and less than 10 percent are over fifty. The United States, by contrast, is an aging society, with only 28 percent of its population under sixteen and 26 percent over fifty. This difference has important

implications for social organization, employment, tax and welfare policies, culture, and politics. Mexico's population continues to expand
quickly, although much less rapidly than in previous decades. In the
United States, the rate of population growth has declined so much that
replacement of superannuated workers could become a problem by the
1990s. The United States is a multiethnic society of immigrants, old and
new. Our society is more conscious of divisions along racial lines than by
class. Mexico, though not without its own very significant ethnic and
cultural splits, is much more deeply divided by class.

Economically, Mexico is still a developing country. It is concentrating
on expanding production, and on improving social equity and welfare.
The United States, comparatively rich, has come to focus more on protecting industries than on growth, and more on ending welfare frauds
and limiting entitlements than on improving social programs.

Politically, Mexico is a highly centralized system with a single dominant party unlikely to relinquish control, despite growing opposition.
The Mexican state in recent years has become somewhat more profi-
cient technically, but its authority has been eroded both by the aloofness
of the new technocracy and by growing public resentment of pervasive
inefficiency and corruption. The government of the United States, in
turn, has lost some of its ability to manage U.S.-Mexico relations because of the complex interplay of business, labor, the media, and other
interest groups.

History also shapes the context for U.S. relations with Mexico. North
Americans typically think little about this history, except perhaps for a
bit of nostalgia about the Alamo. Mexicans, however, learn much about
the "War of the American Invasion" and about the losses of Texas and
what is now the southwestern part of the United States (comprising
more than half of Mexico's original territory). They also study the political and military interventions by the United States during Mexico's
revolutionary process.

Mexicans are taught, as well, about the prolonged efforts by the
United States to prevent their country's nationalization of its oil industry; they still celebrate the date of the oil nationalization as a "day of
dignity." They recall a whole series of frictions in U.S.-Mexico relations: the Chamizal border controversy caused by the change in the
course of the Rio Grande (or the Rio Bravo, as Mexicans call it), the
longstanding problem of salinity in the waters of the Colorado River, and
unilateral U.S. efforts to stop the narcotics trade. They emphasize recurrent U.S. efforts to deport Mexican workers, such as Operation Se-
cado in 1947 or Operation Wetback in 1954, when more than 1 million
Mexicans were rounded up and expelled from the United States within a
few weeks. They focus on egregious instances of violence against Mexi-

can migrants or periodic U.S. interference with traffic across the border, not as isolated episodes but, rather, as examples of a historic pattern.

Mexicans understand relations with the United States to be the central issue in their country's foreign affairs; North Americans often take relations with Mexico for granted. A recent Mexican foreign minister estimated that he spent 85 percent of his time working on the United States. Henry Kissinger's detailed memoir of his *White House Years,* by contrast, mentions Mexico only once.

North Americans generally favor closer relations with Mexico; they typically assume that the interests of Mexico and the United States are easily compatible. Many Mexicans, however, think that the relationship is inevitably exploitative. The perspectives Mexicans and North Americans bring to bear on specific issues often differ fundamentally. Insensitivity from the north and hypersensitivity from the south frequently convert simple differences into great difficulties.

THE ISSUES IN U.S.-MEXICO RELATIONS

The main issues in contemporary U.S.-Mexico relations stem from the juxtaposition of a troubled developing nation and an industrial superpower; from the complex intertwining of the two societies; and from the interactions of their memories, hopes, and fears.

As the interconnections between Mexico and the United States have multiplied, so have the grounds for conflict. The two countries have struggled over issues ranging from the price of gas to the size of tomatoes; from the treatment of Mexican workers in the United States to the treatment of U.S. tourists, law enforcement officials, and private investors in Mexico; from trading rules to oil spills; from air routes to shipping costs; from ground water to fishing zones; from issues of social security to questions of national security; and from divisions over substance to perhaps even more basic differences of style.

Sometimes the issues are highly technical, revolving around the appropriate statistical technique for estimating the fair market price of winter vegetables or the scientific evidence for determining the jurisdictional status of migratory fish. On other occasions, clashes take place over fundamental values: how society should be organized, and the rights and obligations of states and their citizens. But whatever the question, the vast asymmetry between Mexico and the United States—compounded by Mexico's efforts to close the gap and by its profound sense of vulnerability, on the one hand, and by the reassertive impulses of the United States, on the other—feeds tension between the two nations. This tension has been increasing as the stakes in U.S.-Mexico relations rise.

The main issues in U.S.-Mexico relations—trade, investment, and finance; energy; immigration; narcotics; and international relations—are interconnected. Disputes in one realm make it harder to resolve problems in the others. Progress in handling frictions or building accord in one sphere, conversely, can improve the chances of doing so in the others.

On all these issues, both conflict and complementarity are inherent in the differences between the two countries. Mexico needs capital, technology, and access to expanded export markets, but it also has a surplus of unskilled labor and energy and other natural resources. The United States, in turn, is short of oil, some other raw materials, and unskilled labor, but it has both capital and technology and is the largest market in the world. Each country exports products that are in demand, legally or illegally, in the other. Both countries need to expand exports, and both also experience sectoral resistance to imports. Each country both gains and loses from the flow of migration, but the crucial net effect of migration is seen differently by various sectors in each society.

Trade, Investment, and Finance

U.S. investment in and loans to Mexico, as well as trade between the two countries, have vastly expanded over the past twenty years. The sharp decline in U.S.-Mexico economic interaction in 1982–83 should highlight, not obscure, this underlying trend; U.S. exports to Mexico began to pick up again in 1984, as did U.S. investment, which began to expand again in 1985 and 1986 and surged upwards in 1987.

Economic conflicts between the two countries are likely to intensify as Mexico's economy becomes more complex, and as its points of intersection and competition with the U.S. economy multiply. The interpenetration between the two countries makes it increasingly probable that each nation will adopt domestic policies that adversely affect its neighbor.

Domestic economic policies on either side of the border inevitably spill over. Mexican agricultural policy under the last two administrations, for example, has been aimed at modernizing the rural sector to improve productivity. Special attention to irrigated commercial agriculture promoted an export industry in strawberries, tomatoes, and other products to join the long-time exports of cotton and beef. At the same time, however, the squeeze on rain-fed subsistence farming and the increased use of arable land for livestock production in Mexico have resulted in declining food crop production, and consequently in a growing need for imported corn and beans from the United States, and increasing migration of the rural poor in search of jobs. Efforts in the 1970s and early 1980s to correct worsening rural unemployment and falling food-crop production—through the Sistema Alimentario Mexicano (SAM) and other programs—met with very limited success. Pressures to expand the northward export both of people and of produce have increased accordingly.

The tomato controversy exemplifies one kind of trade problem. Mexican growers of tomatoes, green peppers, eggplants, cucumbers, and certain other vegetables during the late 1960s and early 1970s supplied an increasing share of the U.S. market, up to 50 percent during this country's winter season, generating a 500-million-dollar annual business. This success, however, stimulated a protectionist reaction in the United States, spearheaded by the Florida tomato growers. For the Florida farmers, the Mexican imports came to represent a threat to their market, especially in the early spring, when they expected higher prices. The Florida growers mobilized economic, political, and administrative resources to curtail the Mexican inflow. They proposed regulations to restrict the size, shape, color, and packaging of imported produce in order to curb the Mexican competition; most of their suggestions were adopted.

Mexican producers retaliated by mobilizing the U.S. distributors and consumer groups who stood to gain from continued Mexican exports. They stimulated efforts by the Mexican government to link this issue to others in which the U.S. government was more interested, and they undertook sophisticated participation (through Washington law firms) in the bureaucratic and technical processes by which decisions are made and implemented in the United States. Eventually they succeeded in obtaining favorable rulings from some U.S. authorities, reversing previous setbacks, but not before learning that even fervent proponents of free enterprise in the United States make exceptions when the outcome of unfettered competition leaves them disadvantaged.

Mexican producers of other agricultural products (grapes, asparagus, raisins, and pineapples), textiles, shoes, ceramic tiles, various light manufactured products, toy balloons, cement, and petrochemicals have learned similar lessons. Most recently, Mexican (and Brazilian) producers of certain kinds of steel have encountered rising U.S. protectionism.

During the late 1970s and early 1980s (until the 1982–83 recession), Mexico expanded into new product lines and shifted the composition of its exports (other than petroleum) increasingly into nontraditional items, and especially into manufactured goods. If Mexico can resume this process, gain more experience at penetrating the U.S. market and other markets, and achieve greater sophistication in "working the system" of the United States, bilateral trade conflicts will intensify. Development of a vigorous export-oriented automotive industry, for example, was a major component of Mexico's oil-financed industrialization strategy in the late 1970s. Automotive goods have made up a substantial part of Mexican exports to the United States which are eligible for favored market access under the Generalized System of Preferences (GSP). In an effort to improve its trade balance, the Mexican government in 1977 imposed new local-content and export performance requirements on automotive manufacturers. As the U.S. auto industry has fought to regain its competitiveness, frictions in this sector have increased.

Trade issues between Mexico and the United States were complicated during the early 1980s by Mexico's decision not to join the GATT. The "injury test" provision, which limits countervailing duties to cases of actual harm to a U.S. producer, was not applied to Mexico because it remained outside the GATT. As a result, countervailing duties continued to be applied against imports from Mexico which benefited from a Mexican export subsidy.

A bilateral accord in 1985 extended "injury test" protection to Mexico and reduced the incidence of countervailing duties, and in 1986 Mexico finally did apply to join the GATT. But the Trade and Tariff Act of 1984—with its provisions for U.S. retaliation against alleged unfair practices—opened new possibilities for disputes, particularly in the context of the worst commercial deficits in U.S. history. Heated debate over a new omnibus trade bill in the 100th Congress showed that protectionist sentiments in the United States are on the rise, and trade disputes between Mexico and the United States are likely to multiply.

Expanded U.S. investment in Mexico, too, breeds conflict. The complementary interests of a capital-rich and a capital-scarce country do not automatically translate into cooperation. Conflict arises primarily from Mexico's attempts to restrict and regulate capital flows. Mexican law generally limits the share of a Mexican company which can be owned by foreigners to 49 percent; requires that specific shares of the content of particular products be of local manufacture; insists that a certain percentage of the resulting production be exported to produce foreign exchange; limits the share of profits which can be remitted for patents, royalties, and other concepts; and seeks to secure more benefit for Mexico's national economy than would readily be ceded by foreign investors.

Friction over such restrictions will grow as Mexico's capital-intensive development program generates mounting requirements, particularly if capital is expensive. One result of Mexico's current bind has been to cause the government to offer more favorable terms to U.S. investors than had been the case in recent years. The protracted negotiations with IBM and other firms aimed at inducing a U.S. company to establish a major new plant in Mexico to manufacture personal computers illustrate this tendency. But nationalist sentiment to restrict U.S. investment has already been rekindled, and the Mexican state is under strong pressure to bargain hard with foreign companies.

Mexico's massive debt—some $110 billion by the end of 1987—is a major concern for both countries, for Mexico's chances to resume growth and expand its imports depend to a significant degree on renewed credit. Commercial banks, primarily in the United States, have repeatedly had to reschedule Mexico's immediate obligations, but they have only postponed facing the implications of the country's growing external burden. The falling world price for petroleum in the mid-1980s severely undermined some of the assumptions on which Mexico's financial planning was based, and made it impossible for Mexico to meet even the revised repayment schedules. Difficult negotiations have therefore continued over further restructuring of existing debts, over spreads and management fees on the renegotiated loans, and, especially, over how much new credit will be extended and on what terms.

Energy

Mexico's discovery of major reserves of petroleum and associated natural gas, coming after the 1973 Arab oil embargo and the dramatic price hikes thereafter imposed by the Organization of Petroleum Exporting Countries (OPEC), drew immediate attention in the United States. Estimates vary regarding the magnitude of Mexico's reserves. No one doubts, however, that its resources are sufficient to affect the world energy situation measurably. The Mexican government claims total proven reserves of petroleum and natural gas together at over 70 billion barrels oil equivalent; even the official U.S. estimate, 39 billion barrels oil equivalent, would make Mexico the world's fourth-largest source of hydrocarbons.

The first reaction of many in the United States to Mexico's energy bonanza was to posit a perfect natural complementarity of interest between the two countries. U.S. energy specialists as well as social, political, and economic leaders focused quickly on Mexico's potential to become a significant supplier of this country's energy needs. It was argued that Mexico's new oil and gas export capacity and its thirst for capital goods to diversify its economy would neatly fit U.S. energy requirements and this country's own need to export more industrial goods. Some also assumed that the United States and Mexico would share an interest in having Mexico produce as much oil and gas as possible and in selling most of it to the United States. U.S. advisers began to propose special arrangements by which the United States might obtain assured access to Mexico's energy resources in exchange for greater U.S. consideration on other issues. Some even suggested a "common market" based on energy.

It became clear during the 1970s, however, that the potential complementarity on energy would not assure easy cooperation. Mexicans resented the tendency in the United States to see Mexico as a U.S. oil well. They observed that pressure on Mexico to undertake rapid production was insensitive to the social and economic dislocation a quick expansion might stimulate. They expressed concern, too, that if Mexico concentrated its energy exports too much on the United States it would become dependent on the U.S. market. Equally important, they feared that the United States might become excessively reliant on Mexican sources, and that intervention in Mexico to assure access to vital resources might someday be contemplated.

Faced with competing national imperatives—a desire to increase energy exports to make possible a major economic expansion and the simultaneous aim not to increase dependence on the United States—the Mexican government under López Portillo diversified Mexico's energy market so that not more than half of its oil exports would go to the United States. Although Mexico has become this country's largest single foreign source of oil in many years, supplying almost 15 percent of U.S. imports, Mexico has kept the share of its oil exports flowing north to about 50 percent.

Mexico and the United States have also clashed over natural gas. Having encouraged Mexico to expand its gas production and to build a pipeline to ship the gas to the United States, U.S. authorities resisted Mexican efforts to set a high price in 1977. Energy Secretary James Schlesinger vetoed an agreement between six U.S. corporations and PEMEX, Mexico's state oil corporation, on the grounds that the price would adversely affect the lower rate previously agreed on with Canadian exporters and would force up the domestic U.S. price. Schlesinger believed that Mexico could be pressured into lowering its price, given the convenience of the U.S. market. His peremptory manner of communicating the U.S. decision infuriated Mexican officials and reinforced the arguments of Mexico's energy nationalists. Mexico responded by shifting its own energy strategy to make greater use of gas for domestic needs. Renewed negotiation finally produced a U.S.-Mexico gas agreement, but for a reduced quantity (300 million cubic feet, rather than the 2 billion cubic feet originally contemplated) and at a price close to the one Schlesinger had rejected only two years before. In 1984, when gas prices fell, Mexico unilaterally suspended its exports, at least for a while.

The sale of enriched uranium to Mexico has been another source of conflict. The Carter administration's emphasis on nuclear nonproliferation led Washington in 1978 to deny delivery of U.S.-produced enriched uranium for which Mexico had already paid. Washington's decision, part of a world wide U.S. policy shift, heightened Mexico's sense of vulnerability. Mexico then adopted a nuclear energy plan based on domestic uranium supplies (which appear to be considerable), a plan that was actually more proliferation-prone than the previous system. The changing economics of energy have made this controversy moot, but the case illustrates how decisions taken for global reasons and insensitively applied in a particular case can convert potential cooperation into conflict.

Immigration and Employment

More than any other issue, immigration illustrates the double-edged potential for cooperation or conflict between Mexico and the United States. Discussed in the United States as a significant problem, the migration of hundreds of thousands of Mexicans into the United States each year is also a solution, for it responds to needs within both countries. Complementarities undoubtedly exist. Workers who have trouble finding satisfactory jobs in Mexico are gainfully employed in the United States, and the earnings they send home to relatives are a large source of foreign exchange for Mexico. Hundreds of thousands of tasks in the United States are performed at low wages each year by Mexican laborers. Repeated studies show that many of the jobs Mexican immigrants do would not be performed by unemployed U.S.-born workers, and that the pool of such workers is in any case declining because of the low U.S. birthrate since the early 1960s. It has even been argued that the clustering of immigrant Mexican workers in small, lower-tier firms actually protects the higher-paying jobs in industry held by native-born workers, jobs that might otherwise be moved offshore or be lost to automation. Most studies show that both Mexico and the United States overall gain more economically than they lose from migration, though specific individuals or groups lose, at least for a time.

Cost-benefit analyses notwithstanding, the flow of migrants into the United States generates severe tensions. The phenomenon is hardly new, for both Mexican immigration and resulting frictions have been occurring throughout the century. They have ebbed and flowed in rhythm with the U.S. business cycle and, to a lesser extent, with economic changes in Mexico.

United States policy has often encouraged Mexican immigration, openly or tacitly. In periods of recession or depression, however, domestic unemployment rises and native resentment of alien labor increases. Indeed, the historic U.S. stance toward Mexican labor has been aptly termed a "flower petal" policy (I need you, I need you not . . .). The

United States has usually let the flow of migration be regulated, in effect, by the labor market itself. Only when domestic resentment builds up has Washington moved to halt or reverse the flow, often in ways that seem sudden and arbitrary from the Mexican perspective.

Since the mid-1970s, tensions over migration have been worsening. Measures to halt bilingual education programs, attempts to deprive the children of undocumented workers of access to public education, proposals to abolish Spanish-language ballots and voting materials, repeated incidents in which Mexican immigrants have been harassed or abused—all reflect a rising sentiment in the United States to curtail immigration.

For the past several years, the United States has been struggling, therefore, to define a new immigration policy. Consensus has slowly emerged in Congress on the need to adopt a more restrictive approach, one that restores to the people of the United States a sense that the national borders are being protected and controlled. The needs of economic sectors in the United States that depend on alien workers (particularly large agricultural enterprises in the West) were taken into account in the Simpson-Rodino immigration reform legislation adopted in the waning hours of the 99th Congress, in October 1986. So were the rights of many undocumented immigrants who are already well established in the United States and who have been offered lenient amnesty provisions to regularize their immigration status. But beneath all the compromise provisions that finally broke the legislative stalemate and permitted passage of the Immigration Reform and Control Act of 1986, the underlying thrust of the law is restrictive. New means are provided for enforcing immigration controls, including expanded numbers of border patrol officers, improved equipment for frontier protection, and, most important, the imposition of sanctions on employers who knowingly hire alien workers.

How restrictive the new U.S. approach turns out to be in practice, and how strong the pressures to go north become, will determine the intensity of U.S.-Mexico frictions over migration. Stricter control of the U.S. border in the face of increased migration pressure will obviously produce serious bilateral tension. Failure or inability to control the U.S. border, reinforcing a growing perception in certain regions of this country that Latinos will eventually "overrun" Anglo society, could eventually provoke strong nationalist and even racist strains in the United States, however, which might make for even more profound problems.

Narcotics

A long-term problem in U.S.-Mexico relations which has become much more salient in the 1980s is the illegal traffic in narcotics. Drugs are not the only item smuggled from one country to the other; manufactured goods, from stolen automobiles to submachine guns, flow south, while hard currency and undocumented workers come north. But no item of illegal commerce arouses as much concern as narcotics.

The drug traffic from Mexico—principally marijuana and heroin—was heavy in the late 1960s and the early 1970s; some estimates put the share of U.S. imports of these two drugs entering from Mexico at over 80 percent. Intense pressures from the United States on Mexico to curb this flow were epitomized by the Nixon administration's imposition of Operation Intercept in 1969, a source of severe bilateral friction at the time. Eventually, however, the Mexican government's commitment to crop eradication and other measures of effective narcotics control relegated this issue to the back burner. The two countries cooperated effectively on narcotics control during the mid-and late 1970s, especially through Operation Condor. Periodic Mexican arrests of U.S. citizens in Mexico for illegal possession of or commerce in drugs became more of an issue than the flow of narcotics into this country.

The drug traffic from Mexico into the United States has intensified again in the 1980s, however. Stricter eradication programs in Colombia, Peru, and Bolivia; the preoccupation of Mexico's government with critical economic problems; corruption within the Mexican law enforcement apparatus; and a burgeoning demand for drugs from the United States have all combined to expand the flow of narcotics. Throughout the 1980s, Mexican production of marijuana and opium poppy has been increasing, and Mexico has also become a principal conduit for U.S.-bound cocaine from the Andean region. Although narcotics intelligence is a highly imperfect science, and quantitative estimates are rough and perhaps unreliable, there is no doubt that the drug traffic from Mexico to the United States has reached massive proportions; the perception that this is so has become a key ingredient of U.S. public attitudes toward Mexico.

As public opinion in the United States has become increasingly aroused about the menace of narcotics to health and safety, pressures have increased on Washington for more effective programs of drug control; these pressures have in turn been translated into U.S. government efforts to halt the import of narcotics. The intensifying U.S. campaign against the drug trade has been worldwide, affecting countries in Asia as well as in Latin America, but in no country has it produced more intense friction than in Mexico.

For the United States, it is natural to concentrate on Mexico, a prime and visible source of the narcotics traffic, right on the U.S. border. It is politically convenient to show that aggressive and effective measures are being taken to combat drug traders, and that these measures include vigorous activities in Mexico. For Mexico, however, a highly aggressive U.S. posture inevitably sets off nationalist resentments. Mexicans reject the self-serving emphasis in the United States on the supposed efficacy of U.S. enforcement measures, and the converse emphasis on corruption in Mexico; they complain about underreporting in the United States of what Mexican law enforcement agencies have been doing to fight narcotics. They note how strong demand for drugs has become in the United States, and how extensively involved U.S. banks are in the financial aspects of the drug trade. They resist U.S. efforts to export law enforcement personnel and procedures to Mexico, including a plan proposed by Washington to allow U.S. Customs Service planes to give hot pursuit deep into Mexico as they chase the aircraft of suspected smugglers. They wonder whether U.S. efforts to control narcotics might not be more properly concentrated at home.

Tensions between Mexico and the United States on drugs crystallized in 1985 with the murder in Mexico of a U.S. Drug Enforcement Administration Officer, Enrique Camarena, and apparent local police complicity in the escape of Camarena's assassin. Washington's high-profile response to this case—including a two-week slowdown of normal traffic across the U.S. border—provoked strong reactions in Mexico. These were heightened one year later by unprecedented official U.S. allegations of Mexican corruption, allegations presented as testimony in Congress by representatives of the U.S. Customs Commission and the State Department. A summit meeting in August 1986 between Presidents de la Madrid and Reagan, intended in significant measure to be an opportunity to clear the air on the drug issue, was clouded when Mexican police beat up an armed U.S. drug enforcement agent who was traveling in Mexico without official documentation and in an unmarked vehicle. As if this were not enough, press reports in the United States that same day alleged that a cousin of President de la Madrid was involved in the drug trade. A few weeks later, bilateral relations were further set back when the U.S. Congress passed an omnibus anti-drug bill that includes provisions calling on the president to impose punitive measures on Mexico unless Mexico's record on drug control shows "substantial progress."

Such incidents, widely reported and contributing considerably to mutual distrust, illustrate how difficult it has become for Mexico and the United States to cooperate effectively in resolving a problem that neither country can successfully tackle alone. As tensions between Mexico and the United States accumulate on other issues, moreover, this sensitive issue may become even more divisive.

International Relations

The final sphere in which the United States and Mexico are bound to conflict is international politics.

Both governments are reasonably comfortable with the overall structure of the contemporary international system; neither wants to overturn it. The United States and Mexico share many preferences: for a world free of nuclear war and of terrorism; for the peaceful resolution of international disputes; and for facilitating expanded international commercial, technological, and cultural exchange. The two governments share, above all, a strong interest in managing their bilateral relationship to prevent conflict over secondary issues from thwarting cooperation on primary concerns.

But the two countries also differ, often and pointedly. The record is replete with examples: Mexico's criticism of the covert U.S. intervention in Guatemala in 1954 and of the overt U.S. intervention in the Dominican Republic in 1965; its acceptance of Fidel Castro's Cuba, even when all other members of the Organization of America States had broken relations with Havana; its manifest sympathy for Salvador Allende in Chile; its vote in the United Nations in 1975 on the resolution equating Zionism with racism; its refusal to follow Washington's boycott of the Moscow Olympics; its initiative, together with Venezuela, to sponsor the creation of the Sistema Economico Latinoamericano (SELA), a regional organization that excludes the United States and includes Cuba; and resentment in Washington over Mexico's proposal for a UN Charter of Economic Rights and Duties of States, and of Mexico's role in many other discussions on the shape of international economic relations.

Foreign policy differences between Mexico and the United States have focused in recent years primarily on Central America. Mexico supported the Sandinista forces in Nicaragua before the final defeat of Somoza and then led the successful opposition in 1979 within the Organization of American States to the U.S. proposal that an inter-American force be dispatched to Nicaragua to manage the transition. Since 1979, Mexico has provided the Sandinista regime diplomatic and economic support and has publicly opposed U.S. pressures against Nicaragua. In El Salvador, Mexico recognized the leftist insurgents as a legitimate political force in 1981, contrary to U.S. policy.

Most important, Mexico has taken strong initiatives to mediate the conflicts in Central America, particularly through the Contadora process. Although Washington has continuously voiced its support for the Contadora initiative, U.S. actions—covert warfare against Nicaragua, including the mining of its harbors and military support for the anti-

Sandinista insurgents, and the economic embargo announced in 1985—sharply contradict the Contadora approach. As the United States has expanded its intervention in the Caribbean Basin, repeated conflicts between the United States and Mexico have occurred. It has become increasingly evident that one aim of U.S. policy in the 1980s has been to neutralize the Mexican role in Central America.

These various conflicts between Mexico and the United States reflect the contrasting aims of a great power with global interests which is trying to retain and even to restore regional predominance, and those of a middle-tier country with mainly regional engagements which is trying to expand its influence. In part, the tensions also register Mexico's needs as a developing country and those of the United States as an industrialized nation. Some disputes, especially those regarding Central America, also result from divergent historical perspectives on revolution. All these differences have been magnified, in turn, by the temptation felt by some in the United States to take quick advantage of Mexico's debt-induced weakness.

But a fundamental source of U.S.-Mexico clashes on foreign affairs is precisely that many who formulate Mexican policy believe their country requires visible independence from the United States. Mexico's primary foreign policy aim is to consolidate and demonstrate its own autonomy and sovereignty; this is most easily done by disagreeing with Washington. The international reputation and domestic legitimacy of Mexico's government depend, in part, on showing that its policies are not made in the United States.

Every Mexican administration, whatever its general orientation, aims to protect Mexico's independent foreign policy. No U.S. administration, however solicitous or domineering, will successfully co-opt or coerce Mexican foreign policy in an enduring fashion. It is inevitable, therefore, that the United States and Mexico will differ on international issues. What is important is what issues these will be, how seriously the two countries will clash, and whether these conflicts will eventually affect other areas of U.S.-Mexico relations.

PROSPECTS FOR RECOVERY: MEXICO'S SEARCH FOR OPTIONS

Ever since the shortcomings of Mexico's established growth model became painfully evident in the mid-1970s, and with renewed emphasis since the major setback of 1981–82, Mexicans have been debating how to resume the country's development. Fundamentally different diagnoses of Mexico's problems and prescriptions for their treatment emerged during the late 1960s and early 1970s, and were highlighted during the economic and political crisis of 1975–76. The oil boom of the late 1970s allowed the Mexican government to paper over these differences by simultaneously pursuing inconsistent approaches. One of the reasons Mexico ran up such a huge debt in the 1970s was that it invested both in infrastructure and in social services, built up oil production and also strengthened industry, modernized export-oriented agriculture and yet expanded local food production—all at the same time, while also increasing consumption. Instead of making hard choices, Mexico in the late 1970s opted to cover all its bets, albeit with borrowed funds.

The intense financial crises since 1982 have clarified that Mexico needs to make some basic decisions. Debates about the country's future have been renewed as a result.

One stance, favored by the left wing of the governing coalition within the PRI as well as by some groups outside the dominant party, is a radical nationalist stance. This view, foreshadowed during the Echeverría period, gained partial ascendancy in the waning months of the López Portillo administration, with the nationalization of Mexican private banks. The extreme nationalist approach would strengthen the state sector; stress redistributive policies and social programs; orient more production inward, toward the expansion of local markets; and assign priority to generating full employment. It favors a more closed economy, one in which foreign investment would be discouraged or strictly limited, and one that would make Mexico far less reliant on foreign capital than it has been in recent years.

The extreme nationalist approach emphasizes the aim of accelerated recovery from Mexico's depression. It would limit current debt service to levels that will permit Mexico to resume growth. Extreme nationalists would resist IMF advice about curbing spending and would consider unilaterally postponing debt repayment. Some might even contemplate repudiating all or part of Mexico's external debt. Extreme nationalists would strongly reemphasize Mexico's quest for diversified international links and for enhanced international autonomy. They would restrict the sale of oil and gas to the United States, eschew bilateral arrangements on trade or finance with Washington, and withdraw Mexico from the GATT.

Although various influential Mexicans have championed one or more of these nationalist policies, no Mexican regime in the last fifty years has consistently adopted this stance. To do so now would constitute a drastic and unlikely shift, for it would lead to disinvestment and capital flight from the private sector (as occurred during the late Echeverría and López Portillo periods), to a further expansion of the already overgrown state sector, and to polarization and a further fracturing of the loose consensus that has undergirded Mexican politics since the Revolution. The Echeverría regime's emphasis on income redistribution and strengthening the state sector, coupled with its avoidance of tax and fiscal reforms that would have alienated the middle class, led to a galloping deficit, a burgeoning debt, and an intense economic and political crisis that was eased only because Echeverría was at the very end of his term and because the oil bonanza was discovered. The López Portillo government's move toward adopting a national populist approach to the financial crisis of 1982 was no more successful, but, again, it occurred so late in *sexenio* that it could be largely abandoned without great cost within a few months.

These experiences with the extreme nationalist option, however unsatisfactory, serve as a reminder that this approach still has some respected adherents within Mexico's governing coalition. They are not prominent at present, but in the pendular process of Mexican politics they may yet regain influence, especially if Mexico first moves still closer to the United States. A swing toward extreme nationalism in Mexico is not probable, but it could occur as a result of a renewed and more severe financial crisis. If orthodox proposals for resolving such a crisis appeared grossly inadequate, nationalist remedies might well be considered. This would be especially likely, moreover, if ultranationalist impulses in Mexico were exacerbated by direct U.S. military intervention in Central America. These conditions, although not present now, are by no means unimaginable.

A second course for Mexico, the opposite tack, would be to open the country much more fully to the international economy. Under this approach, Mexico would follow all the austerity measures recommended by the International Monetary Fund and the commercial banks. The prime emphasis in this scenario would be on anti-inflation stabilization rather than on immediate recovery. Mexico would return to the private sector parts of the economy, particularly the banking system and various manufacturing enterprises, that have in recent years become part of the state apparatus. It would reinforce its decision to join the GATT by reducing tariff and nontariff protection for its industries. Mexico would adopt exchange rate and other policies to spur its exports further, even at the expense of worsening domestic income distribution still more.

Under extreme versions of the internationalist option, the concessions to foreign investors in Mexico would be significantly increased so as to attract additional capital. More generally, Mexico would stress its comparative economic advantages—especially in the fields of energy, tourism, and light manufacturing—and would rely on free-market pressures to improve its competitiveness. Social policies would receive less attention than measures aimed primarily at stimulating national economic growth.

Some sectors of Mexico's business community, particularly in the northern states, strongly favor an extreme internationalist approach. This approach is also supported by some circles in the United States, particularly in Texas and the Southwest, and it is consistent with the dominant ideology of the Reagan administration.

The Mexican government of Miguel de la Madrid has followed a more internationalist course than any recent Mexican regime. De la Madrid's chosen successor, Carlos Salinas de Gortari, is likely to continue his policies. There is little prospect, however, that Mexico will go much further in the direction of extreme internationalism. The reasons are political, economic, and ideological. Mexico's political stability depends on a governing coalition of labor, peasants, professionals, and intellectuals, most of whom would be hurt by, and virtually all of whom would oppose, opening Mexico up to more intense international penetration. Much of Mexico's national business community, too, would oppose a drastic move away from subsidies, state intervention in the economy, and protectionism on their behalf. Only under conditions of sustained economic disaster and major political upheaval would the extreme internationalist approach be adopted. Even if it were fully put into effect, which is unlikely, it would soon generate nationalist opposition that would probably abort it. Indeed, counterpressures developed against even the moderately internationalist policies of the de la Madrid administration.

Support within Mexico for each of these opposite approaches to Mexico's future—the extreme nationalist and the extreme internationalist (or the "populist" and the "neo-liberal")—is probably stronger now than at any time in the last generation, as the country's prolonged and repeated economic and financial crises have had a polarizing effect. The centrist policies of recent Mexican administrations have increasingly come under attack from both sides. Critics from the business community (supported by some in the United States) fault the regime for leaving too much of the public sector intact, for allowing the government deficit to climb again because of politically motivated spending, and for sending out mixed signals that discourage foreign investors. From the other side, national populists attack de la Madrid for what they regard as obeisance to foreign investors, international banks, and the IMF and criticize what they see as an obsessive concern with curbing inflation, even at the expense of investment and social needs.

Neither the populist nor the neo-liberal view has established itself as likely to provide the basis for a new and enduring national consensus in Mexico, however. Most leaders there support an approach that falls between the two extremes. They want to promote national recovery now, but without restimulating inflation. They want Mexico to continue with its eclectic mix of state intervention and private enterprise, on the one hand, and pragmatic nationalism and selective openness to the international economy, on the other. They seek a balance between promoting and diversifying the country's exports and expanding its internal markets. Similarly, most Mexican policymakers want the country to resume economic growth but also to improve equity and social services. Most Mexican observers believe that the country's foreign debt should be renegotiated on terms more favorable to Mexico, although they differ on how this can be done. And most Mexican policymakers and members of the attentive public agree that Mexico needs to make the most of its proximity to the United States, but they often disagree on exactly what that means.

Much of recent Mexican history can be understood in terms of a search for viable moderate approaches. Mexico's experience from 1968 to the present—particularly during the Echeverría and López Portillo periods but also in the late 1960s and more recently under President de la Madrid—suggests that attempts to pursue elements of a strong nationalist and an extreme internationalist approach at the same time do not work. What is needed in Mexico is a coherent and sustained effort to redirect the country's economic energies so that domestic agriculture and industrial production for an expanded national market are aided, but so that export-oriented industries are also forced to become more efficient and competitive.

THE U.S. STAKE IN MEXICO

It will matter a great deal to the United States how Mexico copes with its problems.

First, the United States has a large direct stake in Mexico's economic recovery. Heavily exposed, U.S. banks want to be sure that Mexico's economy regains strength, that Mexico's exports and foreign exchange earnings resume, and that Mexico continues to honor its international financial obligations. U.S. exporters, whose sales to Mexico fell 49 percent during 1982 and 1983, and fell again in 1986, want Mexico both to recover and to avoid increased protectionism. Mexico's market for U.S. exporters is still very substantial and potentially even more so; it is more than eight times larger than the entire Central American market, for example. The border regions of the United States would also benefit from a significant Mexican recovery.

A second strong U.S. interest in Mexico's economic prospects arises from the interconnection of employment and migration. United States labor, concerned about threats to U.S. jobs both from immigrant workers and from Mexican exports, wants Mexico to recover so that wage levels there increase (unskilled labor in Mexico earns on the average about one-eighth what unskilled labor in the United States does) and the flow of Mexicans to this country abates. Pressures for migration from Mexico have risen because of the economic crisis; detentions by U.S. authorities of illegal immigrants crossing the border with Mexico have doubled during the mid-1980s to almost 1.7 million detentions a year. It is important to avoid uncontrolled Mexican migration that could provoke unmanageable tensions in this country.

Third, as one of the largest and most industrialized of the developing countries, Mexico is sometimes influential in international forums. How it chooses to wield that influence—with regard to commercial and financial negotiations, the strife in Central America, or other issues—will affect the United States.

Fourth, Mexico and the United States have a number of common problems—of which controlling narcotics is the most dramatic—that need to be tackled jointly; other issues that demand bilateral approaches include pollution, ground water, and resource conservation. Because proximity and interpenetration make it impossible for either country to solve such problems unilaterally, cooperation is crucial.

Fifth, the United States has a specific security interest in Mexico as a relatively accessible source of petroleum and several other minerals, primarily strontium, fluorspar, and antimony.

Finally and most important, the United States has a broader strategic interest in Mexico's fundamental stability. The United States would be severely threatened by major and sustained unrest, with its attendant unpredictability, on its southern border. This country could be badly hurt by a deeply hostile Mexican government, the possible result of a profound socioeconomic crisis. The specter of "another Iran" on the border of the United States is remote, to be sure. But its cost would be so high that the United States should help assure that conditions in Mexico do not sharply deteriorate, and that anti–United States sentiment is not compounded.

Each of Mexico's main options for national development—a nationalist or autarchic approach, an extreme internationalist posture, or a more balanced centrist path—has important implications for relations with the United States. The nationalist approach would produce systematic and cumulating conflict between the two countries. The extreme internationalist path, opening Mexico to still greater U.S. penetration, might have some immediately apparent positive effects on bilateral relations, but it could also cause internal social and economic dislocations in Mexico that might eventually increase instability, and it would carry within it the seeds of an ultimate nationalist backlash.

It is in the interest of the United States for Mexico to carry out a viable moderate approach to development that allows for the manage-

ment of conflict and the building of cooperation between the two countries. The United States should aim to have the kind of relationship with
Mexico that, even though asymmetric, is ultimately and increasingly
complementary and interdependent. Expanded cooperation with Mexico would be in the best interests of the United States. Securing that
cooperation should be a major aim of U.S. foreign policy.

THE UNITED STATES AND MEXICO: OPTIONS FOR POLICY

Future relations between the United States and Mexico will depend on
many factors: rates of population growth in each country; levels of inflation and unemployment; whether there is a sustained oil glut or a renewed interruption of energy flows; whether the world economy sags
again or continues to pick up; the weather's effect on the two countries'
agriculture; and the course of Central America's internal turmoil, as
well as other unpredictable developments.

But U.S.-Mexico relations will also be shaped by the approach each
government takes on the main issues facing the two societies. Because
of the complex interconnections between the two countries, neither government can control or manage all aspects of their relationship. Still,
government choices on trade, finance, energy, immigration, narcotics,
foreign policy, and other issues will powerfully affect U.S.-Mexico relations. Policy choices will largely determine whether Mexico and the
United States drift or perhaps even plunge toward greater confrontation, whether they continue to work out specific conflicts within a dis-
tinctly ad hoc framework, or whether they move to restructure their
relationship more comprehensively to make possible enhanced cooperation.

The United States has four major options for dealing with Mexico.
One path would be for this country to adopt a unilateral and nationalist
stance of its own. A second would be to continue the present course:
that is, to work out specific solutions to each bilateral problem on its
own merits, one issue at a time. A third course, very different from the
first two, would be to attempt to construct a meaningful "special relationship" with Mexico, moving consciously and consistently toward
greater integration between the two countries. A fourth option would be
for the United States to design new general policies, not fashioned specifically for Mexico but rather adopted as part of a broader approach,
which respond positively to the major needs of Latin America as a
region and of the more advanced developing countries elsewhere in the
world.

Under a nationalist or unilateral approach, the United States would protect marginal industries and sectors threatened by Mexican competition by restricting imports of products on which Mexico is achieving a competitive advantage. The United States would push Mexico to adopt "energy interdependence" with this country. It would vigorously promote the interests of U.S. investors, despite Mexican sensitivities. It would be sharply restrictive or exclusionary on immigration, moving toward more effectively enforcing border controls, using identity cards and effective employer sanctions, and putting stronger pressures on Mexico to control migration from its side. A nationalist U.S. policy would push Mexico to conform to the U.S. approach in Central America and the Caribbean, and on East-West issues more generally. It would aim for Mexican alignment with the United States on other international questions, and it would be indifferent toward Mexican concerns with broader North-South issues.

A unilateral U.S. approach toward Mexico—in effect, reverting to the days before Mexico's modernization, and perhaps even before its revolution, when Washington could more effectively pressure Mexico—is obviously a recipe for destructive confrontation. No significant observer in the United States openly articulates the nationalist approach—although Senator Helms comes remarkably close—and it can be virtually dismissed as a conscious policy choice.

What is striking about the current period of U.S.-Mexico relations, however, is how many of the nationalist tendencies, each adopted by itself and not as part of a coherent and intentional unilateral policy, are now either already in effect or easily imaginable. If recent trends are not reversed, the United States could find that it is pursuing a strongly nationalist approach toward Mexico by inadvertence. An increasingly destructive period in bilateral relations could well emerge.

The United States and Mexico will probably not allow their relations to drift much further toward outright confrontation without adopting course corrections. Both nations recognize how much they have at stake in avoiding a drastic deterioration in their relations, and they would move to avoid a rupture.

It is more likely, therefore, that Mexico and the United States will pursue the second path, the mostly uncoordinated management of specific conflicts, one issue at a time. This kind of "muddling through" requires continuing compromises among relevant interest groups and between the two governments. Bilateral relations are affected by a general sentiment in the two capitals that some policy coordination is helpful, and that frictions should not be allowed to exacerbate one another. Neither country wants to limit its own autonomy, but each is conscious of the need to be flexible enough to manage this intricate relationship.

Increasing tensions over specific issues, heightened by growing inter-connections, could prove more difficult to handle in future years, how-ever. Nationalist policies on both sides of the border are now conceiv-able precisely because the case-by-case approach to U.S.-Mexico relations has often allowed the resolution of specific issues to be post-poned, to become the captive of special interests, and to be held hostage to domestic political pressures. The United States and Mexico are com-peting more economically, struggling more frequently over debt, trade, investment, migration, drugs, and border issues. A possible confronta-tion over Central America could accelerate this deterioration.

Ad hoc management of U.S.-Mexico relations is no longer good enough. The connections between these two countries have become too multiple, intense, and important to let tensions accumulate until they reach crisis proportions. It is time for conscious, high-level, and sus-tained commitments by both Mexico and the United States to halt the recurrent drift toward conflict and fundamentally to restructure the bilateral relationship in their mutual interest.

The boldest but not necessarily the most effective way to change U.S.-Mexico relations would be to establish a truly preferential "special relationship" between the two countries. Proposals to create such a relationship are hardy perennials, resurfacing often over the years. The idea usually includes privileged Mexican access to U.S. capital, mar-kets, and technology; comparable U.S. access to Mexican markets and exports; sectoral production-sharing agreements; a bilateral accord to regulate migration; U.S. cooperation to increase Mexico's tourist reve-nues; a scheme for meshing the production and distribution of Mexican energy with U.S. needs; and consistent efforts to coordinate approaches to foreign policy, in Central America and elsewhere.

The concept of a meaningful "special relationship" that goes beyond the rhetoric of ceremonial toasts seems attractive. It would translate the unique mutual significance of Mexico and the United States into prefer-ential policies and procedures. For some U.S. policy makers and politi-cal leaders, the notion appeals because Mexico's proximity and size distinguish it so clearly from other nations, and special treatment can therefore be rationalized and explained. Some support also exists within the U.S. business community, particularly in the Southwest, for efforts to integrate Mexico and the United States more fully.

A constituency also exists in Mexico to support closer integration with the United States. It includes business and professional figures, as well as some leaders of the Partido de Accion National (PAN), the lead-ing opposition party. These proponents of a "special relationship" be-lieve that historic Mexican policies are counterproductive, that it is high time for Mexico to adjust to the immutable fact of its location next to the United States.

Building a truly meaningful special relationship between Mexico and the United States is an idea whose time has not arrived, however, and it may never do so. The main flaw of proposals to institutionalize a "special relationship" between the United States and Mexico is that they probably cannot be implemented on a sustained basis in either country.

A truly preferential relationship with Mexico would contradict significant U.S. commitments in other countries and regions, as well as the broad principles of free trade, most favored nation treatment, and other provisions of the liberal international economic order. It is very unlikely, therefore, that a substantial set of special concessions to Mexico would survive the policy-making processes of executive and congressional consideration.

Even if such a policy could be adopted, moreover, it would depend for its effective implementation on a degree of coordination among many private interests and public agencies—municipal, state, and federal—which is unimaginable in the United States except in the throes of dire national emergency. The much more modest efforts of the Carter administration to orchestrate executive branch treatment of Mexico within the U.S. government by appointing a high-level "coordinator" for Mexican affairs foundered precisely because of the diverse interests and actors involved. Any U.S. administration would have great difficulty imposing a centralized preferential policy on the many government agencies that would have to be involved.

Even if the U.S. government could produce and sustain an agreed national policy, this approach would bind only the public sector. Business, labor, the media, and other private groups might dissent, and they control many of the relevant resources. Because of the plurality of actors, it is difficult for the United States to pursue any coherent and coordinated policy toward Mexico, much less one offering special privileges on a long-term basis. A promise to provide Mexico with consistently preferential treatment would be very hard, perhaps impossible, for Washington to keep.

On the Mexican side, it might be even more difficult in practice to sustain meaningful, detailed bilateral cooperation on a preferential basis. The many objective conflicts between U.S. and Mexican interests are compounded by profound political sensitivities in Mexico.

Many Mexicans—especially government officials, political leaders, technocrats, and intellectuals—are intensely wary of proposals for constructing a special bilateral relationship. They recognize (increasingly, in many cases) the importance of U.S. policies for Mexico's development, but they do not want to heighten or highlight their country's dependence on Washington. Nor do they want to be set apart from other advanced developing nations with whom they believe they share fundamental interests.

A strongly pro-interdependence posture by a Mexican regime might well trigger an extreme nationalist reaction. "Silent integration" between the United States and Mexico may well continue to occur, but articulated and explicit integration will almost certainly be abortive.

The best U.S. approach toward Mexico, indeed, might be not a Mexico policy at all but rather an overall U.S. stance toward Latin American and, indeed, toward advanced developing countries in general. Many of the principal issues of interest to Mexico are shared by other advanced developing countries, most of them in Latin America and some elsewhere in the Third World. Mexico and other such nations want improved access to capital, markets, and technology; more foreign investment on terms conducive to national development; a greater say in international organizations; and generally enhanced influence and status. An overall U.S. policy that responds positively to these general Third World concerns would contribute significantly to improving U.S.-Mexico relations, for Mexico is the developing country with which U.S. ties are by far the strongest.

Chapter 7 spells out more fully how the United States could respond positively to the concerns of Mexico and other advanced developing nations. First, I call for a strong U.S. government initiative to work with the commercial banks, the international financial institutions, and the governments of the developing countries to help assure that significant net new flows of capital will enter these nations in coming years. U.S. government decisions are required to augment the resources available to the International Monetary Fund, the World Bank, and the Inter-American Development Bank so that the advanced developing countries can obtain capital in amounts and on terms that will permit them to resume and sustain economic growth. The commercial banks should extend the maturities of existing debts, limit repayment obligations to a reasonable share of export earnings, reduce spreads and eliminate fees on renegotiated loans, and capitalize some interest payments and/or put a cap or ceiling on interest rates. The U.S. government, other industrial country governments, international financial institutions, and the commercial banks should together assure that new, incremental financing flows to the potentially dynamic countries of Latin America and the Third World.

Second, it is vital for the United States to put its own fiscal house in order, to reduce substantially the public sector deficit, which creates a strong inflationary pressure on interest rates. Each 1 percent rise in the interest rate adds approximately $700 million to Mexico's immediate debt service requirements. Only when the United States controls its own deficit can Mexico and other debtor nations hope for sustained relief from high interest charges.

Third, a strong effort is needed by the United States and other industrial nations to beat back protectionist pressures and to make their markets increasingly open to exports from the advanced developing countries. For the developing countries to trade themselves out of their financial distress, it will be necessary for the United States and the other industrial countries to sustain commercial policies that reward developing nations for achieving a comparative advantage in various products. For Mexico, in particular, the key export market is the United States.

A general U.S. policy that helps the advanced developing countries would be very positive for Mexico. It could be made even more positive by adding to it specific measures, substantive and procedural, that respond to the unique issues that Mexico poses for the United States. Within a positive overall framework of relations, the two countries would be more likely to be able bilaterally to expand and regulate the legal flow of migration through a mutually agreed guest-worker arrangement. Special programs to deal with the problems of the border regions could also be facilitated. It should be possible to relate Mexico's energy production to evolving U.S. requirements without threatening Mexico's autonomy, through long-term supply arrangements.

On these issues and others, the challenge is to take into account Mexico's location on the border of the United States without undermining the broader policies of either government and without provoking a strong nationalist reaction in Mexico. A U.S. posture that responds positively to the financial and commercial needs of all developing countries, without singling out Mexico for special treatment, would make it easier to fashion such bilateral arrangements.

Mexico's future depends fundamentally on Mexican decisions, and in particular on the country's ability to reshape and strengthen its economy after the devastating setbacks of the 1980s. Decisive and courageous leadership is required in Mexico—in government, in politics, in the private sector, and in the labor unions—to make the country's economy more efficient and productive, its public administration more effective and less corrupt, and its political system more responsive. Mexico's national confidence needs to be rebuilt after a period that was doubly traumatic because the oil-induced euphoria of the late 1970s was so quickly dashed, and because of the further twin blows of natural disaster and sharply declining oil prices.

The United States cannot solve Mexico's tough problems. A positive U.S. approach toward advanced developing countries, particularly sensitive to Mexico's needs without being obtrusive, could make a major contribution to Mexico's national recovery, however. It could help Mexico resume its economic growth, resolve its social problems, and refurbish its political institutions without turning toward either the extreme nationalist or the extreme internationalist course—paths that would be self-defeating for Mexico as well as harmful to the United States.

No quick fix will resolve the many issues that arise between the United States and Mexico each year. Some procedural steps might greatly improve the management of this complex relationship, however. Existing means should be reinforced to be sure that public and private leaders in the two countries are more systematically exposed to one another's views. Binational task forces, including both public officials and private citizens, should be formed to seek joint solutions on issues such as pollution, resource management, or even migration. It would be particularly useful to foster attempts in both countries to develop policies that transcend the immediate and particular interests of private groups. The recently launched nongovernment Binational Commission on the Future of United States–Mexico Relations, sponsored by the Ford Foundation, is one such effort. Equally important would be sustained work, both in Mexico and in the United States, to improve mutual public understanding. Attempts to improve attentive public consciousness of Mexican problems and their implications for the United States might be particularly valuable beyond the New York–Washington corridor.

The most important single change we in the United States could undertake to improve relations with Mexico would be one of attitude. Washington is repeatedly tempted to handle conflict with Mexico either by ignoring it or by pressuring Mexico to accept U.S. positions. It is crucial for leaders in the United States always to bear in mind, as Mexicans necessarily do, that conflict is built into the U.S.-Mexico relationship.

The interests of Mexico and the United States are often compatible, but they are seldom identical. Legitimate differences of interest are complicated, moreover, by nationalist impulses on both sides of the border, and by longstanding and deep-seated mutual suspicion. Only when the people and the government of the United States understand that Mexico's interests are different from those of the United States and yet also appropriate—as Mexicans must and do understand that U.S. interests are global—will the prospects for effective cooperation between these uneasy neighbors be improved.

CHAPTER FIVE

The United States and Brazil

Managing Conflict

Relations between the United States and Mexico have long been complex and conflictual. Until recent years, by contrast, U.S. relations with Brazil were usually relatively limited in extent, uncomplicated in content, and cordial in tone. Despite its vast size, Brazil seemed a distant country with which the United States had few problems. Maintaining friendly relations with South America's largest nation did not often require much consideration.

The U.S. government, so intently interested in the domestic politics of the countries close to its borders, only rarely concerned itself with Brazil's internal situation. The international interests of the governments of Brazil and the United States, when they overlapped, were easily compatible. From the turn of the century on, U.S. and Brazilian officials periodically proclaimed a "special relationship" between the two countries. But the quality of that relationship, like that between blood relatives residing at a great distance from each other, was not often tested.

Beginning in the 1930s and then with greater speed from the 1950s to the 1980s, Brazil has undergone a sustained period of industrialization. Brazil's transformation and its correspondingly greater international involvement have changed Brazil's internal structure, enhanced its power, and redefined its interests. Relations between Brazil and the United States, consequently, have gradually become more complicated. During the last thirty years, Brazil has become a significant international actor with foreign policy objectives that often differ from those of the United States.

The United States has reacted to Brazil's emergence sometimes by accommodating, sometimes by resisting, and sometimes by ignoring Brazil's divergent international interests. The Kennedy administration welcomed Brazil's President João Goulart to Washington but cooperated little with his regime. The Johnson administration hailed the advent of a military government to replace Goulart but did not provide the preferential economic treatment Brazil's military rulers desired. The Nixon-Ford administration sought to placate Brazil by showing it some procedural deference but did not make major substantive changes in policy. The Carter administration initially attempted to force Brazilian policies to conform with Washington's, thus provoking nationalist resentment. Later, the Carter administration tried to mollify Brazil but failed to introduce significant modifications in relevant U.S. policies.

The Reagan administration attempted from the start to restore what a key adviser had called a "beautiful relationship," but it found Brazil's government skeptical and standoffish. The Reagan administration has pushed U.S. preferences more tactfully than the Carter administration did, but it has done so without significantly altering the basic U.S. stance on issues of concern to Brazil. During each of the past several U.S. administrations, bilateral frictions between Brazil and the United States have been evident.

Brazil today has emerged—albeit unevenly and with the possibility of a relapse—from a severe economic depression. This crisis, which first became obvious in 1981, was in part a result of the country's fuller integration into the world economy, for Brazil's international involvements made the country more vulnerable to external shocks.

Brazil's economic difficulties not only interrupted the country's rapid growth but also threatened its welfare and social cohesion. The difficulties have also affected the international financial system, for Brazil owes more than one-fourth of Latin America's staggering total debt. The temptation in Brazil to blame foreign bankers and the governments of the advanced industrial countries for the country's prolonged difficulties raises the possibility of an extreme nationalist reaction if economic problems worsen again. An extended recession within Brazil producing an ultranationalist response would damage the economy of the United States and the international economy more generally.

The United States can no longer afford to take Brazil for granted. Policies are needed that combine a respect for Brazil's increased stature with heightened sensitivity to the intense growing pains Brazil has suffered during the past several years.

A NATION TO BE RECKONED WITH

Brazil's sheer size and its abundant resources have endowed it with great potential.

Brazil is, by area, the fifth-largest nation in the world; it is larger than the United States excluding Alaska. It shares borders with ten other nations; only the Soviet Union has more neighbors. Brazil is the sixth most populous country in the world, with a population approximately equal to those of Mexico, Argentina, Chile, and Venezuela taken together. Brazil's economy has become by far the largest in Latin America, the largest in the entire Third World except for China, and the ninth or tenth largest in the world (the seventh or eighth among market economies). Its gross domestic product—some $280 billion in 1987—exceeds those of all other South and Central American countries combined.

Brazil's resources are legion. The country's reserves of iron ore are the world's largest or second largest. Brazil ranks first in hydroelectric potential; its total electric-generating capacity is already tenth in the world and doubles every eight years. Its utilized, underutilized, and unutilized lands are vast. Brazil has one of the world's few remaining habitable frontiers. Mineral riches—uranium, bauxite, manganese, copper, iron, and, most recently, gold—are still being discovered (or rediscovered, in the case of gold). Of the resources needed for modern industry, only petroleum has been missing in Brazil in significant quantities, and important deposits have been discovered in recent years.

Brazil is already a major actor in the international economy. It exports more agricultural commodities than any country except the United States. In coffee it ranks first; in soybeans, sugar, and cocoa, second; and in tobacco, fourth. Brazil is the world's largest exporter of iron ore. Next to Korea, it is the largest industrial exporter among developing countries, and it is the developing world's second-largest steel producer. In 1980, Brazil produced 26 percent more steel than Great Britain, the original industrial power. As a producer of automobiles, Brazil ranked in 1985 with Spain and close to Canada and Britain.

Brazil is also among the world's major exporters of weapons. It sells aircraft, tanks, missiles, armored personnel carriers, and similar items worth well over $1 billion a year to more than thirty countries. Brazilian-made airplanes fly many commuter-line routes in the United States and are used in more than twenty other nations. Brazilian-built ships sail in many parts of the world. Brazilian-manufactured engines run many U.S.-built cars. Brazilian computers are used in China. Brazilian engineers and contractors have been undertaking major construction projects elsewhere in Latin America, in the Middle East, and in Africa.

Brazil is a significant force in various other aspects of international affairs. As the developing world's largest borrower (with more than $110 billion in outstanding loans), Brazil obviously affects the global financial system. As one of the Third World's main exporters and importers, Brazil is important for international commerce. As one of the nations most seriously committed to seeking alternatives to fossil fuels,

Brazil influences world energy prospects as well as the climate for nuclear nonproliferation efforts. Brazil also affects international negotiations on matters ranging from coffee and sugar to the Law of the Sea and the future of southern Africa, as well as international energy, finance, and trade. Although Brazil has not traditionally sought a visible leadership role in international forums, its influence has steadily grown.

Brazil's scope eclipses that of any other Latin American nation. Brazil accounts for almost 35 percent of all of Latin America's gross output of goods and services, foreign investment, and trade in manufactured goods. Brazil's cultural activities project the country's image abroad; some fifteen thousand Latin American, African, and other foreign students have come to Brazil in recent years on official programs, for example. No other nation in South America approaches Brazil's degree of industrial development, the extent of its international involvements, or the strength of its military establishment (although the size and budget of the armed forces are low in per capita terms). Brazil's large, professionally skilled diplomatic corps is prominent at the United Nations, the Organization of American States, and elsewhere.

Brazilians have long seen their country as an emerging world power, endowed with a kind of "manifest destiny." Brazil's leaders (and many Brazilians of all levels and sectors) expect their country to be taken seriously, to be consulted and even courted internationally. They want to ensure that Brazil's interests will be taken into account, that the established world powers will not freeze Brazil and other emerging countries out of a chance for more power, prosperity, and status. They have become increasingly frustrated at what they see as external constraints on Brazil's prospects for growth.

Until a generation ago, it was a wry commonplace that "Brazil is the country of the future—and always will be." The country's sheer size inevitably gave it some international significance even then. But Brazil was not really powerful, and its foreign policy aspirations could usually be met by essentially symbolic gestures.

Until the 1960s, Brazil had never managed to harness its material and human resources effectively. During the late nineteenth century and for the first decades of the twentieth, neighboring Argentina, although a considerably smaller country in area and population, consistently outranked Brazil on most indicators. By 1960, Brazil had caught up with and even surpassed Argentina, but this was due at least as much to Argentina's postwar decline as to Brazil's progress. Brazil was still a sleeping giant.

All that has been changing in the past generation. Few nations have grown so much, so quickly, and on such a grand scale as has Brazil in the last thirty years. Even with its current problems, Brazil is a nation to be reckoned with.

Brazil has been altered, first, by the explosion of the country's population from about 70 million in 1960 to some 135 million today. Although the rate of population growth in Brazil has begun to fall, by the end of the century Brazil's population should reach 180 to 200 million, equal to that of the United States in the 1960s, and it may reach 300 million by the second half of the twenty-first century. Four out of ten Brazilians are under age fifteen, so that Brazil's work force continues to expand enormously.

Brazil has also been reshaped by urbanization. Although major traditional rural enclaves remain, the modern and urban nation within Brazil has grown apace. The urban share of Brazil's population spurted from 32 percent in 1950 to more than 70 percent in the 1980s, up to the level found in several advanced industrial societies. Between 1970 and 1980, the rural population decreased in absolute numbers for the first time in Brazil's history. São Paulo, a city of restless dynamism, has an estimated population of 14 million; eight other cities now have populations greater than 1 million, compared with two just twenty-five years ago.

Brazil's increasingly urban population has entered the modern era. The number of Brazilians with access to electricity in their homes, sewage facilities, and potable water has nearly doubled in a generation, although many people still lack these amenities. The number of radios, televisions, telephones, and telexes has exploded.

Education, a major contributor to modernization, has boomed. Adult literacy jumped from just over 40 percent in 1948 to about 60 percent in 1960 and to well over 70 percent (almost 80 percent by some estimates) in the 1980s. The number of Brazilian youths in secondary schools multiplied almost ninefold between 1960 and the late 1970s, to over 2.5 million. University enrollment is now well over 1 million.

These social and demographic changes have contributed to a fundamental transformation of Brazil's politics. Almost 59 million persons went to the polls in November 1982 in the gubernatorial and congressional elections, almost four times as many as participated in the legislative elections of 1962. Major sectors of Brazilian society—industrial workers, shanty-town dwellers, women, and lay participants in local religious movements, as well as business executives and professionals— have immersed themselves in electoral politics. Although they are still weak, professional associations, labor unions, neighborhood organizations, and political parties have all been gaining institutional strength in recent years, even during the prolonged period of authoritarian military rule.

The Brazilian state has also been transformed. Brazil's public sector (including state-controlled enterprises) now accounts for a large share of the national economy; some 46 percent of the country's financial resources are under the direct control of the federal government. Some five hundred Brazilian firms, including nine of the ten largest, are state controlled. The dramatic growth of Brazil's public sector has increased the state's capacity to plan, tax, invest, and control—if also to waste. A new and powerful technocratic class has built a dense network of relations between private business and the public bureaucracy.

In the 1950s, Brazil's economy was still largely organized around coffee. Fifty-six percent of Brazil's export earnings in 1960 derived from that crop, which shaped the country's international concerns. In the 1980s, however, coffee contributes less than 10 percent of Brazil's export earnings. Agricultural diversification accounts for some of this dramatic difference, to be sure. Brazil has captured the largest share of the world trade in frozen orange juice concentrate. It has also become a massive exporter of frozen poultry and soybeans, competing successfully with the United States in third markets.

But the most striking shift in Brazil's economy has been its rapid and pervasive industrialization, based mainly on import substitution in the 1940s and 1950s, and also on export promotion since the late 1960s. The share of Brazil's work force employed in agriculture has declined by one-half within one generation (to about 30 percent), while the industrial work force now comprises almost 20 percent of the economically active population. Industry now accounts for almost 35 percent of Brazil's GDP.

Within one generation, Brazil transformed itself from an importer to an exporter of steels, heavy machinery, petrochemicals, weapons, and other industrial products. For example, Brazil imported 4.3 million tons of steel in 1974; ten years later it exported over 4 million tons. The share of Brazil's exports accounted for by manufactured goods exploded, incredibly, from 3 percent in 1960 to more than 65 percent in 1985. As if to symbolize the country's new economic role, Brazil's exports of automobiles and auto parts now exceed in volume its exports of coffee.

As Brazil's economic structure has evolved, its involvement in the world economy has become much more complex. Exports grew an average of almost 10 percent annually in real terms from 1965 to 1980. Brazil's imports, meanwhile, climbed about as fast as exports, as the country came to depend increasingly not only on imported petroleum but also on many capital goods. Foreign investment in Brazil has risen sharply to over $26 billion, the highest level in the developing world. Most important, Brazil's foreign debt surged from a negligible $2 billion in 1960 and a modest $21 billion in 1975 to the present enormous sum. Annual debt service charges jumped from 33 percent of exports in 1974 to more than 80 percent by 1982, with interest payments alone comprising more than 55 percent. Although debt service charges dropped to less than 40 percent of exports by 1986, this figure is still high by historic standards. Brazil has been paying out some 4 percent of its GDP each year to service the debt; this drain is not long sustainable, economically or politically.

During the 1960s and 1970s, Brazil significantly diversified its markets and its sources of capital and other imports. The share of Brazil's exports bound for the United States declined steadily from 1960 to 1980; the proportion going to Western Europe and to Japan significantly increased. Brazil's exports to other Latin American countries more than doubled, and trade with African countries, with Asian countries other than Japan, and with Eastern Europe also increased steadily in the late 1970s, albeit from a much lower base. Brazil's commerce with the Soviet Union expanded, as well.

Although U.S. investment in Brazil has climbed in absolute terms, the U.S. share of overall foreign investment in Brazil declined from about 45 percent in 1960 to about 30 percent in the 1980s. This was largely a result of rapidly increasing European and Japanese investment and some investment from the Arab Middle East. Brazil also significantly diversified its debts; the share of Brazil's debt owed to European banks increased from 27 percent in 1971 to 44 percent in 1980. As in most other Latin American countries, official U.S. aid came to represent a tiny share of Brazil's external financing, while commercial bank lending rapidly increased.

One immediate result of the economic crisis of the 1980s has been to halt or even reverse temporarily Brazil's long-term trend toward diversifying its trade, debts, and sources of investment. Brazil's export revenues declined substantially in 1982 because many industrial countries, as well as most of Brazil's new trading partners in Latin America and elsewhere in the Third World, could not maintain the level of their imports. Major reductions, more than 40 percent in each case, occurred during 1982 and 1983 in Brazil's exports to Argentina, Chile, Mexico, Uruguay, Poland, and Algeria; Brazil's exports to all Latin American non-oil exports in 1983 were at 49 percent of their 1981 level. The share of Brazil's trade accounted for by the United States consequently shot back up; in 1984 and 1985, the United States accounted for about one-third of Brazil's exports. This bulge is likely to be temporary, however, a result of the overvalued dollar and the slump of Brazil's other trading partners.

Brazil increased its autonomy during the 1970s by broadening its international links, but it remains vulnerable to world economic conditions. The country's prosperity depends more than ever on trade and, especially, on external capital. As interest rates change, for instance, Brazil is powerfully affected; a 1 percent increase in the London Interbank Official Rate (LIBOR), a standard base for international lending, adds almost $1 billion to Brazil's external obligations for a year.

Brazil is still quite vulnerable to international economic reverses, but it also has more power to affect the world economy. If Brazil's economic recovery of the mid-1980s can be sustained, this could significantly expand the market for exports from the United States and other advanced industrial nations. A return by Brazil to a prolonged and severe depression, on the other hand, could harm the chances for economic recovery in several major industrial countries, because of both the contracted Brazilian market and the impact a Brazilian depression would have on international commercial banks.

A Brazilian default on its debt or even an extended moratorium on payments would have serious repercussions for several major U.S banks; the nine largest U.S. money center (as distinct from regional) banks have some 37 percent of their capital on loan in Brazil. Even a one-year delay by Brazil on payment of the interest and principal due on its foreign debt could significantly reduce the profits of these banks. A major setback for these U.S. banks, in turn, could adversely affect the banking system of the United States and international finance more generally.

Because of its generation-long export-led growth, the diversification of its international economic ties, its severe debt and trade problems of the early 1980s, and its incipient recovery since 1984, Brazil is an important part of the world economy. An effective U.S. policy toward Latin America needs to take fully into account Brazil's new economic significance as well as its difficulties.

FROM MIRACLE TO CRISIS

Brazil's experience during the past generation was widely heralded, until the 1980s, as a "miracle" of rapid economic growth. More recently, since 1981, some observers have come to regard Brazil's course as deeply worrisome. Each of these contrasting visions of Brazil needs to be corrected, for each is only partially valid.

Brazil's extraordinarily rapid economic transformation—especially in the late 1960s and early 1970s—seemed miraculous at the time because no developing country of Brazil's size had previously grown for so long at such a pace. Critics pointed out, even while Brazil's dazzling spurt was still occurring, that whole regions of the country were largely unaffected or adversely affected by the expansion of Brazil's industrial heartland, and that income distribution remained badly skewed or was worsening. But a widespread perception of Brazil until the early 1980s was that it had taken off, that its economic growth had become self-sustaining, and that the benefits of growth would eventually "trickle down" to all, or at least most, elements in Brazilian society.

Brazil seemed a notably positive example of the authoritarian capitalist path to national development. No one claimed that this course was without cost, for the fact of systematic political repression was obvious, but this was often portrayed as a temporary, if unfortunate, side effect of economic progress. The harshest aspects of Brazil's authoritarian rule—the exile of dissidents, the detention of political prisoners, the banning of leading political figures from public office, physical torture and other gross and systematic violations of fundamental human rights—began to diminish in intensity and frequency after 1974. A gradual process of political opening (*abertura*), a phased restoration of democratic politics, began then under President Ernesto Geisel.

The country's continued rapid rate of economic growth, even after the first oil shock of 1973, gave the Brazilian approach considerable domestic and international legitimacy for a time. Brazil's evident economic accomplishments contradicted the arguments of those dependency theorists who had suggested that stagnation inevitably results when international capital penetrates the Third World. No one could deny in the 1970s that Brazil was growing rapidly and that it was adding considerably to its national power. The continuing if somewhat uneven process of *abertura,* moreover, countered the arguments of those who claimed that Brazil's regime lacked political appeal. Brazil seemed to be well launched toward national progress. Discussions of U.S. policy options during the 1970s were usually based on the premise that Brazil's course was established and successful.

Even while it was occurring, however, the Brazilian "miracle" was partly illusory in three respects.

First, Brazil's rapid economic growth from 1968 to 1973 was due in part to special circumstances that were unrelated to the regime's approach to development. The economic spurt was made possible by a temporary confluence of highly favorable factors: pent-up internal demand and underutilized productive capacity due to the 1963–67 recession, coincident with an unprecedented increase in international trade and world capital flows. No Brazilian regime could sustain these advantages forever, for they arose not mainly from government policies but from the context of Brazil's expansion.

Second, the transformation of Brazil's economy had human costs well beyond the sacrifice of civil liberties. The Brazilian approach, especially during the "miracle" years, was based on a strategy of development which left a wide gap between rich and poor. Economic production in Brazil during the boom period was consciously directed toward a narrow, high-income slice of the domestic market and toward export markets, not toward broadening national participation in the economy. The regime's economic policies thus had the effect of concentrating income, investment, and purchasing power. The poorer half of Brazil's population received 17.4 percent of national income in 1960, 13.5 percent in 1976, and only 12.6 percent in 1980. The poorest 20 percent of Brazil's population saw its share of national income fall from 3.4 percent in 1970 to 2.8 percent in 1980, while the top 1 percent was raising its share from 14 percent to 17 percent in the same decade, and a new middle class was also greatly expanding.

Poverty in Brazil was not substantially alleviated, even during the boom period. Widespread deprivation persisted. Infant mortality, malnutrition, and illiteracy remained high. Brazil's "miracle," in short, did not reach all, or even most, Brazilians. Some, in fact, became its victims. Two different countries have come to coexist within the borders of Brazil: a modern industrial power and a large nation of the rural and urban poor.

Third, the political appeal of the military regime proved impermanent. To the extent that Brazil progressed economically, repression and authoritarianism came to be seen as less excusable. To the extent that growth slowed, on the other hand, the regime's main justification for harsh and inequitable policies was undercut. Over the course of several years, the initial coalition that favored the military takeover in 1964— the Church, industrial and commercial leaders, middle-class professionals and technocrats—began to split, to become disaffected, and to press for changes. President Geisel's moves toward *abertura* in the mid-1970s, and the subsequent acceleration of that process under President João Figueiredo, reflected the weakening of public support for Brazil's military leadership.

Changes in the international economic environment after 1973 combined with and reinforced the structural flaws inherent in Brazil's approach to development to plunge Brazil into increasingly serious difficulties in the late 1970s. Brazil's Second National Development Plan, released in 1973, had postulated an annual growth rate of 10 percent for the next few years. Although this rate was unprecedented for a nation of Brazil's size, it seemed a natural projection of Brazil's experience from 1968 through the early 1970s. These optimistic expectations, however, soon clashed with sharply changing realities. The 1973–74 oil shock abruptly increased Brazil's oil import bill, bringing it to about one-half the level of the country's total exports. Brazil's export potential was simultaneously cut by slowing growth, also a result of the oil shock, in the industrialized market economies of North America, the Far East, and Western Europe.

Faced with unanticipated balance-of-payments difficulties, Brazil's first response was to increase its international borrowing vastly, engage in a major new effort at import substitution, cut back its imports and consumption somewhat, and continue diversifying and promoting its various exports. These tactics seemed to work well for a while, as Brazil took full advantage of petrodollar recycling and of its own export growth potential. Economic expansion was renewed in Brazil, after a brief lull in the mid-1970s, at higher but still tolerable rates of inflation. International bankers had confidence in Brazil's prospects and management, and they had large petrodollar surpluses to invest, both in Brazil and in other developing countries that might import Brazilian exports. Brazil was able for a time, therefore, to finance continued growth at low (sometimes even negative) real rates of interest, although shortened maturities and variable interest rates made these new loans potentially much more costly and thus increased Brazil's vulnerability.

The second oil shock, in 1979–80, resulting in a 200 percent increase in the price of petroleum, was far more painful, however. Brazil's import bill soared again, while real interest rates began to climb. The lethal combination of higher petroleum prices and substantially increased interest rates consumed virtually all of Brazil's export revenues, setting off a downward slide.

Brazil's government then chose to up the ante: to borrow still more in order to cover immediate needs while moving vigorously to stimulate even more exports and, at the same time, trying to curb domestic inflation. International commercial bankers still favored Brazil, making its approach appear viable for a time, although the banks began to increase their "spreads," the charge they imposed above the cost to them of obtaining the capital. The fact that Brazil managed from 1978 to 1981 to double its exports to Latin America, Africa, the Middle East, and Eastern Europe temporarily masked the degree of its accumulating financial burden. By 1981, however, the limits of this approach were becoming readily apparent.

The bubble finally burst in 1982. The immediate pinpricks were largely provided by events unrelated to Brazil. Indeed, one was noneconomic: the South Atlantic conflict touched off by Argentina's attempted takeover of the Malvinas-Falkland Islands in April 1982. The uncertainties precipitated by the South Atlantic War, by Argentina's badly aggravated financial situation, and by the deep rift in hemispheric relations that resulted from the U.S. support of Britain strongly reinforced the newly hesitant attitude that commercial banks in the United States and

Europe were beginning to adopt in their dealings with all Latin American debtors.

A second and more important immediate pinprick, this one economic, was also unrelated directly to Brazil. When Mexico recognized in August 1982 that it could not meet its international financial obligations (in part, ironically, as chapter 4 points out, because Mexico's oil revenues had fallen unexpectedly in 1982), commercial bankers became even more cautious about the entire Hemisphere. New loans to Latin America were delayed or denied, so that the total flow of resources to Latin America, including Brazil, dropped precipitously. Loans to Brazil, which had reached $10.5 billion in 1980 and $15.6 billion in 1981, averaged $1.5 billion a month during the first eight months of 1982 but then plummeted to just $400 million a month for the rest of the year. To make matters much worse, Brazil's exports, far from continuing to expand, declined sharply as the sustained world recession caused many of Brazil's trading partners to restrict their imports. The gap between Brazil's revenues and its financial requirements became correspondingly larger.

The third external reason for Brazil's worsening crisis in the early 1980s was the substantial rise in the real cost of capital, arising in large part from the fiscal and monetary policies adopted toward the end of the Carter administration and then strongly reinforced by the Reagan administration. The sharp increase in real interest rates in 1981 (what some have called the Reagan shock) subjected Brazilian loans to even higher costs.

Brazilian authorities responded slowly to the gathering financial crisis. In part, they were inhibited by their understandable desire to project a successful image to the voting public before the November 1982 elections, the first direct elections for state governors since 1966. The regime's efforts made much sense politically but weakened the government's capacity to conduct national economic policy at a crucial juncture.

A proud but futile effort was made to avoid recourse to the International Monetary Fund during the preelectoral period. Instead, Brazil attempted to renegotiate its commercial debt with the private banks on the basis of the country's record and prospects. One cost of that strategy was a substantial underestimation of Brazil's needs for debt restructuring. In order to earn the continued confidence of the financial community, Brazil depicted its plight as less serious than Mexico's. As a result, when Brazil finally was obliged to go to the IMF shortly after the congressional elections, it received less international credit than it might well have received if its requirements had been accurately portrayed.

Brazil's effort to solve its economic problems with modest measures failed, and the delay in facing reality exacerbated matters. Brazil's economic managers lost credibility at home and abroad. As the months passed, Brazil's predicament was recognized by a widening circle of Brazilians; by commercial banks in the United States, Europe, and Japan; by foreign governments; and by relevant international agencies.

As the extent of Brazil's financial troubles became clear, the underlying structural factors that contributed to Brazil's quandary became more widely understood. The Brazilian strategy of economic growth has primarily emphasized industrial development, much of it in capital-intensive sectors that have been largely dependent on imported materials, equipment, and technology. Subsidies have been extended to stimulate agricultural and industrial exports, both through direct subventions and through tax exemptions and other indirect devices. Public enterprises have also been favored as a means of rapidly expanding Brazil's production in a number of sectors. Various private enterprises have also been protected through tariffs and nontariff barriers. Massive public investments in infrastructure and in meeting consumer needs (for example, housing for the middle class) have led to a significant public deficit, fueling inflation.

As a consequence of all these policies, Brazil's food production for domestic consumption has lagged, many public enterprises have become bloated, and some sectors have been allowed to become inefficient.

These economic problems were exacerbated after 1979 by Brazil's response to its worsening balance-of-payments difficulties. Proposals by Finance and then Planning Minister Mario Henrique Simonsen and others to restrict credit and other subsidies as part of a standard inflation-fighting strategy were at first rejected. Instead, Brazil chose the approach of the new planning minister, Antonio Delfim Netto, who favored stimulating more rapid growth through cheap credit and various other incentives. From that decision on, Brazil became locked into a series of measures that depended for their efficacy on a world economic recovery.

After 1979, Brazil repeatedly heightened its structural vulnerability by betting on a prompt improvement in the world economy. Each year Brazil came to depend even more on new loans (often at still higher real rates of interest) and on expanding still further its export of products that were subject both to falling world demand and to increasingly protectionist policies in the industrial countries. In 1981, a number of Latin American and European countries imposed import restrictions. As a result, Brazil's export earnings suddenly fell by more than 13 percent (after average annual increases of about 19 percent in the previous two years), and the country's balance-of-payments deficit grew rapidly. Brazil's financial crisis followed ineluctably.

The extent and gravity of Brazil's economic debacle should not be underestimated. Inflation from 1983 through 1985 went over 200 percent a year, a rate unprecedented in Brazil's history. Efforts to curb inflation, moreover, reinforced a severe national depression. Real per capita income fell almost 11 percent from 1980 through 1983 (even more, if the terms of trade effects are included). Brazil's industrial output in 1983 was at or below the 1977 level. Employment in manufacturing was more than 10 percent below the 1976 level. New investment in Brazil, domestic and foreign, fell dramatically. A record number of firms, including some of the country's largest as well as many smaller companies, filed for restructuring or bankruptcy. State governments and government-run institutions also became very shaky financially. Major export promotion efforts helped Brazil begin to recover in 1983, and national economic growth resumed in 1984 and accelerated in 1985 and 1986, but major problems resurfaced in 1987, and a new decline is possible.

Even without further deterioration, poverty in Brazil has reached critical dimensions. Infant mortality, life expectancy, and nutrition indicators show that for many Brazilians, conditions have become worse in the 1980s.

Brazil's grim economic situation has had social and political consequences. Food riots and other disturbances rocked São Paulo, Rio de Janeiro, Salvador (Bahia), and other cities in 1983. Such outbreaks have not been sustained, but street crime in urban areas has reached epidemic proportions. The numbers of homeless and abandoned youths are growing. Brazil's social problems are a source of increasing concern.

The process of *abertura,* begun in the 1970s, became an important outlet for national frustration in the early 1980s. In the 1982 elections, antigovernment parties won the governorships of ten (out of twenty-three) of Brazil's states. These states comprise two-thirds of the nation's population and account for almost 70 percent of its economic production and tax base. Opposition parties carried the capital cities in nineteen of the twenty-three states in the gubernatorial elections of 1982, and they won in almost all of Brazil's eighty largest cities.

Widespread repudiation of the military regime—and especially of its civilian economic team, which only a few years ago had been so widely hailed—became obvious. Polls conducted in September 1983 showed that more than 80 percent of the Brazilian public opposed the regime's economic policies. Millions of Brazilians went further in 1984 and demonstrated in mass rallies, the largest in the nation's history, calling for direct presidential elections, a fundamental reform that almost passed in congress despite the military regime's intense opposition.

In January 1985, Brazil's first civilian president in twenty years was selected, albeit through indirect elections by an electoral college composed of members of the senate and the house. The choice of Tancredo Neves, a longtime opposition leader with widely recognized political skills and a capacity for consensus building, seemed to augur well for the restoration of democracy in Brazil. Tragically, Mr. Neves—chosen precisely because of the nearly universal respect he personally commanded—became mortally ill on the eve of his scheduled inauguration and was never able to assume the presidency of the New Republic, the restored civilian regime.

The strength of Brazil's commitment to restoring democracy was demonstrated by the unhindered succession to the presidency of Vice-president José Sarney, until a few months earlier a member of the pro-military party. It was reinforced by Sarney's almost immediate indication that he would be willing to limit his term to fewer than the mandated six years.

The Sarney administration quickly undertook significant economic reforms to fight inflation, promoted economic growth policies, initiated an agrarian reform, and began to attack the problems of gross socioeconomic inequity. The Plano Cruzado, an innovative attempt to reverse inflation without inducing recession through strict wage and price controls and a package of related reforms, had promising initial results. Efforts to expand Brazil's trade surplus proceeded well in 1985–86, as did negotiations with the commercial banks to stretch out Brazil's financial obligations. These efforts were well launched, but failure to make the necessary adjustments in 1987 brought a new economic downturn.

Although Brazil's rampant inflation was dramatically slowed after April 1986, the mandated controls caused bottlenecks and shortages; labor unrest and inflation resumed late in the year. The industrial recovery caused plants to function at a level that could not be sustained for long; a long-term expansion of industrial capacity will require major investment in a period when external flows of capital are negligible. Unless Brazil can somehow harness adequate resources for investment and growth on a sustained basis, further economic difficulties are likely before the end of the decade.

PROSPECTS FOR RECOVERY: BRAZIL'S SEARCH FOR OPTIONS

After a generation of remarkable if uneven growth, Brazil was severely shaken in the early 1980s by long-cumulating economic difficulties.

The Brazilian military government's efforts to induce further recession, drastically cut back public expenditures, and sharply reduce imports—all to rebalance the country's payments, curb inflation, and regain the confidence of foreign investors and lenders—were only partially successful. Brazil's exports recovered, and impressive trade sur-

pluses were achieved, but domestic production and employment continued to fall, and government revenues and expenditures declined. High
inflation persisted and social problems mounted.

Brazil's economic situation began to improve during 1984, thanks
largely to further reductions in petroleum imports (owing to expanded
hydroelectric power, use of gasohol and pure alcohol fuel, conservation,
and, especially, expanded domestic oil production), a decrease in the
cost of oil, an improvement in the terms of trade of Brazil's agriculture
exports, and a surge of exports to the United States. But modest advances in 1984 and even more impressive growth in 1985 and 1986,
aided by the drop in the price of oil, have not solved Brazil's fundamental problems. Brazil's economic recovery has been somewhat fragile
because it has been based partly on an unsustainable sharp reduction of
imports and an unusually large increase in exports to the United States,
and because inflation has been a difficult problem.

Brazilians are aware that their nation has been paying out more in
interest and amortization than it is receiving in new loans and suppliers'
credits. Some recent studies suggest, indeed, that even if worldwide
economic recovery occurs, Brazil may continue to be a net exporter of
capital well into the 1990s, unless the terms of its external debt are
substantially renegotiated. Growing protectionist tendencies in the
United States and the OECD countries further complicate Brazil's prospects, as does the possibility that world interest rates will rise again.
Understandably, skepticism is growing in Brazil that orthodox means
can extricate the nation from this pass. A search for a viable national
development policy has been taking place.

Brazilians of many different views agree that the costs of adjusting to
the international financial crunch should be shared by the lenders and
not absorbed wholly or even primarily by Brazil and other developing
countries. They argue that Brazil should seek to restructure its debt
substantially, to stretch the debt out over a number of years, and to
make the terms of the debt less onerous.

Within this overall consensus, considerable debate has taken place
about how to extricate the country from its economic difficulties. Brazil
has four choices: moderate or extreme variants of either an essentially
nationalist or a fundamentalist internationalist stance.

One option, essentially the one followed by the Figueiredo regime to
its end, is to play for more time, to "muddle through" until an eventual
international upturn eases the external constraints that contribute to
Brazil's plight. To pursue this "moderate internationalist" course, Brazil would continue to constrict its economy without fundamentally
changing its overall orientation. Some state enterprises would be
trimmed or sold to the private sector, though the privatization would not

be rapid or drastic. Real wages would be cut again as they were in the early 1980s. Brazil would negotiate periodically with commercial banks and international institutions in order to obtain relief if and when a gap redevelops between the country's earnings and its international financial obligations. Brazil would count on world economic recovery to expand markets for its exports and facilitate access to additional external capital. In the meantime, Brazil would continue to accept the established rules of the game in international trade and finance. It would not default, delay payments inordinately, or declare a unilateral moratorium, nor would it erect higher protectionist barriers.

Because this course demonstrably failed to achieve economic recovery, domestic resistance to the policy rose steadily during the latter years of the Figueiredo government. In August 1983, the Brazilian congress indicated for the first time in fifteen years that it would reject a government proposal—specifically, a new wage law intended to be part of the austerity package then being negotiated with the IMF. In October 1983, the congress actually rejected a government-decreed austerity wage law, despite the regime's imposition of state-of-emergency restrictions in Brasilia that would have intimidated members of congress in previous years.

Both presidential candidates in the indirect election of January 1985 won nomination in 1984 on platforms critical of the Figueiredo regime's economic policies; a move by the new civilian regime to revert to those policies would be strongly opposed by the same congressional coalition that produced a civilian victory. In short, the economic policies Brazil followed from the beginning of the crisis until mid-1985 are no longer politically feasible. The resignation of Brazil's finance minister and the president of the Central Bank in August 1985, early in the Sarney administration, in fact, signified the rejection of the moderate internationalist course on which Brazil had relied for a generation.

A second theoretically possible but also probably unfeasible course would involve opening Brazil's economy much more fully to international competition by sharply reducing protectionist policies and cutting back the public sector. This "extreme internationalist" policy, akin to the approach adopted in Chile, Argentina, and Uruguay during the mid-1970s, would shake down the Brazilian economy through the relentless discipline of the free market. The aim would be to force Brazil to emphasize sectors of production for which it has a natural comparative advantage, thus enabling it better to survive the ups and downs of the world economy. Expansion of foreign investment would be encouraged by lifting restrictions on the operations of foreign firms and on the remittances of profit.

Although some elements of Brazil's private sector are attracted by this approach and external pressures are occasionally exerted on its behalf, it is noteworthy how little support this recipe has in contemporary Brazil. Organized labor, the Church, the state technocracy, and much of the entrepreneurial community would all strongly oppose such a policy, which could, therefore, be adopted only by reversing the political opening. Brazil's military hierarchy understands, however, that it would be much harder to take over the government today than it was in the 1960s, particularly now that the *abertura* process has finally brought a civilian president to power. Because Brazil's society is so much more modern, mobilized, integrated, and complex than it was in the 1960s, and because the institutions of the civil society are much more highly developed, a restoration of hard-line authoritarianism would be difficult and costly.

Adoption of the extreme internationalist economic approach would be unlikely, even if elements within the armed forces were to reintroduce harsh authoritarian rule. The military officers who are most disposed toward opening up Brazil's economy are precisely those who are most committed to political opening. The officers who would be brought to power by an unlikely reversal of *abertura* would be against an extreme internationalist policy and inclined instead toward autarchic economic policies.

Brazil is turning, therefore, away from its strongly internationalist economic orientation and toward a somewhat more inward-oriented, nationalist approach to stimulating growth. The elements of such a new economic strategy have been widely discussed in Brazil during the past several years, particularly during the 1984 presidential election campaign. Although he presented no detailed economic plan, Neves as a candidate associated himself with the moderate nationalist approach, as has President Sarney, especially after his first three months in office.

Advocates of a more nationalist Brazilian development strategy argue that Brazil's internal market should be significantly expanded through redistributive measures that, if implemented over several years, should not be inordinately disruptive or expensive. Such reforms, they claim, could significantly raise the standard of living of Brazil's poorest people and of its lower middle class within one generation. Basic services would also be improved, enabling millions of Brazilians to produce and consume more.

According to this view, sustained public investment in primary education, urban and rural water supplies, health care, nutrition, and public transportation, as well as sustained public effort toward strengthening the agricultural sector through agrarian reform and investment in irrigation and infrastructure, could immediately provide increased employment. Over time, this investment could contribute to enhanced productivity and could considerably expand the domestic market for Brazilian-made goods. Such measures would also require much less energy and import requirements per unit of output than the capital- and energy-intensive growth strategy Brazil has been pursuing. Finally, this approach to development, it is argued, would leave Brazil less vulnerable to external factors—commercial, financial, or political.

Proponents of a nationally oriented shift in Brazil's economic strategy share two basic assumptions: that the country's size makes a more inwardly directed policy viable, and that international exigencies now make this tack advisable. In this view, the trends during the past generation toward urbanization, mass education, infrastructural improvements, and the reduction of regional disparities have set the stage for an appreciable expansion of the local market. Brazil's continuing inequities and lags in development provide considerable potential for further expansion. On the other hand, international conditions are such that no demonstration of Brazilian austerity can possibly induce a major net inflow of long-term capital. Efforts to contract Brazil's economy faster than that of the rest of the world are not only useless but counterproductive. They hurt Brazil, they make the repayment of debt even more difficult, and they help to stifle world recovery.

Advocates of a new Brazilian growth strategy disagree on a number of issues: how much emphasis should be given to the export sector; what kind of foreign exchange policy to pursue; how far to cut back the public sector; how and to what degree to realign wages; how to treat multinational corporations; how to deal with technology transfer issues; and, especially, how to handle Brazil's staggering debt. Differences on these issues exist at many points on a spectrum, but the basic options cluster around two distinct positions.

The "moderate nationalist" approach recognizes the continuing importance to Brazil of a strong export sector, foreign investment and technology, and access to international capital markets. Moderate nationalists, including most of the leadership of the PMDB (the Brazilian Democratic Movement, Brazil's main opposition party during recent years and now the major force in the Sarney government), seek not to isolate Brazil from the international economy, but rather to improve the terms of Brazil's interaction with creditors and commercial partners. They do not propose repudiation of the debt or even a prolonged unilateral moratorium. They push, instead, for a negotiated delay in repayment and a considerably restructured debt. In place of the combination of tacit moratoria and short-term adjustments which has characterized Brazil's policy during past years, they seek a multiyear extension of the debt, lowered interest rates, and repayment at a pace that

will leave Brazil with enough export earnings to permit sustained investment and growth. Moderate nationalists recognize that export imperatives require continued austerity for Brazil in the coming years. But they
propose to limit the costs of Brazil's sacrifice by extending the debt to
gain breathing space, sharing the necessary sacrifices more equitably
within Brazil, and compensating somewhat for these sacrifices with
welfare and redistributive policies.

Moderate nationalist policies differ from the moderate internationalist policies of the Figueiredo regime mainly in emphasis. Moderate in-
ternationalists by now recognize that full integration into the world
economy is not sufficient to resolve Brazil's development problems,
whereas moderate nationalists increasingly accept the need to retain an
export orientation. The elements of a consensual position on Brazil's
economic future have begun to emerge, therefore.

More extreme nationalists, on the other hand, doubt that continued
dependence on international finance and trade still serves Brazil's interest in this period of sustained global recession. They emphasize that
without major changes in policy, Brazil is likely to be a net exporter of
capital for the next fifteen years, even if the industrial economies do
well. Under these circumstances, they point out the potential benefits of
repudiating Brazil's debt, either unilaterally or in agreement with other
major debtors, as part of a debtors' cartel. They favor adopting much
tougher policies toward multinational corporations to make them serve
Brazil's interests. They propose populist approaches to wages, exchange rates, and public spending—all to encourage nationally oriented
production.

Proponents of this autarchic approach recall that Brazil reacted to the
Great Depression of the 1930s by turning sharply inward, and with very
favorable results. Brazil insulated itself from many of the depression's
costs and began a period of import substitution that provided a long-
term boost to the country's economy. Arguments for a return to an
inward-oriented stance, however, tend to underestimate the changes
that have occurred in the last half-century. Because of its new reliance
on sophisticated imported technology and on exports, as well as on
external capital, Brazil is far more dependent on the international economy than it used to be. Even so, a nationalist stance of withdrawal from
the world economy would strike a responsive chord in some sectors of
Brazil, especially if prolonged recession loomed on the national horizon.

Economic and political circumstances in Brazil and elsewhere make
more nationalist and inward-oriented economic policies increasingly
probable. The most likely course, under currently foreseeable circumstances, is a moderate nationalist approach of the sort put forward by
the PMDB, endorsed by significant segments of the PDS (the Social

Democratic party, the government party during the years of military rule), and then initiated by President Sarney's government. Under this moderately nationalist course, Brazil will seek to expand its domestic economy and make it more equitable without neglecting the export sector or isolating the country from the international economy. Brazil will endeavor to expand its domestic market, to respond more actively to social needs, to strengthen agriculture, and to increase domestic savings.

If Brazil sustains a moderate nationalist approach, it will continue to engage in tough bargaining with its international creditors, foreign investors, and trading partners over the exact terms of the country's continued integration into the international economy. Brazil will increasingly insist that a satisfactory rate of national growth is its primary economic objective and that other goals are subsidiary. United States banks, investors, and exporters will be forced to struggle with Brazil over rates of interest, spreads, fees, remittances, protectionist barriers, export and local content requirements, reserved sectors, transfer pricing, and a host of similar details. Brazil's insistence on more favorable terms will be greater in the light of increased public pressure. It is likely, therefore, that more conflict, not less, will characterize U.S.-Brazil relations.

THE CHANGING SHAPE OF U.S.-BRAZIL RELATIONS

Brazil has historically interacted with the United States much less than have Mexico or the nations of the Caribbean Basin. Until this last generation, U.S. investment in and trade with Brazil was relatively modest. Migration between Brazil and the United States has been scant, and tourism has never been significant. Few U.S. groups or institutions have been so deeply engaged in Brazil as to make Brazil's domestic economic or political orientation important to U.S. politics and policymaking. In short, the consequences for the United States of Brazil's internal trends have never been very great.

Until the past few years, United States–Brazil relations have primarily involved cooperation on foreign policy. For most of this century, the two countries were closely aligned on a wide range of international issues. Brazil's great foreign minister, Barão do Rio Branco, built his country's international posture early in the twentieth century around an avowed "special relationship" with the United States, and this stance was often reinforced over the years.

For its part, the United States also singled out Brazil. The United States was the first country to recognize Brazil's independence in 1824, and the first power to recognize the Brazilian Republic in 1890. Brazil was the first (and long the only) country in Latin America with which the

United States exchanged full-fledged ambassadors. In the mid-1930s, Brazil was the first nation with which the United States negotiated a reciprocal trade agreement to lower tariffs.

Washington intensified its interest in relations with Brazil in the late 1930s, when the hemispheric ramifications of the deepening European crisis became clear. Increasing German trade with Brazil (rising from 14 percent of Brazil's trade in 1935 to 25 percent in 1938, slightly more than the U.S. share in that year) aroused Washington's concern, as did Brazilian purchases of arms from Germany. The United States was also alarmed at the possibility of increasing German cultural and ideological influence in Brazil, especially within the armed forces. The United States began actively to seek Brazil's cooperation in order to curb Nazi influence, assure U.S. access to Brazil's natural resources (and deny it to Germany), protect Brazil against German attack, and secure the right to build military bases and other facilities in northeast Brazil.

For a while, the Brazilian regime of Getulio Vargas played Germany and the United States off against each other, but by 1940 Brazil opted for a closer relationship with Washington. The United States responded to this decision by supporting the price of coffee, supplying economic assistance for the Volta Redonda steel mill project, transferring significant amounts of weapons, and aiding in the construction of airfields and other facilities. In addition, Brazil enjoyed enhanced domestic and international status as a close ally of the United States. After the United States entered World War II, Brazil on its own initiative became the only Latin American nation to send troops (more than 20,000) to fight in the European theater.

During World War II, three-fourths of all U.S. military aid to Latin America went to Brazil. United States forces were based in Brazil, U.S. military and economic missions proliferated, and extensive bilateral public and private sector economic cooperation occurred. Public opinion in Brazil supported this alliance, as did Brazil's military leaders. Washington took note of Brazil's sensitivities and accorded Brazil enough symbolic and rhetorical attention to meet Vargas's own political needs.

Following World War II, however, differences between Brazil and the United States began to appear. One source of friction was political, as the U.S. worldwide commitment to the Four Freedoms strengthened pressures against the Vargas regime and contributed to his ouster in October 1945.

More important, differences of economic interest arose. Brazil sought to parlay its supposed special relationship with the United States into meaningful economic assistance, through aid, loans, or preferential trade arrangements. Washington, however, was by then more concerned with Europe and the Far East than with Latin America. The

United States government wished to rely mainly on the private sector to promote U.S. interests in the Western Hemisphere, and on free trade to promote world commerce. Washington was unwilling to provide substantial economic or trade concessions to Brazil; only $184 million was extended to that country in economic assistance and loans from 1946 to 1952, compared with more than $13 billion provided to European nations under the Marshall Plan. Some symbolic attention was still paid to Brazil, but its substantive aims were largely ignored. When the worldwide economic and political interests of the United States clashed with Brazil's expectations, the latter got short shrift.

Nationalist resentment of the United States began to accumulate in Brazil during the late 1940s and early 1950s. That resentment did not build even faster owed in part to Brazil's rapid postwar economic advance, which was fueled by the large dollar, gold, and sterling balances accumulated during World War II and by the increased value of Brazil's exports after the war and during the Korean conflict. The postwar period also saw rapidly growing U.S. investment in Brazil, bringing U.S. firms into a dominant position among foreign investors for the first time. The new U.S. prominence in Brazil's economy made bilateral relations closer but also provided an additional source of friction. The Brazilian government under Vargas—now back in office as an elected president—began to undertake restrictive measures to control foreign investment and, particularly, to build up state corporations.

From the late 1950s to the present, U.S. relations with Brazil have changed fundamentally, primarily as a result of Brazil's internal transformation. As Brazil's economic structure has changed, the role of the United States in Brazil's economy has been altered, Brazil's international interests have become more complex, and U.S.-Brazil relations have been affected. Except for a brief parenthesis immediately following the military takeover in 1964, Brazil has moved during the past generation toward an increasingly independent and assertive stance. Tensions have grown between Brazil and the United States on specific issues, mainly economic in content. Usual (if not automatic) alignment between Brazil and the United States has been replaced by frequent conflict, limited and managed, but nevertheless real—and growing.

During the 1950s and early 1960s, the United States began to become concerned about signs of rising economic nationalism and political independence in Brazil, first under Getulio Vargas, then under Juscelino Kubitscheck, more intensely under Janio Quadros, and finally and most dramatically under João Goulart.

During the Vargas presidency, pressures within Brazil against U.S. investment grew, and splits developed within the Brazilian military between pro-U.S. officers and a more nationalist cadre. These splits, in turn, eventually contributed to the weakening of the Vargas regime and, ultimately, in August 1954, to the suicide of Vargas, who left behind a note blaming outside "forces and interests" and "international groups" for his downfall.

The Kubitscheck period saw an improvement in U.S.-Brazil relations but also deliberate efforts by the Brazilian government to diversify its economic, political, and military ties in the Hemisphere and in Europe. The latter trend was carried much further during the brief presidency of Quadros, who opened diplomatic and commercial relations with the Soviet Union, Cuba, and various other Communist countries, and vigorously expanded Brazil's contacts with the Third World, especially with Africa. The Quadros regime ended abruptly, however, when the president resigned, warning that "terrible forces," including "foreign ones," were trying to frustrate Brazil's progress.

Frictions between the United States and Brazil deepened during the presidency of João Goulart, Quadros's vice-president. These tensions mounted over Brazil's nationalization of certain U.S. public utility investments, Brazil's restrictions on profit remittances, U.S. conditions for economic assistance, and broader international issues. More important, the Kennedy administration was deeply troubled by the inclusion in Goulart's entourage of alleged Communists and Communist sympathizers. As the Goulart regime moved to more radical domestic and foreign policies and retained personnel whom the U.S. government considered suspect, Washington increased its distance from the Brazilian government. By March 1964, the U.S. government was sympathetic toward, and seems to have been prepared to support, if necessary, the military coup that overthrew Goulart in favor of General Humberto Castelo Branco, an officer in the Brazilian unit that had fought alongside the United States in Europe during World War II.

Under the Castelo Branco government, Brazil returned to a closely collaborative relationship with the United States. The new ties were exemplified by Brazil's decision to send troops to join the U.S. occupation of Santo Domingo in 1965, and to accept having a Brazilian general appointed to head the Inter-American Force there. Brazil's new military rulers not only shared U.S. ideology and concepts of security but also accorded these issues the same salience U.S. policy makers did.

By the end of the 1960s, the reconstructed U.S.-Brazil alignment began to unravel again. Domestic opinion in Brazil and world rejection of the U.S. role in Vietnam contributed to attenuating the U.S.-Brazil bond, as did the replacement of General Castelo Branco, an especially close friend of the United States, by General Artur da Costa e Silva. The key reason for the emerging bilateral frictions, however, was Brazil's pursuit of its own concrete interests on a widening range of issues.

Despite the ideological and even the personal predilections of its military rulers, Brazil found itself by the 1970s differing with the United States, within an amicable framework, on numerous specific questions.

The particular circumstances of bilateral conflict have varied, but there has been a common thread. Brazil and the United States have clashed repeatedly over Brazil's determined efforts to secure maximum scope for its expansion as an independent industrial power.

—Brazil has pushed—in the United Nations, in the General Agreement on Trade and Tariffs, in the International Monetary Fund, in the World Bank, and elsewhere—to restructure international organizations to provide greater participation and influence for developing countries.

—Brazil has been active in various international negotiations on trade and finance and on basic commodities, as well as in broad North-South economic deliberation. It has acted increasingly as a Third World power, often critical of the approach of the advanced industrial countries.

—Brazil has resisted efforts led by the United States and other industrial countries, through the United Nations and otherwise, to impose ecological and population policies that Brazilians fear would restrict their nation's options for growth.

—Brazil has played a leading role in pushing for international agreements on the Law of the Sea which would strengthen the position of developing countries in the management of and revenues from ocean resources.

—Brazil has refused to put into effect the Tlatelolco accords against nuclear proliferation in the Hemisphere and has opposed U.S.-led attempts to restrict its access to certain types of nuclear materials and technology, restrictions the United States claims are necessary to prevent the spread of nuclear weapons.

—Brazil has also differed with the United States on several political matters. It has expanded (albeit slowly) its diplomatic, commercial, and cultural relations with the Soviet Union and various Eastern European nations. Brazil ignored the U.S.-inspired grain embargo imposed on the Soviet Union in 1980 as well as the U.S.-sponsored boycott of the Moscow Olympic Games in that year. Brazil has contradicted the U.S. approach to the Middle East by voting at the United Nations in the mid-1970s to condemn Zionism as a form of racism, by accepting the Palestine Liberation Organization as a legitimate representative of the Palestinian people, and by developing close commercial links (including the export of arms) with Libya, Iraq, and several other Arab nations. Brazil was the first non-Communist nation to recognize the

MPLA regime in Angola in 1974, and it has subsequently kept its distance from U.S. policy regarding the Cuban presence there. In the early 1980s, Brazil reportedly resisted U.S. proposals that a South Atlantic Treaty Association, including South Africa, be formed. In the mid-1980s, Brazil pushed the idea of a nuclear-free zone in the South Atlantic, a concept strongly resisted by the United States.

—Most important, Brazil and the United States have been in conflict on a variety of specific economic concerns. The United States has objected often to Brazil's practice of subsidizing exports and to Brazil's protection of its own domestic markets through tariff and nontariff barriers. Brazil has complained with equal vehemence about U.S. protectionism, including the use of countervailing duties and quotas to limit imports on a range of products such as sugar, footwear, textiles, ethyl alcohol, and specialty steels. Brazil and the United States have clashed, as well, on profit remittances by U.S. firms; on the terms of technology transfer; on regulations affecting U.S. banking and other services; on Brazilian efforts to bar foreign firms from particular sectors of the economy (commuter aircraft as well as small computers and "informatics" more generally); and on trade competition in third markets.

All these bilateral tensions—exacerbated since 1979 by continuing negotiations over the terms, timing, and cost of refinancing Brazil's massive foreign debt—arise naturally from the changing economic interests of the two countries' firms, banks, consumers, and trade unions. The interests of all these economic actors are competitive, not automatically compatible, and the intensity of conflict among them increases as the level of economic interaction rises. The resulting frictions are manageable through negotiation on specific matters. But the conflicts are far from trivial, for they involve the allocation of costs and benefits between the two nations and among sectors within each country.

Washington has been slow to understand how deeply rooted are the issues in contemporary U.S.-Brazil relations and how firmly committed Brazil is to pursuing its own interests. At the onset of significant tensions with Brazil in the early and mid-1970s (actually a return to the pattern preceding the military takeover in 1964), the United States failed to recognize their fundamental nature and therefore used mainly procedural devices to improve the relationship. The Kissinger-Silveira "memorandum of understanding" (1976) epitomized this U.S. reaction, for it concentrated almost entirely on visible bureaucratic procedures for dealing with bilateral concerns. This tack did, in fact, temporarily improve the climate of bilateral relations. Substantive frictions between the two countries persisted, however. Neither country significantly modified its policies affecting trade, finance, technology, or related matters, and Brazil was determined to continue enhancing its autonomy in foreign policy.

Tensions between Brazil and the United States were exacerbated early in the Carter administration. First the U.S. government attempted, without consulting the Brazilian government, to persuade West Germany to break its contract to provide sensitive nuclear technology to Brazil. Then Washington aggravated relations by heralding its human rights policy in ways Brazil's government found offensive. These two specific irritants were considerably alleviated in the course of the Carter period, but the underlying economic conflicts continued, and the nuclear issue also remained divisive. The United States and Brazil were still at odds at the end of the 1970s.

The Reagan administration entered office in 1981 avowedly committed to restoring the erstwhile "beautiful relationship" by revising U.S. policies that were particularly irritating to Brazil. The new administration quickly tried to improve bilateral communication. General Vernon Walters, a favorite of Brazil's military leaders ever since his service as liaison officer with the Brazilian forces during World War II, was dispatched as a special emissary. Vice-president Bush announced in Brasilia that U.S. firms would be granted an exception to allow them to transfer nuclear fuel to Brazil. Reciprocal state visits by Presidents Figueiredo and Reagan were arranged.

It soon became evident, however, that Washington's main aim was to gain Brazil's cooperation regarding Central America, the South Atlantic, Cuba, and East-West relations in general, and that the United States was not prepared to alter policy on the underlying economic issues important to Brazil. The classic pattern of U.S.-Brazil relations thus repeated itself. Washington ostentatiously adjusted its symbols and its rhetoric but did not meaningfully amend its substantive economic policies toward Brazil. On matters importantly affecting Brazil, such as the pleas for substantial additional resources made by the International Monetary Fund in the autumn of 1982, U.S. policy did not change much.

As the acuteness of Brazil's financial crisis became evident late in 1982, the Reagan administration finally responded, as it had earlier in the case of Mexico, with an emergency package of ad hoc assistance. Bridge loans (short-term loans to help meet an immediate need while an IMF pact was being negotiated) to Brazil totalling $1.2 billion were announced by the U.S. Treasury in December 1982 and early 1983 to help ease the immediate shortfall of foreign exchange. But the loans barely compensated, in effect, for the adverse impact on Brazil of the high interest rates produced by Reaganomics, a combination of lower taxes and higher budget deficits. Additional loans and guarantees were also provided by the Export-Import Bank of the United States, but these have been of very limited relevance to Brazil; they were infrequently utilized.

The basic economic issues that concern Brazil in the 1980s—improving the terms of its massive foreign debt and expanding the market for its exports in advanced industrial countries, including the United States—have not yet been squarely addressed by the U.S. government. On the contrary, protectionist sentiments have been intensifying in the United States, and Washington has so far been largely unresponsive to calls for a broad restructuring of international finance. The "Baker Plan" of 1985 was a step in the right direction, but much more international credit than called for in the Baker initiative will be required if Brazil and other developing countries are to resume and sustain growth.

THE U.S. STAKE IN BRAZIL'S FUTURE

Brazil, by far the largest country in Latin America and one of the most important countries in the Third World, is at a crossroads. Rapid growth and fundamental transformation during the 1960s and 1970s made Brazil increasingly powerful, self-confident, and assertive. Basic flaws in Brazil's approach to development, as well as sustained adverse conditions in the world economy, however, produced a deep economic and social crisis in the early 1980s. Brazil's politics have evolved toward greater popular participation and government responsiveness. But Brazil's first civilian president in more than twenty years must govern at a time when economic problems and constraints are challenging.

The political and economic choices Brazil makes now will not only shape Brazil's course but also affect the future of Latin America as a whole as well as the interests of the United States.

Whether Brazil continues the process of redemocratization, as it has for a decade, or reverts instead to authoritarianism will influence all of South America. The renewed appeal in Latin America of democratic processes has been strongly reinforced in recent years by Brazil's slow but steady return to democracy. Conversely, the regional climate for democracy and for the protection of fundamental human rights would deteriorate sharply if Brazil returned to authoritarian practices.

The regional effects of Brazil's choices regarding finance, trade, investment, technology, and related issues will also be important. Brazil's choice of a moderate nationalist approach, particularly if that approach is worked out in concert with international actors, would help other Latin American countries adopt similar policies, which, in turn, would support the reexpansion of the international economy. An extreme nationalist turn in Brazil, on the other hand, would no doubt legitimize that option elsewhere in the region; it might even lead to a debtors' cartel and other forms of South-South cooperation at the expense of the established international system. The chances that nationalist, populist, and anti-American movements might gain strength elsewhere in Latin America would be increased if Brazil veered in that direction. Populist and anti-American currents already evident in Peru and Argentina (and latent in Chile) would gain internal credibility and external support if Brazil adopted an extreme nationalist course.

Brazil's choices regarding democratic politics, general economic orientation, debt and trade, foreign investment, and technology transfer will significantly affect the United States. This is true both because U.S. banks, exporters, and investors have major direct interests in Brazil and because Brazil's international weight and influence have become so substantial. Brazil's economic difficulties have already reduced U.S. exports, slowing economic growth and increasing unemployment in the United States. More U.S. investment is concentrated in Brazil than in any other Latin American country, and most of it depends for its profitability on a Brazilian economic recovery. U.S. banks, obviously, have an enormous stake in Brazil's economic future. How Brazil behaves and fares will also affect the future of many other Third World nations.

THE UNITED STATES AND BRAZIL: OPTIONS FOR POLICY

United States policy, in turn, will be significant for Brazil. The United States is still Brazil's single largest market, its biggest supplier of goods and services, and its primary source of investment and finance. Although Brazil is far from a U.S. dependency, it is influenced strongly by U.S. policies on fiscal and monetary issues, trade, energy, technology transfer, resource development, and, above all, debt.

The United States has three broad options for structuring its future relationship with Brazil. It can maintain its long-established stance, one that combines rhetorical deference with actual disregard for Brazil's substantive needs. It can attempt instead to establish a new and truly preferential bilateral relationship with Brazil, significantly changing U.S. policies to meet Brazilian aims. Or the United States can design new general policies, not specifically directed at or limited to Brazil, to deal with the basic problems faced by Brazil and other advanced developing countries.

When it follows the traditional U.S. policy, the United States pays special verbal and procedural attention to Brazil but stops short of making commitments involving significant costs to the United States or any of its sectors. Brazil's economic development continues to be encouraged rhetorically, but Brazil encounters protectionist reactions when it demonstrates a competitive advantage in a specific product of some importance. Under this approach, the United States occasionally makes ad hoc concessions to Brazil on specific items, but these are considered exceptions; the emphasis is on restoring "business as usual" between the two countries. This has been the case so far, for instance, with regard to Brazil's overwhelming external debt. Washington helped to arrange emergency bridge loans at the height of Brazil's liquidity crisis at the end of 1982, but it has preferred since then to let commercial banks work out their own relations with Brazil.

If the United States persists in this approach to Brazil, relations may well continue much as they have for the last few years: generally cordial in tone, increasingly conflictual on specific matters, mostly lacking in creative efforts to develop mutual interests, but usually free of intense struggle.

It is possible, however, that a continuation of the classic U.S. approach could inadvertently help push Brazil toward an extreme nationalist course that would cause much deeper conflict between the two countries. Many Brazilians have come to perceive that U.S. fiscal and monetary policies in effect tax Brazil and other countries through high interest rates to pay for the U.S. federal deficit. Protectionist U.S. and OECD trade policies are thought to thwart some of Brazil's export possibilities. The United States has on several occasions opposed increased resources for the World Bank and the IMF, blocked reforms that would make those agencies more responsive to Third World demands, and resisted broad proposals to restructure the external debt of developing countries. If the United States continues to pursue such policies, Brazilians may blame the resulting stress not on neutral market forces but on the United States.

Under these circumstances, Brazil would surely intensify its pleas for relief, particularly in the form of improved access to capital and markets. If the United States and other international actors then remain unresponsive, Brazil's internal political dynamics could push that country toward extreme nationalism. Brazil's political history includes a substantial tradition (epitomized by the suicide of Vargas and his references to "outside forces") of pointing to external causes for Brazil's troubles. If Brazil's situation worsens, an extreme nationalist turn could eventually occur. Brazil might consider a long-term or perhaps indefinite moratorium or even a repudiation of the foreign debt, highly protectionist trade policies, harassment or expropriation of foreign investments, or radical policies on other international issues. Such a "beggar thy neighbor". approach is not now favored by most Brazilian leaders, for they understand that it would probably be self-defeating and ultimately unviable. But if the United States continues to pursue policies that many Brazilians regard as insensitive or punitive, such a response could be provoked—and that would certainly hurt the United States.

The second option, the proposal that the United States and Brazil resurrect a "special relationship" comparable to that briefly experienced during World War II, is favored by a few Brazilian and U.S. business executives, and it would be consistent with periodic U.S. rhetorical deference to Brazil. This approach would provide Brazil with preferential access to U.S. finance, technology, energy, arms, and markets in exchange for privileged U.S. access to Brazilian markets, raw materials, diplomatic support, and security cooperation. Brazil unsuccessfully sought to establish this type of relationship after World War II, and Brazil's military government of 1964 also wished to achieve it.

By now, however, the interests of both Brazil and the United States are too diverse and complex to sustain a truly preferential arrangement for long. Both nations have too many other commitments to cut meaningful, lasting bilateral deals. The United States has major involvements throughout the world, while Brazil now has important ties in Africa, East Asia, and the Middle East and a growing stake in improving its relations with the rest of Latin America. Neither country could afford to make genuinely preferential agreements that would undermine its interests and commitments elsewhere.

A "special relationship" would predictably break down, as it did after World War II, because other interests would get in the way of a sustained U.S. commitment. Brazil, too, would find its own reasons to escape such provisions. Moreover, a Brazilian government would be especially vulnerable politically if it sacrificed Brazilian interests to keep a bargain on which the United States eventually might welch. In any case, the special relationship path is currently moot at best. The Sarney government wants to assert its independent foreign policy stance, not to align more closely with Washington.

It would be in the best interest of the United States to take the third course. New general policies are needed to address fundamental needs Brazil shares with Mexico, other major Latin American nations, and advanced developing countries elsewhere in the Third World. The United States should help reform international economic relations so that Brazil, Mexico, and other advanced industrializing nations in the Third World can resume economic growth and development, regain solvency, and work cooperatively with the industrial countries to reexpand international economic exchange. Instead of reacting to economic setbacks in newly industrialized countries with niggardly attempts to protect the faltering old order, the United States should move boldly and positively to help refurbish and thereby strengthen the international system.

The general approach the United States should take to improve international economic relations in the mutual interest of the United States and of Brazil, Mexico, and other advanced developing nations is more fully discussed in chapter 7. Three specific steps are highlighted here.

First, the United States government should take a leading role in resolving the problem of Third World debt. As is discussed more fully in chapter 7, plans are needed to extend the maturities of current Third World debt; to expand official flows of capital through the IMF, the World Bank, and the regional development banks; to reduce interest rate spreads above market rates to a level closer to the commercial lenders' costs of securing capital; to reduce or eliminate management fees for refinancing; to capitalize or else reduce interest payments that Third World debtors cannot repay without disrupting their chances to resume growth; and, in general, to help provide the breathing space necessary for Brazil and other developing countries to resume economic advance. None of these steps is beyond the innovative capacity of current governments, international institutions, and commercial banks, but they are unlikely to occur unless the government of the United States takes a strong initiative. The Baker Plan must be followed by more concrete and extensive measures to reverse the flow of resources from Brazil and the rest of Latin America to the United States and other industrialized countries.

The second step is related to the first: the United States must reduce its enormous public sector deficit, which inevitably affects international interest rates. Until the United States puts its own economic house in order, the strain that high real interest rates place on the solvency of Brazil and other Third World debtors cannot be relieved.

Third, the United States should continue to resist protectionist pressures, and it should open up its markets more fully and consistently to exports by Brazil and other developing nations. No scheme for the repayment of Third World debts can be viable unless it provides a means for these countries to earn foreign exchange through increased exports. Brazil achieved a trade surplus after 1983 mainly by cutting imports to an unsustainably low level, by taking advantage of the strong dollar to expand exports to the United States, and at times by imposing excessive export subsidies. If Brazil's productivity is to remain high and sustainable growth is to be resumed, imports of capital goods will have to rise again in future years. For that to happen, however, Brazil's exports must continue to expand.

Brazil has amply demonstrated its dynamism, ingenuity, and productivity by winning increased export markets in many different products, including agricultural ones (soybeans, orange juice, sugar, and frozen poultry), footwear, textiles, light manufactures, automobiles and auto parts, steel, and various specialized products, such as commuter aircraft. The United States and other OECD countries, however, have increasingly imposed various kinds of market restrictions when Brazil or another exporter shows a competitive advantage. It is vital for Brazil's national development that this protectionist tendency be reversed.

A U.S. economic policy that responds to the needs of advanced developing countries for debt relief and expanded market access would enhance Brazil's economic strength and improve the prospects of U.S. investors, banks, and exporters. It would greatly strengthen Brazil's renewed democratic political stability and would thus support the emergence of a regional climate for the protection of human rights. It would reward Brazil for its generally cautious and pragmatic policies to date and would thus reinforce them. It would also strengthen the position of moderate policy makers in Brazil and would undermine the potential appeal of extreme nationalists who might take Brazil on a destructively autarchic course. The United States would then also be in a much stronger position to persuade Brazil to fight its own protectionist tendencies and to open itself more fully to world trade, and to U.S. exports in particular.

If the United States and Brazil could help resolve the hemispheric crisis of debt and trade, they could build on other important mutualities of interest. Each country wants to find safe and reliable sources of energy. Each wants to protect and develop natural resources without doing ecological damage. Each wants to make international organizations and institutions more effective, and to strengthen regional mechanisms for resolution of conflict. Each also wants to prevent threats to hemispheric security by limiting Soviet involvement in the region.

Within each of these shared interests, elements of tension also exist. These have become more evident in recent years as Washington and Brasilia have begun to clash over energy, ecology, and policy toward the Middle East, Africa, and, to a limited extent, Central America. If economic relations between Brazil and the United States deteriorate in the coming period, such discrepancies would become much more contentious. Brazil could become a formidable obstacle to the achievement of the international objectives of the United States.

Within the context of positive cooperation to resolve the Hemisphere's economic crisis, however, the United States could regain in Brazil an important and effective international partner. Achieving and maintaining that partnership should be a major aim for U.S. policy. Brazil is still, fundamentally, our natural ally, but improved cooperation will only be possible if Washington recognizes that Brazil's needs require concrete policy adjustments by the United States.

CHAPTER SIX

The United States
and the Caribbean Basin

The Politics of National Insecurity

The small nations of the Caribbean Basin—the islands of the Caribbean and the countries on the isthmus of Central America—are once again at the heart of U.S. foreign policy in the 1980s, as they were sixty years ago.*

During the first quarter of the twentieth century, U.S. troops landed more than twenty times in Caribbean Basin countries: in Cuba, the Dominican Republic, Guatemala, Haiti, Honduras, Nicaragua, and Panama. In several of these countries, U.S. troops remained for years. In many cases, the United States became a predominant actor in local politics. It made and unmade governments, organized elections, trained military units, and fought against insurrectionary movements that were allegedly being aided from abroad. An intense debate took place in the United States sixty years ago about U.S. interventionism. Powerful voices demanded that the United States end its occupation of several countries in the Caribbean Basin.

Franklin D. Roosevelt's Good Neighbor Policy and the U.S. commitment, formalized in 1934, to eschew unilateral military intervention,

---

*Analysts differ on how to define the Caribbean Basin, or even whether the concept makes any sense at all.

For the purpose of U.S. policy, I believe the most useful concept of the Caribbean Basin comprises that set of dependent countries, in or near the Caribbean Sea, concerning which the United States has historically felt a special security interest, arising primarily from their proximity and from their presumed vulnerability to external penetration. All the Caribbean islands, all the nations of the Central American isthmus, and Guyana, Suriname, and French Guiana on the South American mainland fit this definition of the region. Mexico, Colombia, and Venezuela—regarded as Caribbean Basin countries by some observers—are not included within this concept; nor is the United States, as much a Caribbean nation as any of these three.

ended this chapter in the diplomatic history of the United States. For the next generation, the Caribbean Basin countries no longer received priority in U.S. foreign policy, as the United States concentrated on advancing its interests elsewhere in the world.

Beginning with the Carter administration, and with greater attention during the Reagan period, official Washington has rediscovered the Caribbean Basin in the 1980s. President Reagan has probably spoken more often about Central America and the Caribbean than about any other single foreign policy issue. His Caribbean Basin Initiative (CBI)—a plan for extensive economic assistance, unveiled at the end of February 1982—was the president's major foreign policy proposal during his first two years in office. Mr. Reagan's speech on Central America to a joint session of Congress on April 27, 1983, was only the fifth such presidential foreign policy message since 1950. After his reelection in 1984, President Reagan continued to focus insistently on this region, particularly on Nicaragua.

Economic and military assistance from the United States to the countries of the Caribbean and Central America has multiplied more than tenfold since 1977, even while overall foreign aid figures have been declining. Except for Israel and Egypt, the countries of the Caribbean Basin receive the largest amount of U.S. assistance worldwide. El Salvador alone receives the fourth-highest amount of U.S. foreign aid. The military and economic involvement of the United States in Nicaragua's civil war escalated during the 1980s.

The Reagan administration has already intervened militarily in the Caribbean Basin, deploying some seven thousand Marines and army paratroopers to occupy tiny Grenada in October 1983. Although the troops were ostensibly sent to protect U.S. citizens, their primary aim without doubt was to reverse the island's alignment with the Soviet Union and Cuba. In addition to the operation in Grenada, the Reagan administration has repeatedly undertaken extended military and naval exercises, involving several thousand U.S. troops each time, in Honduras and off the coasts of Nicaragua. It has also built new military bases and airfields in Honduras and has pre-positioned thousands of tons of materiel. The Reagan administration engaged the United States in a prolonged and hardly covert, albeit indirect, war against the Sandinista government in Nicaragua, overwhelming or flaunting congressional resistance to U.S. military involvement, and there is good reason to believe that the United States government has prepared itself for eventual direct military intervention.

Lack of public and congressional support for a more active U.S. role in the Caribbean Basin led the Reagan administration in 1983 to establish the National Bipartisan Commission on Central America, with former Secretary of State Henry Kissinger as chairman. The commission's report, released in January 1984, called for stepping up U.S. involvement in Central America to an extent unprecedented since the 1920s. The Kissinger report proposed sending $8 billion in U.S. economic assistance to the region during the ensuing five years, as well as the creation of a new Central American Development Organization, with the United States at its center. The report also suggested making trade concessions, increasing military assistance, offering ten thousand scholarships, establishing a Literacy Corps for Central America, and many other forms of U.S. engagement. Coming on the heels of the Caribbean Basin Initiative, the recommendations of the Kissinger commission amounted to a brief for intensifying the U.S. government's focus on the border region.

Neglected by Washington for so many years, the Caribbean Basin countries are today receiving lavish attention from the United States. This chapter analyzes what is at stake for the United States in this region now, and how U.S. aims can best be advanced.

THE CARIBBEAN BASIN

The very concept of the Caribbean Basin has been resurrected in recent years from the writings of the nineteenth-century geopolitical theorists, particularly Admiral Alfred Thayer Mahan and Sir H. Halford MacKinder. These writers emphasized the strategic and tactical importance for the United States, then emerging as a world power, of controlling its border region and of securing the naval passages through the Caribbean. From their standpoint, the entire circum-Caribbean region (including the Central American isthmus) was of vital significance to the United States because of its proximity.

In most respects, however, the islands of the Caribbean are very different from the countries of the isthmus of Central America. The two regions have distinct cultural and national histories, as well as different economic structures, demographic compositions, social organizations, and politics. The Central American countries share a common history, and their citizens interact frequently across national boundaries. Similarly, the islands of the Caribbean (and especially the former British colonies of the Commonwealth Caribbean) share many experiences and traits among themselves, and project a common regional identity. But interchange, even communication, between these two regions is rare. Policies that treat the Caribbean and Central America together in an undifferentiated way are bound, therefore, to miss the mark.

The Insular Caribbean

The insular Caribbean includes some twenty-eight separate political entities with a population totalling about 32 million people. Eighteen of these units are now independent countries, four having achieved their independence since 1960 and eleven since 1970.

The Caribbean islands are remarkably diverse, yet in some ways they are overwhelmingly alike. Except for Cuba and Hispaniola (the island that includes both the Dominican Republic and Haiti), most are very small. Two-thirds of the Caribbean islands could fit together into the King Ranch in Texas, or inside the Everglades in Florida. Grenada is not much larger in area than the District of Columbia or Martha's Vineyard, and its entire population could fit into the Rose Bowl. Trinidad is smaller than Rhode Island. Jamaica is the size of Connecticut. The total population of all the Windward and Leeward islands is less than that of South Dakota. Even Cuba, by far the largest Caribbean island, is smaller in area than Ohio; it is about the size of Virginia.

None of the insular Caribbean territories is ethnically or culturally homogenous. Five racial groups (black, white, oriental, native Indian, and East Indian) and their numerous subgroups and combinations mingle with varying degrees of integration and hostility, and with considerable consciousness of color and shade. Numerous languages and dialects are spoken within the region, including Dutch, English, French, and Spanish and their derivatives, plus the Creole mixtures with African and Indian tongues. Caribbean religious sects are similarly diverse.

The economic organization of the Caribbean islands runs the gamut from the tax havens of the Bahamas, reportedly the largest single Eurocurrency market outside London, to Cuba's brand of socialism, with all manner of hybrids in between. In the Dominican Republic, longtime dictator Rafael Trujillo's personal fiefdom passed to government ownership after his assassination in 1961, and the country has a large public sector as a result. Jamaica's previously strong private sector became massively disgruntled during the 1970s; both Jamaica and Guyana, which chose to build mixed economies with a heavy dose of state ownership in the 1970s, have been trying since then to reattract and stimulate private investment. Tiny Grenada—where the principal exports are cocoa, nutmeg, and bananas, and the main economic potential is tourism—opted from 1979 to 1983 for "socialism," although no form of economic organization could much alter the obviously strict constraints on growth: poor resources and small scale.

Economic productivity in the Caribbean ranges from the depths of Haiti ("the land of unlimited impossibilities," the only nation of the Americas to be among the very poorest countries in the world) to the uneven but impressive performance of Martinique and Guadeloupe, the Bahamas, Puerto Rico, Trinidad-Tobago, and Barbados. The region includes four of the six countries with the lowest per capita GDP in the Americas (Haiti, Dominica, Grenada, and Guyana), but also eight territories with among the highest (Martinique, Trinidad-Tobago, Netherlands Antilles, Guadeloupe, Puerto Rico, Suriname, the Bahamas, and Barbados).

Although the per capita income in some Caribbean islands is high by Third World standards, poverty is widespread in much of the region. Two-thirds of Haiti's rural population have annual per capital incomes below forty dollars; 50 percent of children under five are said to suffer from protein calorie malnutrition, with 17 percent classified as severely malnourished. Seventy-five percent of preschool children in the Dominican Republic reportedly suffer from malnutrition, 4 percent severely. An estimated one-third of Jamaica's people have annual per capita incomes under two hundred dollars.

Overall, the regional economies are in deep trouble. World demand for two major Caribbean exports—sugar and bauxite—is stagnant, and prices are low. The region's share of world tourism revenues fell in the late 1970s and has not recovered.

High prices for petroleum and other vital imports placed additional strains on most Caribbean economies in the 1970s and into the 1980s. Jamaica had seven consecutive years of negative growth during the 1970s and has been unable to sustain a strong recovery. Haiti's per capita income is now at the 1960 level. The Dominican Republic grew rapidly during the early 1970s but has been very hard hit since the mid-1970s, first by the exploding price of oil and then by high interest rates. Despite huge Soviet subsidies, Cuba has also suffered economic reverses.

The Caribbean units share a number of painful characteristics. Almost all are heavily dependent on exporting a few primary products and are vulnerable to international market fluctuations and to the vagaries of disease and weather. Most of the islands have only a few known resources, apart from the sun and the sea. All have limited domestic markets and small local savings. Agriculture is weak and declining throughout most of the region. Per capita food production has dropped in most of the insular Caribbean, and regional imports of food have risen.

But while agriculture has declined, so has the push toward industrialization. The regionwide burst of "industrialization by invitation" during the 1960s reached the limits of import substitution and market scale and quickly ran out of steam. Unemployment and underemployment, consequently, are high throughout the Caribbean. Most of the islands are

TABLE I. THE CARIBBEAN COUNTRIES AND DEPENDENCIES

Country	Year of Independence	Area (Square Kilometers)	Population/ Annual Increase (Number/ Percentage)	Population Density (Per Square Kilometer)	Population under 20 Years of Age[2] (Percentage)	Literacy Rate (Percentage)
Anguilla	(United Kingdom)	91	6,000/—	72.0	—	80
Antigua & Barbuda	1981	280	82,000/2.6	293.0	—	90
The Bahamas	1973	13,934	235,000/1.8	17.0	49.6	89
Barbados	1966	430	253,000/0.5	588.0	41.1	99
Belize	1981	22,963	168,000/2.2	7.3	—	90
British Virgin Islands	(United Kingdom)	153	12,000/1.0	78.4	—	98
Cayman Islands	(United Kingdom)	259	22,000/2.8	85.0	35.0	97
Cuba	1902	114,471	10,221,000/1.1	89.3	39.7	96
Dominica	1978	753	74,000/0.4	98.3	—	80
Dominican Republic	1844	48,734	6,785,000/2.5	139.2	58.7	68
French Guiana	(France)	90,909	88,000/4.1	1.0	42.2	73
Grenada	1974	334	86,000/−0.4	250.0	—	85
Guadeloupe	(France)	1,779	334,000/0.5	187.7	43.9	70
Guyana	1966	214,970	771,000/0.3	3.6	—	85
Haiti	1804	27,749	5,870,000/1.9	211.5	48.9	23
Jamaica	1962	10,991	2,288,000/1.0	208.2	50.6	76
Martinique	(France)	1,100	328,000/0.1	298.2	41.6	70
Monserrat	(United Kingdom)	—	12,000/0.2	117.6	41.3	77
Netherlands Antilles[1] (Including Aruba, independent since 1986)	(Netherlands)	1,821	300,000/1.3	270.0	—	88
Puerto Rico[1]	(United States)	8,897	3,283,000/1.5	369.0	42.1	88[3]
St. Kitts–Nevis	1983	261	40,000/−1.2	153.3	50.2	80
St. Lucia	1979	619	123,000/1.1	198.7	59.2	78
St. Vincent and the Grenadines	1979	389	103,000/0.9	264.8	—	82
Suriname	1975	163,265	381,000/1.7	2.3	52.7	65
Trinidad and Tobago	1962	5,128	1,204,000/1.5	234.8	46.6	89
Turks and Caicos	(United Kingdom)	430	7,436/1.9[2]	22.1	53.7	99
U.S. Virgin Islands	(United States)	344	110,800/1.3	324.0	29.9	—

SOURCE: Unless otherwise stated, figures are from the Central Intelligence Agency, *The World Factbook, 1986* (Washington, D.C., 1986).

[1]Figures on Netherlands Antilles and Puerto Rico, and figures on tourist receipts, are from Caribbean/Central American Action, *Caribbean and Central American Databook* (Washington, D.C., 1986).

[2]Population growth rate for Turks and Caicos, and figures on percentage of population under 20 years of age, are from the United Nations, *UN Demographic Yearbook, 1984* (New York, 1986).

[3]Puerto Rican literacy rate is from the 1980 U.S. Census.

TABLE I. *(cont'd.)*

Infant Deaths (Per 1,000 Births)	Per Capita GDP in U.S. Dollars (Year)		Imports c.i.f. (In Millions of U.S. Dollars)	Exports f.o.b. (In Millions of U.S. Dollars)	GDP Growth[4] (Percentage; Same year as for Per Capita GDP)	Average Annual Per Capita GDP Growth, 1965–84[4] (Percentage)	Tourist Receipts, 1985[1] (In Millions of U.S. Dollars)
—	1,000	(1983)	—	—	—	—	—
31.5	1,990	(1984)	147.0	41.0	( )	−0.1	158.0
20.2	7,950	(1984)	3,000.0	2,300.0	4.5	−1.6	1,428.0
26.3	4,650	(1984)	656.0	390.0	0	2.5	3,089.0
56.0	1,200	(1985)	126.0	93.0	1.5	2.5	23.0
—	6,425	(1983)	50.0	2.0	( )	—	65.0
—	8,333	(1983)	140.0	2.4	—	—	19.0
15.0	1,530	(1982)	8,100.0	6,200.0	1.4	—	82.0
24.1	1,034	(1984)	56.0	26.0	4.3	0.3	4.5
63.0	1,090	(1984)	1,400.0	866.0	−2.0	3.2	371.0
—	1,940	(1976)	246.0	35.4	—	—	—
16.7	940	(1984)	55.6	18.9	0.6	1.7	—
18.6	3,760	(1980)	560.0	89.2	15.7	—	95.0
41.0	510	(1984)	222.0	212.0	4.0	—	—
107.0	240	(1984)	284.0	168.0	2.0	1.0	69.0
16.8	890	(1984)	1,100.0	706.0	−1.0	−0.4	583.0
12.6	4,540	(1980)	703.0	123.0	( )	( )	—
124.0	2,760	(1983)	20.0	1.6	2.0	—	4.8
—	9,140	(1983)	4,500.0	4,400.0	1.0	—	—
18.6	4,301	(1985)	10,100.0	10,500.0	2.8	—	710.0
—	1,563	(1985)	47.3	30.6	4.0	3.2	13.0
27.4	1,105	(1984)	106.8	49.7	5.0	3.1	56.0
—	781	(1983)	71.4	42.0	3.0	1.9	35.0
23.0	2,980	(1984)	346.0	356.0	−1.0	4.2	—
197.0	7,370	(1984)	1,900.0	2,200.0	−7.4	2.6	197.0
—	2,020	(1980)	20.9	2.5	—	—	12.0
—	7,780	(1985)	3,700.0	3,300.0	( )	( )	698.0

[4]Figures on percentage GDP growth and average annual per capita GDP growth are from the World Bank, *World Development Report, 1986* (Washington, D.C., 1986).

extremely overpopulated, and emigration from all of them is high. Most of the migrants enter the United States, legally and illegally. Some 20 percent of legal immigrants to the United States, and an equal or higher percentage of illegal entrants, come from the Caribbean. Five of the six countries in the world with the highest per capita rates of migration to the United States in the 1980s are in this region.

Most of the Caribbean nations have been politically stable in recent years and have managed to sustain functioning democratic institutions. Even the Dominican Republic, where rampant political instability prevailed but twenty years ago, has managed to hold six consecutive free and contested national elections, with power being transferred peacefully on several occasions. Grenada's coups, in 1979 and 1983, have been unique in the Commonwealth Caribbean.

Most of the Caribbean islands, except for a few of the smallest ministates, did reasonably well economically in the 1960s and early 1970s. Even then, however, growth was not equitable in most countries. Land concentration continued to be high, wage differentials remained great, income distribution was badly skewed, and structural unemployment and underemployment remained a fundamental problem. And practically all the Caribbean nations have been seriously hurt since the mid-1970s by the rapid increases in the price of oil and by the overall international economic downturn. The decreased cost of oil in the late 1980s has not made up for the effect of sagging commodity prices.

Although a few of the Caribbean islands have been politically independent since the nineteenth century, many have achieved their independence only during the past few years, and a few are still colonies today. All the Caribbean islands, even the long-independent ones, rely to some degree on close relations with a metropole; they are satellites in search of an orbit, requiring a regularized pattern of relationship with a central power. Increasingly, in recent years, that power has been the United States, which has seen its influence grow as the presence of Great Britain and other former colonial mentors has receded. The United States is closely involved with practically all the Caribbean islands, increasingly dominating their trade and investment. United States trade with the insular Caribbean totalled almost $10 billion in 1985; U.S. direct private investment, though harder to estimate reliably, is also important.

The most significant ties between the United States and the insular Caribbean are human ones. Hundreds of young Americans are attending "last chance" medical schools in the Dominican Republic, Dominica, and Grenada. Thousands of older Americans are living out their retirement years in the Caribbean sun. Hundreds of thousands more vacation in the region. American culture and technology, both high and low, pervade the islands.

The most dramatic link between the insular Caribbean and the United States is the steady stream of Caribbean immigrants to the mainland. Since World War II, close to five million Caribbeans have entered the United States. Almost two million Puerto Ricans have come in, as well as more than one million Cubans, about one million West Indians, over half a million Dominicans, and more than three hundred thousand Haitians. This flow is a response both to regional overpopulation and poverty and to the magnetic attraction of the U.S. economy. To a large extent, the Caribbean islands have become demographically integrated with the United States.

The Caribbean territories are insular, not just geographically, but socially and culturally, as well. Even in those physically situated on the mainland (Belize, Guyana, Suriname, and French Guiana), 90 percent of the population lives in coastal enclaves. Caribbean nations are searching for identity and meaning, trying to draw on the shared experience of slavery, migration, and colonialism to derive an acceptable heritage. Their social structures, economies, race relations, and interaction with the external world all bear the mark of centuries of colonial rule and plantation societies. Ninety percent of today's population in the insular Caribbean descend from the four million African slaves who were imported in the sixteen through nineteenth centuries.

Caribbean history has always been shaped, and even written, largely from outside; the very concept that the Caribbean is one region is mainly an externally imposed idea. A few outstanding Caribbean intellectuals—V. S. Naipaul, Frantz Fanon, Aime Cesaire, C. L. R. James, Eric Williams, Juan Bosch, William Demas, Lloyd Best, and Arthur Lewis among them—have reinforced the notion of the Caribbean as a region whose countries share common problems and opportunities despite different cultural and colonial backgrounds. Their work, and numerous institutional efforts to promote regional cooperation, have not overcome the area's tendency toward political fragmentation, however.

The Caribbean islands have been restless during the last few years. Regional economic difficulties have been a factor, to be sure, but underlying the Caribbean's unease has been conflict among fundamental goals.

Caribbean people, of whatever race, religion, or nationality, want economic growth, improved equity, full employment, political participation, enhanced national autonomy, and more self-respect. These understandable goals may not be simultaneously attainable in the Caribbean today, however. Cuba has achieved nearly full employment and consid-

TABLE 2. THE CENTRAL AMERICAN COUNTRIES

Country	Area (Square Kilometers)	Population/Annual Increase (Number/Percentage)	Population Density (Per Square Kilometer)	Population under 20 Years of Age[1] (Percentage)	Literacy Rate (Percentage)	Infant Deaths[3] (Per 1,000 Births)	Total Net Official Development Assistance, 1984[2] (Millions of U.S. Dollars)	Preliminary GDP Growth Estimates, 1985[3]	Average Annual Per Capita GDP Growth, 1965-84[1] (Percentage)	Per Capita GNP[2] In 1984 U.S. Dollars
Costa Rica	50,700	2,714,000/2.6	53.5	46.7	93	18.8	217	1.6	1.6	1,190
El Salvador	21,041	5,105,000/2.5	242.6	55.3	65	35.1	263	1.6	-0.6	710
Guatemala	108,780	8,600,000/5.0	79.1	55.6	50	56.0	65	-1.1	2.0	1,160
Honduras	112,088	4,648,000/3.3	41.5	58.4	56	78.6	290	3.0	0.5	700
Nicaragua	130,000	3,342,000/3.3	25.7	58.8	66	87.0	114	-2.6	-1.5	860
Panama	77,080	2,227,000/2.1	28.9	49.9	90	20.0	72	3.3	2.6	1,980

SOURCE: Unless otherwise stated, figures are from the Central Intelligence Agency, *The World Factbook, 1986* (Washington, D.C., 1986).

[1] Figures on percentage of population under 20 years of age are from the United Nations, *UN Demographic Yearbook, 1984* (New York, 1986), except for figures on El Salvador, which are from the United Nations Population Division, *World Population Prospects: Estimates and Projections as Assessed in 1982* (New York, 1985).

[2] Figures on total net official development assistance, average annual per capita GDP growth, and per capita GNP are from the World Bank, *World Development Report, 1986* (Washington, D.C., 1986).

[3] Figures on infant deaths and preliminary GDP growth estimates are from the Inter-American Development Bank, *Economic and Social Progress in Latin America: 1986 Report.*

erably improved equity, but at the cost of personal freedoms. Martinique is relatively prosperous, but in large part because it is not autonomous. Barbados has grown rapidly but not equitably. Puerto Rico, which once was thought to be advancing on most of these dimensions, has in recent years found progress hard to sustain.

No strategy for development has been very successful in the insular Caribbean. Progress has everywhere been elusive. Increased frustration, understandably, has resulted.

Central America

The Central American nations are quite different from those of the insular Caribbean.* They are somewhat larger in territory than most of the Caribbean islands: most are equivalent to small- or medium-sized states of the United States. Except for Guatemala, where half the population is Indian (and the Miskito Indian enclave in Nicaragua and the Kuna Indian region in Panama), they are ethnically more homogeneous and less influenced by African immigration than are the Caribbean islands. They are all Spanish speaking, and they have many cultural, economic, and political links with one another; indeed, they are in a sense "a nation divided," for all but Panama once formed a regional unity. Their economies are more industrialized than those of the insular Caribbean and are more diversely integrated into world markets.

The Central American nations have been independent since the nineteenth century, and their cultural and political identities are more secure. Although they are export oriented and are tied primarily to the U.S. market, they are less exclusively tied to the United States than are the Caribbean islands. Although several of the Central American countries are very densely populated—El Salvador's figure of 580 persons per square mile is among the world's highest—their resource base is richer than that of most of the Caribbean islands. Their rate of emigration historically has been considerably lower than that of the insular Caribbean, though it is rising fast as a result of the bitter conflicts now underway.

Most of the Central American nations experienced very rapid economic growth and social change during the 1960s and until the mid-1970s. From 1950 to 1978, the nations of Central America averaged an annual real rate of economic growth of 5.3 percent. Real per capita income doubled over those years. Physical infrastructure in Central America, including roads, port facilities, electrical energy, and mass communications, expanded remarkably. The rate of adult literacy rose

*This section discusses Costa Rica, El Salvador, Guatemala, Honduras, and Nicaragua, plus Panama. Belize (formerly British Honduras, granted independence in 1981) is more Caribbean than Central American in background, culture, and tradition.

from about 44 percent to 72 percent over these years. Urbanization increased at a similar pace, from 16 percent in 1950 to 43 percent urban in 1980.

In the mid-1970s, however, the economic expansion in Central America slowed and in some countries reversed. The easy phase of import substitution was exhausted in most of these countries by about 1970. The economic benefits of the Central American Common Market, of considerable importance in the early 1960s, gave way in the late 1960s to intraregional tensions that were exemplified by the 1969 "Soccer War" between El Salvador and Honduras. And Central America, without any oil resources except in Guatemala, was hard hit by the worldwide increase in energy costs; the region's oil bill climbed from $189 million in 1973 to about $1.5 billion in 1980, while the prices of the region's main exports lagged.

Central America's economic woes have worsened dramatically since the late 1970s. The region's terms of trade have deteriorated severely, by almost 50 percent from 1977 through the mid-1980s. The volume of Central America's exports has decreased by some 20 percent since 1980, and intraregional trade has dropped almost 35 percent. Central America has been very hard hit, too, by other consequences of the international recession. These include the dramatically increased regional debt of $14 billion and the burgeoning debt service costs, which reached $1.5 billion in 1982, equivalent to 33 percent of the region's export earnings. Capital flight has also increased, to an estimated $3 billion since 1979. Per capita incomes in Costa Rica and Guatemala are down to the 1972 level, and incomes in Honduras are back to the 1970 level, while in Nicaragua and El Salvador—wracked by civil strife—they have fallen to the levels of the early 1960s.

As economic difficulties have mounted, the striking socioeconomic inequities in most Central American nations (except for Costa Rica) have become more extreme and have aggravated internal tensions. The size of the average plot owned by the highland Indians in Guatemala was cut in half from 1955 to 1975, and the number of landless peasants in El Salvador grew from 11 percent of the rural population in 1961 to 40 percent in the late 1970s. In most Central American countries, the real per capita incomes of the poorest 20 percent of the population fell during the 1970s and has continued to fall in the 1980s. Estimates from the UN Economic Commission for Latin America and the Caribbean (ECLAC) suggest that 65 percent of Central America's population should be classified as "poor," and 42 percent as "critically poor." Fifty-two percent of Central America's children, according to ECLAC, are malnourished.

The desperate poverty and the increasing concentration of land ownership and income in Central America are part of a syndrome. Small groups have monopolized political power (often with U.S. support) and have used it to reinforce their dominance over the export-based economies. Production of cash crops for export has been crowding out small-scale agriculture since the late nineteenth century. The process intensified in the 1950s and 1960s, when the oligarchies manipulated their control of the banking and judicial systems (and the local militaries) to cash in on booming world prices for cotton and beef. While a few plantation owners and ranchers enriched themselves, small farmers lost their lands and were forced to become rural wage-laborers. The Central American Common Market stimulated some foreign investors in the 1960s to set up industries that produced for the expanded regional market, but migration to the cities by landless peasants outstripped industrial employment.

As income distribution in Central America has worsened, conflicts have intensified. As a consequence, both political repression and insurgency have increased. Central America has been wracked since the late 1970s by bitter internal struggles.

Nicaragua's broke out first, in part because of the excesses of the Somoza dynasty. A powerful, broadly based national opposition to the Somozas grew during the 1970s, culminating in the overthrow of General Anastasio Somoza in 1979. But the removal of Somoza did not end Nicaragua's civil war, for opposition quickly developed to the victorious Sandinista movement. The fact that the military opposition to the Sandinista government has been made possible in part by U.S. support for this campaign is evident, but it is equally incontrovertible that thousands of Nicaraguans became sufficiently disaffected by the Sandinistas to fight a guerrilla war.

El Salvador has for several years also experienced an intense civil war, pitting Marxist-led guerrilla groups against the country's armed forces. Leftist groups in El Salvador, like those in Nicaragua during the late 1970s, have received some Cuban encouragement and support (as well as some Nicaraguan assistance since 1979), but the main impetus has been local. Guatemala has experienced prolonged bloodletting, as well, more violent in some years than in others, but with little respite since the 1950s. Honduras, the poorest of the Central American nations, teeters on the edge of violence. Even Costa Rica, long tranquil, has begun to experience incidents of terrorism.

The disruption that accompanies civil turmoil, moreover, has further clouded economic prospects in most of Central America. Central America's internal wars during the past decade have killed almost 150 thousand people, displaced at least 1½ million more, and caused billions of dollars of damage. The crumbling of Central America's remaining oligarchies and the further polarization of Latin America's most bitterly divided countries contrast with the muted unease of most of the insular Caribbean.

Although the United States has historically exerted considerable influence on the Central American isthmus, the region is less closely tied to the United States, and to any other metropolitan power, than are the Caribbean islands. United States economic involvement in Central America has remained modest in recent decades. After a surge in the 1960s, direct U.S. investment in the countries of Central America except Panama slowed again in the 1970s and decreased in the early 1980s. It now amounts to less than $800 million: about 2.5 percent of U.S. direct investment in Latin America, 10 percent of U.S. investment in the insular Caribbean, and less than 0.3 percent of worldwide U.S. investment. The financial involvement of U.S. banks in Central America is less than 2.3 percent of their total exposure in Latin America and the Caribbean, and it has been declining further in the face of the region's turmoil. Nor is U.S. trade with Central America very significant; it comprises only 5 percent of U.S. trade with all of Latin America, about 30 percent of U.S. trade with the insular Caribbean, and less than 1 percent of the worldwide commerce of the United States. The economic stake of the United States in Central America today is modest. It is more limited than the U.S. economic stake in the Caribbean islands, and it is much smaller than that in Mexico or Brazil.

THE POLITICS OF NATIONAL INSECURITY

Although they are different from each other, the countries of the Caribbean and Central America are similar in one very important respect. Clustered around the Caribbean Sea—America's Mediterranean—they comprise the "Third Border" of the United States. The proximity of the Caribbean Basin to the United States has been that region's defining characteristic ever since this country burst onto the international scene as a significant power in the nineteenth century. The United States rose to international prominence precisely by exerting its influence in the circum-Caribbean region, starting with Cuba and Puerto Rico. The region remains fundamental to the perception many U.S. leaders have of this country's world standing. As President Reagan put it in his April 1983 address to the joint session of Congress: "The national security of all the Americas is at stake in Central America. If we cannot defend ourselves there, we cannot expect to prevail elsewhere. Our credibility would collapse, our alliances would crumble, and the safety of our homeland would be put in jeopardy."

The belief that tight U.S. control of the small nations of the Caribbean Basin is vital to the national interest of the United States has long been widely accepted. During the late nineteenth and early twentieth centuries, the Caribbean Basin was necessarily a major focus of U.S. foreign policy. A considerable share of U.S. foreign investment and trade was then concentrated in the Caribbean and Central America. This nation's most important overseas military installations were the network of coaling stations and naval bases established to protect U.S. interests in the region—especially to assure access to the Panama Canal, constructed at the turn of the century. A primary aim of U.S. foreign policy, therefore, was to prevent extra-hemispheric powers from expanding their influence in the Caribbean Basin. The annexation of Puerto Rico, the Platt amendment imposed on Cuba, the promulgation of the (Theodore) "Roosevelt corollary" to the Monroe Doctrine, the repeated U.S. military interventions in the Dominican Republic, Haiti, and Central America—all were part of a sustained effort by the United States to secure absolute control of its border region.

By the time Franklin Delano Roosevelt launched the Good Neighbor Policy in 1934 to shore up hemispheric relations in a troubled international context, the United States could afford to change its approach toward the Caribbean Basin. This shift was possible, in part, precisely because the United States was not being effectively challenged in its border region. The destroyer-for-bases deal with Britain, secured early in World War II, further solidified U.S. influence in the region, as did the establishment of the Caribbean Commission in 1946.

The United States emerged from World War II dominant in the whole Western Hemisphere—indeed, in much of the world. The United States extended its sway throughout Latin America and spread its investment, financial, commercial, diplomatic, military, and cultural presence across the globe.

Because the United States undertook such a large international role in the postwar period, its involvement in the Caribbean Basin paled into relative insignificance and was largely taken for granted. The U.S. government paid very little attention to the Caribbean Basin from the mid-1940s until the mid-1970s except when it appeared to Washington that leftists aligned with the Soviet Union were actually taking power: in Guatemala in 1954, Cuba from 1959 on, British Guiana in the early 1960s, and the Dominican Republic in 1965. In Guatemala, a covert military operation removed the left-leaning Arbenz government and installed a client regime. In British Guiana (later Guyana), clandestine U.S. involvement helped to frustrate the political ambition of Cheddi Jagan. In the Dominican episode, some twenty-two thousand U.S. troops were landed to prevent what some in Washington feared might become a Communist takeover, and many remained to stabilize the local situation until national elections could put a trusted Dominican political figure back into power.

The case of Cuba was different, however, and it has helped to change the nature of U.S.-Caribbean relations. Beginning in 1959 and especially from 1960 on, Washington tried a variety of techniques to co-opt, reverse, abort, or destroy the Cuban Revolution, but to no avail. The strategic and tactical skill of Fidel Castro, blunders in U.S. policy, and a Soviet decision to provide unstinting assistance to Castro's regime—all combined to permit the firm consolidation of an anti-U.S. government in what had formerly been a U.S. client-state. Unchallenged U.S. dominance of the Caribbean Basin ended for all practical purposes in April 1961, when the U.S.-supported invasion at the Bay of Pigs collapsed. The "understandings" reached between the United States and the Soviet Union at the end of the October 1962 missile crisis—when the Soviet Union agreed to remove its missiles and not to reintroduce a strategic threat to the United States, in exchange for a U.S. pledge not to invade Cuba—reinforced the end of U.S. hegemony. Many opinion leaders in the United States still do not accept the loss of absolute U.S. control over the Caribbean Basin, but it has been a fact for nearly thirty years.

From the mid-1940s to the mid-1970s, tangible U.S. interests in the Caribbean and Central America changed a great deal. The region's military importance diminished as new technology (especially intercontinental ballistic missiles and nuclear submarines) drastically reduced the significance of proximity. Preserving U.S. access to the Panama Canal remains an important U.S. aim, but (as is pointed out in chapter 3) it is no longer as vital an interest as it used to be. Today's aircraft carriers and supertankers are too large to transit the canal, and the share of U.S. commerce passing through the canal has declined to less than one-sixth of this country's total ocean-bound trade. Some U.S. bases and other military assets in the circum-Caribbean region are still useful, especially for training purposes and as listening posts. Their diminished significance in the 1970s was made evident by the Pentagon's decision to downgrade or close several Caribbean facilities, and by the reduction in the number of U.S. military personnel stationed in the region.

The sea lanes that pass through the Caribbean remain important to the United States, for almost half of all foreign cargo tonnage and of the crude oil imported into the United States transit them. But absolute control of each Caribbean Basin country is no longer needed to protect these lanes. A Caribbean Basin nation (such as Cuba or Nicaragua) which sought to disrupt the sea lanes would find itself instantly vulnerable to the overwhelming power of the United States, only minutes away.

It is hard to imagine a credible scenario in which the Caribbean sea lanes would be disrupted. Even if the Soviet Union were to undertake the risky enterprise of interfering with U.S. shipping, it would be more likely to do so in the North Atlantic than in the Caribbean, where the relative disparity in easily projectable power is so favorable to the United States.

U.S. economic interests in the Caribbean Basin have also declined, both in absolute and in relative terms. U.S. investment in the insular Caribbean accounts for less than 2.5 percent of the total book value of all direct U.S. foreign investment; even that figure would be much lower if the essentially paper investment in the Bahamas were excluded. United States investment in the Caribbean islands may eventually be increased somewhat by the incentive provisions of the Caribbean Basin Initiative, but if that does occur it will be primarily a result, not a cause, of official U.S. interest in the region. The U.S. investment stake in Central America, as has been noted, is even smaller. Moreover, it has been declining in recent years and is unlikely to expand significantly while conditions of violent instability prevail. Likewise, the relative importance of Central America and the Caribbean as sources for products and materials has diminished, as the worldwide involvements of the United States have produced multiple suppliers, and synthetics have replaced natural products. The main items exported from Central America—bananas, coffee, cotton, cocoa, and sugar—are all items for which the U.S. market is very important to the producers, but on which the United States surely does not depend. The United States does import 85 percent of its bauxite and 25 percent of its processed aluminum from the Caribbean Basin, mainly from Jamaica, but there are other sources for these materials.

Two newer U.S. interests in the Caribbean Basin have emerged in recent years, particularly with regard to the insular Caribbean. One is diplomatic: the Caribbean nations wield many votes in the United Nations, the Organization of American States, and other bodies. The Caribbean democracies have consistently supported U.S. positions on a number of international issues; their hostility would be irritating.

A second U.S. stake in the insular Caribbean, and to a lesser extent in Central America, is demographic: the interest created by immigration from these regions into the United States. The much-publicized flight of more than 10 percent of Cuba's population to the United States since 1959 tends to overwhelm an even more impressive statistic: the percentage of people from the rest of the Caribbean who have entered the United States during the same period is as high. This massive flow affects the economy, politics, and culture of the United States. The United States and the Caribbean import from each other music, dance, crime, cuisine, literature, and political ideas and techniques. Large Caribbean communities are visible in Florida, New York, New Jersey, and other regions of this country. Because these increasingly large groups of immigrants are a source of local anxieties and tensions, the United States has an interest in regulating migration from the Caribbean Basin.

In sum, traditional U.S. interests in the insular Caribbean and Central America have declined over the last generation, although they are still emphasized in official documents and discussions. Newer U.S. interests in these regions, particularly the diplomatic and demographic concerns, have increased in significance but not yet in salience; President Reagan's key address to the OAS on the Caribbean Basin Initiative did not even mention migration, for instance. The main reason U.S. policy makers have rediscovered the Caribbean and Central America arises instead from an almost reflexive U.S. aim to retain overwhelming predominance in the border region.

Washington's strong interest in retaining absolute control of the Caribbean Basin is axiomatic, having been inculcated ever since the late nineteenth century through years of repetition in internal documents and public pronouncements. It is reinforced by most U.S. political leaders' perceptions of domestic public opinion. These leaders believe that an administration identified as having "lost" a country previously in the U.S. orbit, having permitted a "second Cuba," would suffer a high domestic political cost. And the urge to retain tight control is further strengthened by a calculus about international prestige. United States officials do not want the United States to be perceived abroad as being unable to maintain dominance so close to home.

To some extent, recent U.S. administrations have been caught in a credibility trap of their own making, as they have voluntarily raised the declared stakes for the United States in the Caribbean Basin and then escalated U.S. involvement to match the stakes. But the underlying perception that U.S. influence in the world would suffer greatly if hostile states emerged in this country's border region has been widely accepted for many years. The costs to U.S. credibility and prestige of divisive and ineffectual U.S. efforts to reimpose U.S. control in a country like Nicaragua, conversely, have rarely been assessed.

Official discussions of U.S. policy in the Caribbean Basin are laced with assertions of a vital U.S. "national security interest" in the region, although the exact nature of the interest is rarely specified. The 1984 report of the National Bipartisan Commission on Central America (the Kissinger report) states, for instance, that preventing the Soviet Union from establishing military bases or facilities in the region is not the sole or even the primary security concern; but where a convincing statement of exactly what is, in fact, at stake would have been appropriate, the report trails off into vague generalities. Repeated presidential assertions of a U.S. national security concern in the Caribbean Basin have been similarly imprecise.

It may be, to underline a point made in chapter 3, that the underlying rationale of recent U.S. policy can be understood best not in terms of "national security" as it is usually discussed, but, rather, in terms of "national *in*security." What is fundamentally at issue, more than any tangible challenge, may be the psychological or psychopolitical difficulty of coping with loss of control in the border region. United States policy makers have considered it important to retain U.S. control of the internal politics of Caribbean Basin countries, even though the object of this control is far less significant than it used to be. And the United States has sought to retain its overwhelming control, even though the domestic and international costs of perpetuating this stance are increasingly high in the face of nationalist and revolutionary movements. That is the heart of the matter in the Caribbean Basin.

THE U.S. STAKE IN THE CARIBBEAN BASIN

Discussions of U.S. relations with the Caribbean Basin often suffer from a tendency to treat ideal visions of the region as realistic objectives of U.S. policy, and thus to confuse unattainable preferences with core U.S. interests.

The vision that the Kissinger report holds out as the correct aim of U.S. policy in Central America, for example, is one of securing and supporting peaceful, democratic, reform-oriented, stable, prosperous, and congenial neighbors. This goal is utterly unrealistic, however. Except for Costa Rica, Central America's nations are conflict wracked, repressive, polarized, economically depressed, and unstable, and they harbor deep resentments of the United States. No U.S. policy could soon change these grim realities. On the contrary, part of this country's problem in Central America stems from the paradox that an increased U.S. presence may well heighten the very nationalist and revolutionary sentiments that make Washington uncomfortable. In this sense, the goals posited by the Kissinger report and other recent official articulations of U.S. policies toward Central America and the Caribbean are not merely unrealistic; they are like a mirage, receding inevitably as they are approached.

To fashion a successful U.S. policy toward the Caribbean Basin, it is essential to define the core objectives of the United States.

The primary U.S. interest in the Caribbean Basin, today as in the past, is to prevent hostile extra-hemispheric forces from using the Basin as a platform for directing damaging activities against the United States or its allies. In contemporary terms, this means assuring that no bases, strategic weapons or facilities, or combat forces are introduced by the Soviet Union or its allies into the border region of the United States.

In fact, given the presence of missile-toting Soviet submarines off the Atlantic coast, such facilities or forces would probably not very markedly increase the Soviet military threat to the United States. But threatening bases or facilities in the Caribbean Basin would pose some additional danger, at a margin where each increment matters. Equally important, in a world where perceptions can themselves create realities, the United States would appear weak if it could not keep provocative direct challenges to its military security out of its immediate vicinity.

The second core interest of the United States in the Caribbean Basin today is to assure continuing access to the assets of Central America and the Caribbean, primarily the Panama Canal but also the sea lanes. It has historically been important for the United States to maintain secure access to these assets without making a major investment of resources, and this objective remains a priority. Trying to maintain tight control of the internal affairs of Caribbean Basin nations may no longer be the most effective means of achieving this goal, however. On the contrary, the Panama Canal treaties of 1978 suggest that accommodating nationalist impulses in the Caribbean Basin region is sometimes a more effective means of protecting U.S. interests than is resisting such nationalist currents. It is also important for the United States to reduce the risk of a regional conflagration in the Caribbean Basin, for such an outbreak would be far more likely than any domestic political change within the individual Caribbean nations to disrupt U.S. access to the region's assets.

The third important U.S. interest in the Caribbean Basin is to decrease the pressure for immigration into the United States, a pressure created by continued economic decline and violent turmoil in the region. The causal connections between development and migration are complex, and the United States cannot be confident that pressures for migration from the Caribbean Basin will diminish just as soon as economic development in the region picks up. It is clear, however, that worsening economic conditions will heighten pressures for emigration, and that increasing polarization and strife will increase migration, regardless of the results of a civil war.

This interest in stemming the flow of migration from the Caribbean Basin leads to a fourth and broader U.S. interest: promoting economic development and long-term political stability in the Caribbean Basin countries so that they can become self-sufficient. Assuring access to Caribbean Basin resources is no longer the issue most important to the United States. Rather, the United States has an increasing interest in

helping Caribbean and Central American nations use their own resources to achieve regional development.

These four U.S. interests in the Caribbean Basin are fundamental,
and other aims of U.S. policy, though oft repeated by Washington officials, are or ought to be less important. Although the United States
should support democracy in the Hemisphere (as is more fully discussed
in chapters 3 and 7), U.S. policy cannot create instant democracy in
countries that lack the traditions and institutions required or that are in
the midst of civil wars. It is not vital for the United States that democracy soon emerge in Central America, where (except in Costa Rica) it
has never heretofore taken root.

Moreover, although the United States would prefer that its neighbors
share its perceptions of world problems, favor free enterprise and foreign investment, and disdain the Soviet Union and its policies, such
regional conviviality is not crucial. If countries in the Caribbean Basin
choose to adopt socialist economies or even to embrace the Soviet
Union, that can be tolerated by the United States as long as these
countries do not offer military advantages to the Soviet Union or Cuba.

THE UNITED STATES AND THE CARIBBEAN BASIN: OPTIONS FOR POLICY

The United States has four main options for advancing its core interests
in the Caribbean Basin: intermittent intervention; sustained disengagement; activist expansion of immediate U.S. influence; or a long-term
developmental emphasis. Intermittent intervention combines a low degree of interest in Caribbean socioeconomic development with a high
degree of concern for U.S. security interests, narrowly defined. Sustained disengagement features a low degree of U.S. concern with the
Caribbean Basin on both socioeconomic and traditional security dimensions. The activist policy involves a high degree of U.S. concern with
both socioeconomic and security aspects. The developmental approach
combines a high degree of U.S. concern for socioeconomic questions
with a reduced preoccupation with classic security issues.

Intermittent Intervention

Intermittent intervention was, in effect, the traditional policy of the
United States toward the Caribbean Basin from the turn of this century
until the late 1970s. A long-term cycle of indifference and panic characterized U.S. relations with the countries of Central America and the
Caribbean. The historic stance toward these regions combined neglect
of their underlying economic and social realities with keen sensitivity to
any potential challenge to U.S. hegemony.

In practice, the traditional stance meant ignoring the Caribbean Basin countries most of the time; sending diplomats without stature to the region; offering few, if any, economic concessions; and, often, letting private interests dominate national concerns. Whenever change threatens to undermine U.S. control, or even to generate significant unpredictability, the traditional policy called for U.S. power to restore this country's domination. Sometimes intervention by the United States was covert, as in Guatemala in 1954 and British Guiana in the early 1960s. On other occasions, the United States sent in its troops, as in Santo Domingo in 1965. The traditional approach might well be called a "Hallmark" policy, after the greeting cards that, according to their advertisements, you send when you "care enough to send the very best." From time to time the United States sends in the Marines, but between such extravagant displays, it avoids indicating much interest.

The intermittent interventionist approach to the Caribbean and Central America had its advantages. It tied up few resources most of the time, and it freed policy makers to concentrate on other matters unless they thought key U.S. interests were directly engaged.

One main difficulty always plagued the traditional U.S. approach to the Caribbean Basin, however. Although weak and dependent entities like those dotting the Caribbean are precisely those most vulnerable to instability and hence to outside influence, traditional U.S. policy did little to help the Caribbean Basin territories (aside from Puerto Rico) overcome their disadvantaged condition. By themselves, these territories have never been able to resist the encroachments of external powers which Washington considers threatening; but neither have they been able to undertake the development and integration that might make them less vulnerable to foreign penetration.

Historically, the United States has taken an exceptional interest in domestic political changes within the Caribbean Basin, but it has resisted more fundamental and sustained engagement. Although the United States has traditionally regarded the area as strategically important, it has never adopted the positive, long-term measures this concern might imply. That is why the United States has so often been drawn into unpleasant Caribbean entanglements, including military interventions. The seeds of future interventions germinate in the underlying conditions that Washington persistently ignores.

The periodically intrusive nature of U.S. policy toward the Caribbean Basin has had its costs. Each U.S. intervention tends to undermine local development. Each distorts the distribution of power and resources, often in ways unsupportive of long-term and self-sustaining growth. Each U.S. intervention, whether overt or covert, fuels anti-U.S. movements not only in the affected country but also elsewhere in the region.

These episodes often strain the domestic consensus on foreign policy within the United States. And each makes more distant the day when international laws against military coercion will have real force.

The traditional approach, in sum, has been shortsighted, counterproductive, and ultimately expensive. It amounts, in effect, to putting out fires in the region without removing the flammable material and even, indeed, leaving some lit fuses behind. Increasingly it is an unfeasible approach. The large Caribbean diaspora in this country makes it hard for the United States to ignore the region. Most important, both domestic and international constraints make it impossible for the United States to exercise force in Central America and the Caribbean as easily and effectively as it once did. The brief U.S. intervention in Grenada was, in some ways, the exception to prove this rule, for it involved sending U.S. forces into a ministate with a makeshift armed force of less than one thousand men, and under optimal political circumstances. In Nicaragua since 1979, on the other hand, the United States government has felt the constraints limiting the possibility of armed intervention. These limits have also sharply narrowed U.S. options in dealing with the Marxist groups in El Salvador, and, most obviously, with Castro's Cuba.

Sustained Disengagement

Although it has never been attempted, the option of sustained U.S. disengagement from the Caribbean Basin is at least a theoretical possibility.

The argument for disengagement is that the Caribbean and Central America are no longer objectively important to the United States in economic or security terms, and that U.S. political interests in these regions would be better served if the United States left the Caribbean Basin countries alone than if it became embroiled there. Under this approach, the United States would limit its involvement in the Caribbean Basin to conventional diplomatic and commercial interchange. This view holds that U.S. economic interests in the Caribbean Basin are not overwhelmingly important and would probably remain largely unaffected even if some governments in the area became hostile to the United States. These countries would almost inevitably maintain economic relations with the United States, unless Washington itself imposes economic sanctions, as it has on Cuba and Nicaragua.

Under this option, U.S. policy makers, the attentive public, and eventually the electorate at large would be educated to accept a substantial U.S. withdrawal from the Caribbean Basin. United States officials would rid themselves of their traditional nervousness about Caribbean turbulence and leave the people there alone, to develop or to stagnate, to revolt or to ally, or to stew in their own juices, whatever the flavor. The

United States would not preoccupy itself with either the economic development or the political direction of the Caribbean Basin countries, but would treat them with the kind of benign neglect it usually accords to small countries in central Africa.

The disengagement formula has some abstract appeal, for frenetic U.S. intervention in Caribbean Basin affairs has often been counterproductive. But the disengagement option is blatantly unfeasible. The United States cannot simply withdraw unilaterally from involvement in its border region.

Geography—strongly reinforced by history, politics, economics, and culture—makes the United States a major presence in the Caribbean Basin. The countries of this region cannot escape the shadow of the United States, whether it be benign or stifling. Nor can the United States escape involvement in the Caribbean, with which this country is so interconnected. Whatever policy an administration adopts, immigration from the Caribbean Basin would not stop, tourism would continue, and other business flows would prompt fuller U.S. involvement. More importantly, people in the United States, both at the attentive public and at the mass level, would feel uncomfortable if Washington abandoned these countries to their fate. The international reputation of the United States, among both allies and rivals, would also be damaged by such a passive U.S. stance. Great powers simply do not behave that way; disengagement would prove impossible to sustain.

Activist Expansion of U.S. Influence

The third approach—the active expansion of U.S. involvement in both the internal politics and the economies of the Caribbean Basin countries—was the policy of both the Carter and Reagan administrations, although each adopted different emphases. The basic tenets of this approach are that the United States should concern itself with the immediate situation in the Caribbean Basin, acting to shore up current U.S. influence wherever possible, and that it should increase longer-term economic and technical assistance in order to contribute to the region's long-range social development and political stability. Rather than wait for instability, revolutionary conditions, and anti-U.S. movements to intensify, it is argued, the United States should head off problems in the Caribbean Basin by helping these nations cope with their problems, while moving at the same time to counter Cuba's influence.

From the beginning of its term, the Carter administration favored the activist approach to the Caribbean Basin and took a number of steps to expand the U.S. presence in the insular Caribbean. High officials (Rosalynn Carter, Secretary of State Cyrus Vance, UN Ambassador Andrew Young, Undersecretary of State Philip Habib, and others) were sent to the Caribbean to indicate interest and to show that Washington accepted "ideological pluralism" there. The Latin American Bureau of the State Department was reorganized to assure greater concern for the Caribbean, and the contingent of U.S. officials assigned there was expanded. United States economic assistance to the Caribbean was doubled, and Washington took the lead in establishing a multilateral consortium to channel aid. The Carter administration sponsored the creation of Caribbean/Central American Action, a business lobby. It greatly expanded the number of friendly port calls made by U.S. Navy warships, and it established a powerful new radio transmitter and antennae capable of beaming medium-wave broadcasts throughout the Caribbean. The Carter administration also began to explore the possibilities for a limited improvement in bilateral relations with Cuba, while making it clear that Cuba's efforts to support revolutionary movements would be strenuously opposed.

The Carter administration's response to the simmering turmoil in Central America was comparatively slow. In its first years, the Carter administration nominated inexperienced personnel to some of the main Central American posts and generally ignored that region. The gathering strength of the anti-Somoza movement in Nicaragua and the insurrectionary groups in El Salvador, however, eventually convinced the Carter administration to include Central America in a broader Caribbean Basin policy. Significant economic aid packages were designed for Nicaragua, El Salvador, and the other Central American countries in the hope of preempting revolutionary movements or co-opting them where they had emerged.

The Carter approach failed to produce quick results. Cuba remained actively involved in Africa despite the administration's overtures and signals. The revolutionary governments in Nicaragua and Grenada refused to be co-opted. Leftist insurgents in El Salvador, in turn, stepped up their attacks. During its latter period, the Carter administration responded to these developments by backing away from its forthcoming posture toward change in the Caribbean Basin region. Gradually it moved back toward a more conventional anti-Communist approach.

The Reagan administration was preoccupied from the start with the Caribbean Basin. The administration's first official visitor was Jamaica's newly elected prime minister, Edward Seaga, whose views epitomized the free-enterprise, anti-Communist approach the Reagan team wanted to assist. Attention soon focused, however, on El Salvador. Secretary of State Alexander Haig devoted his first full-scale briefing on

Capitol Hill to the situation there. He and others in the new administration drew a line in El Salvador against the expansion of Soviet and Cuban influence.

From its first days, the Reagan administration intensified its war of words and at least a few actions against Cuba. Although it would not go as far as Haig says he recommended, the Reagan administration stepped up anti-Castro propaganda efforts, especially by establishing Radio Marti, a new communications venture aimed exclusively at the island. Washington resumed air surveillance of Cuba, tightened restrictions on commerce and cultural exchange with the island, and repeatedly threatened to "go to the source" to stop Cuban support for insurgent movements in Central America.

The Reagan administration's overall approach, unveiled by the president in his Caribbean Basin Initiative of 1982, has been to beef up the U.S. presence throughout the Caribbean and Central America: militarily, politically, economically, and culturally. As originally proposed, the CBI included major adjustments in trade and tariff policy—even "one-way free trade" on a number of products—as well as tax incentives to stimulate U.S. investment in the region. Significant public resource transfers were also proposed, mainly through bilateral channels. The U.S. Congress, however, removed the investment tax incentives and excluded selected products from the free trade provisions, thus reducing the economic impact of the CBI.

An East-West focus has characterized every aspect of the CBI. Allocations for assistance have depended much more on a country's attitudes toward Cuba and the United States than on its economic need or development prospects. The insignificant aid offered to Haiti, the poorest country in the Caribbean region, illustrates this point, as does the outright exclusion from the plan of Nicaragua—and of Grenada, until the leftist government there was ousted. Moreover, the entire aid supplement has taken the form of Economic Support Funds: simple transfers of funds to recipient countries' treasuries, without reference to specific development projects. The CBI's thrust has been to shore up immediate U.S. political influence; it is not primarily a strategy for the region's long-term economic and social development.

When it comes to combating leftist gains in Central America and the Caribbean, the Reagan administration's approach has been avidly to support anti-Communist governments and movements.

The United States channeled covert aid to counterrevolutionaries in Grenada during the period of the New Jewel Movement, and it seized the opportunity to unseat the leftist regime there in October 1983. The United States is deeply involved in the politics of El Salvador, in addition to providing arms, training, and advisers to that country's military.

Honduras has been converted into a major base for U.S. military training and for operations against neighboring Nicaragua. The Reagan administration has revised the Central American Defense Council (CONDECA) and has sought to restore military aid to Guatemala. Military equipment and training has also been provided to Costa Rica, despite that country's misgivings.

Most dramatically, Washington has become ever more deeply involved in supporting the armed partisans (the *contras*) fighting against the Sandinista government in Nicaragua. Despite congressional opposition, the Reagan administration steadily built up its aid to the *contras* to a level equivalent to that going to several Central American governments and has given every indication that it would request still more assistance. Mindful of congressional and public opinion, the administration has frequently reiterated that it does not plan to send U.S. combat forces into Central America. Some U.S. officials have begun openly to discuss the possibility that U.S. troops may eventually be used there, however.

The Carter and Reagan variants of the activist approach to the Caribbean and Central America are somewhat different, and the differences ought to be noted. The Carter stance toward leftist regimes in the Caribbean Basin area was (especially at first) more accommodating; Washington was willing to accept ideological diversity, even in this border region. The Reagan administration, on the contrary, made it plain from the beginning that it favored regimes oriented toward free enterprise and foreign investment, supportive of U.S. foreign policy and opposed to Cuba, and that it would reward such governments and ignore or punish the others. The Carter administration (again, especially at first) gave priority to multilateral economic and technical assistance; the Reagan administration from the start downplayed multilateral aid, preferring visible bilateral assistance. The Carter administration, although willing to commit U.S. resources to counter undesired trends in the Caribbean and Central America, respected the sovereignty of the Caribbean and Central American nations. The Reagan administration, on the contrary, made it plain from the start that it might use force as a means of reversing unacceptable developments in this region.

These significant differences should not obscure important similarities between the Carter and Reagan variants of the activist approach, however. Both administrations lumped together the insular Caribbean and Central America. Both showed a high degree of concern with socioeconomic development as well as immediate security issues. Each emphasized short-term political considerations and the aim of countering Cuba. Both proposed that the United States take the lead in orchestrating regional security and development initiatives in order to combat revolutionary inroads. Both administrations sought to perpetuate, or to restore, U.S. control of Central America and the Caribbean.

The recommendations of the National Bipartisan Commission on Central America (The "Kissinger commission") epitomize the activist approach by calling for more U.S. involvement in practically all aspects of that region. The commission argued that Central America needs major social changes and massive economic development, as well as considerable security assistance, in order to beat back the challenge of Marxist-oriented insurgent movements. It urged the United States to play a pivotal role in promoting economic growth, social change, and political democracy, as well as to provide a "security shield" behind which progress could occur. It called for the United States to lead a process of regional transformation in order to preempt revolutionary movements.

The activist approach to the Caribbean Basin has obvious advantages over both the interventionist and the disengagement options. Focusing sustained attention and resources on the Caribbean Basin should enable the U.S. government more effectively to influence U.S. relations with the region. The scale of Caribbean Basin entities is such that even limited U.S. moves can have an impact. Many Caribbean countries are so dependent that an infusion of U.S. resources is likely to fix the region even more firmly in the U.S. orbit, at least in the short run.

But the activist approach involves important risks. First, it may arouse unrealistic expectations within the region. Prime Minister Seaga, for instance, called for a long-term program of aid to Central America and the Caribbean at the level of $3 billion per year, and the Kissinger commission called for $8 billion over five years. In a period of massive U.S. federal deficits, aid transfers to the Caribbean Basin will be much more modest, however. Aid to shore up military regimes, moreover, often produces a need for more aid. The activist approach may thus produce a troublesome gap between rhetoric and expectations, on the one hand, and implementation and impact on the other. The U.S. public will surely not long support an expensive effort to transform Caribbean Basin realities.

Second, the preoccupation of U.S. policy makers with Fidel Castro's Cuba exacerbates severe political strains. Caribbean leaders typically perceive Castro as primarily a regional actor, not a Cold War instrument. At times they have found "playing the Cuban card" useful to increase legitimacy with domestic constituents or to strengthen Third World ties. The persistent failure of U.S. government officials accurately to assess Caribbean perceptions of Castro, and the recurrent U.S. readiness to focus on Cuba rather than on the region's underlying needs, inevitably breeds resentments. To the extent that U.S. interest in the Caribbean Basin appears to be purely instrumental, the chances increase that an activist U.S. presence in the region will backfire, triggering nationalist reactions.

The activist approach has three other drawbacks. First, despite the Reagan administration's repeated assurances that U.S. combat forces will not be used, the risks of an escalating U.S. military involvement in Central America are inherent in the policy of direct confrontation with insurgent movements and unrelenting hostility toward Cuba and Nicaragua. The prospect that the United States will eventually have to choose between humiliation and escalation in Nicaragua is built into the policy of aid to the *contras*.

Second, the more fully the United States is engaged in the internal affairs of the Caribbean Basin nations, the greater is the likelihood that this country will have to absorb larger flows of refugees from the continuing civil wars. As the United States involves itself more deeply in the region, it creates increasing political and moral imperatives to assist the victims of violence.

Third, an increasingly interventionist U.S. stance, even if it stops short of direct military action, contradicts the respect the United States must show Latin America if this country is to secure greater cooperation from the Hemisphere's major nations. Gunboat diplomacy in the Caribbean Basin may win back Grenada or perhaps even Nicaragua, but such "successes" may well alienate Brazil, Mexico, Colombia, Argentina, Venezuela, and other Latin American nations. As chapter 4 emphasizes, the one event that could conceivably push Mexico into a strongly nationalist, anti-U.S. mode would be U.S. military intervention in Central America. The consequences throughout South America of such an intervention would also be harmful; throughout the region, a direct U.S. military involvement would fuel insurgencies, provoke urban terrorism, and generally stimulate nationalist reactions.

The Developmental Alternative

A fourth approach to Central America and the Caribbean would involve a sustained U.S. commitment to the economic and social development of the nations in the Caribbean Basin without a corresponding attempt to exercise tight control of their internal affairs.

The developmental approach posits that the core U.S. interest in its border region is to exclude tangible security threats—to keep hostile bases, combat forces, and strategic facilities out of the area. It would accept diverse sociopolitical and economic approaches, even Marxist ones, in the Caribbean Basin, as long as no direct security threats were introduced into the region. This aim would be accomplished not by controlling the domestic politics of the area, but by making it clear to the Soviet Union or other potential adversaries that the introduction of threatening forces and facilities would trigger an immediate U.S. response, and by negotiating verifiable and enforceable regional agreements to exclude such items.

The second assumption of the developmental approach is that the United States will benefit if the countries of the Caribbean Basin are able to grow economically and build effective social and political institutions. The improved viability of Caribbean Basin nations would decrease pressure for migration to the United States and would facilitate expanded economic exchange between the United States and those nations.

The developmental approach assumes as well that geography, history, and economics will tie the countries of the Caribbean Basin to the United States as long as the United States does not choose to expel them from its orbit. Caribbean Basin nations, regardless of their domestic or even their international politics, will send most of their exports to the United States and buy most of their imports from this country as long as they are permitted to do so. They have an interest, therefore, in avoiding deeply hostile relations with the United States.

The developmental approach to the Caribbean Basin would concentrate on long-term economic and social progress rather than on immediate political alignment. It would distinguish between those countries ready for significant economic advance (presently most of the Caribbean islands, along with Costa Rica, Panama, and perhaps Honduras and Guatemala on the Central American isthmus) and those where civil turmoil precludes effective economic progress in the near future.

With regard to the former group of countries, those ready for economic and social development, the United States would extend the provisions for free access to the U.S. market contained in the originally proposed Caribbean Basin Initiative to all that refrain from military alliance with the Soviet Union—regardless of ideology, domestic social or political organization, and foreign policy. An attempt would be made to reverse congressionally imposed restrictions that have reduced the impact of the CBI for precisely those products on which Caribbean Basin nations have achieved a comparative advantage. The United States would revise its sugar program so that the U.S. market would be more open to Caribbean producers, and it would allow Caribbean producers to take fuller advantage of their proximity on such products as textiles and small electronic appliances.

Under the developmental approach, the United States and other interested countries would provide assistance for infrastructural and human resource development in the Caribbean Basin. Foreign assistance would be provided mainly through multilateral rather than bilateral channels, in order to reduce politicization and to extend time horizons beyond the U.S. electoral cycle. Rather than increase its visibility in the Caribbean Basin, the United States would gradually lower its profile. Washington might then be less of a focus for nationalist impulses.

With regard to the strife-torn nations of Central America, the United States would cut back its intense involvement of recent years. The United States would aim primarily to stop any of the Central American conflicts from providing an occasion for the introduction of extra-hemispheric military threats, and to prevent the Central American conflicts from escalating, broadening, or contributing to a general East-West confrontation. The main instrument of U.S. policy would be diplomatic, not military. In particular, Washington would genuinely support efforts—such as those of the Contadora nations (Colombia, Mexico, Panama, and Venezuela) and, more recently, of Costa Rica's Oscar Arías—to mediate Central America's conflicts.

The United States would fully back attempts to negotiate a regional political solution to protect the territorial integrity of existing states (including Nicaragua and El Salvador) against insurgent movements. Such an accord would bar both overt and covert attempts to overthrow established governments. It would also, by regional agreement, keep threatening bases, forces, and facilities out of the Caribbean Basin. As part of the agreement, the United States would assure the government of Nicaragua that U.S. efforts to overthrow the Sandinistas would end as long as Nicaragua refrains from attacking or subverting its neighbors or providing a military base to the Soviet Union or Cuba.

Such an accord would extend to the whole Caribbean Basin the basic principles embodied in the U.S.-Soviet understandings of 1962, 1970, and 1979 affecting Cuba: Soviet strategic bases or facilities will not be introduced into the region, conventional forces will not be augmented so as to threaten regional security, and the territorial integrity of every state in the region will be respected by all. The draft treaties presented by the Contadora nations in 1986 go a long way toward this kind of regional solution. Still more work is needed on monitoring, verification, and enforcement of the proposed treaty provisions, but the underlying concept would protect core U.S. interests.

With regard to Cuba itself, the developmental approach would counsel restoring conventional diplomatic relations and trying to engage Cuba constructively in regional peace agreements. Pragmatic attempts to resolve immediate problems between the two countries—regarding migration, fishing rights, hurricane tracking, hijacking, narcotics control, and other issues—would proceed. As long as Cuba remains militarily aligned with the Soviet Union, the United States would not warm its relations with Havana or include Cuba in the proposed regional provisions for preferential economic treatment. In time, however, as the improved regional relationships took hold, it might become possible, in effect, to threaten Cuba with peace. Cuba might be induced to weaken its close relationship, and particularly its military ties, with the Soviet Union in exchange for access to U.S. markets, capital, and technology.

Finally, the United States would work with all the countries of the Caribbean Basin to regulate migration. The United States would consult with Caribbean Basin nations on means of keeping migration to this country within legal bounds and preventing exploitation of illegal aliens. The United States would target U.S. foreign investment, trade policy, and foreign assistance to foster labor-intensive development in the region. Local family-planning programs would also be supported.

The developmental approach to the Caribbean Basin—concerned both with preventing direct strategic threats to U.S. security and with the long-term viability of the Caribbean islands and Central America—would protect the core interests of the United States, immediately and in the longer term. It would do so without engaging the United States unnecessarily in these regions' internal struggles. It would keep the U.S. focus on the problems of the Caribbean Basin that should matter most to us, and that we can best affect. Most important, this approach would enable the United States to deal with its border region without distracting this country's attention from the major economic and political issues affecting its relations with Mexico and South America. The challenge for U.S. policy in Central America and the Caribbean in the 1980s is less a test of national will and credibility than of our sense of perspective and priorities.

A NOT-SO-HYPOTHETICAL ILLUSTRATION

To illustrate how the Carter approach, the Reagan approach, and the developmental approach differ from one another, consider how each would handle the following not-so-hypothetical case: the takeover by revolutionaries aligned internationally with Cuba and the Soviet Union of a tiny Caribbean island about the size of Washington, D.C. The island's population is about one hundred thousand; the main export products are cocoa and nutmeg; the principal economic potential is tourism, but even that potential is limited by the country's inadequate airport and hotel facilities.

The Carter administration's first response to a leftist takeover of such an island would have been to send Rosalynn Carter and/or Ambassador Andrew Young on diplomatic visits. When these expressions of sympathetic interest failed to co-opt the revolutionary leadership, the

Carter administration might have sent the U.S. Navy on friendly port calls to all neighboring islands, pointedly failing to call on this one island. When this gesture also failed to produce results, Carter would have curtailed bilateral aid while allowing multilateral assistance to continue. Eventually, as a sign of real displeasure, the Carter administration would have refused to permit its ambassador to pay a farewell visit to the island on leaving the region. Finally, as it became obvious that none of these pressures would reverse a political development regarded as undesirable, the Carter administration would have considered the feasibility of avoiding future problems of this sort by setting up an anti-Communist training camp where young political leaders from the Caribbean would receive pro-democratic, pro-capitalist, and anti-Communist indoctrination.

The Reagan administration's approach to the same case would be very different. Rather than sending high officials, it would hurl verbal bricks from the beginning. It would also send the fleet to the region, but to stage mock invasions intended to intimidate the island's leadership. It not only would terminate bilateral economic assistance, but would try to end multilateral aid, as well. It would refuse to accept the credentials of an ambassador from the island, or to accredit a new U.S. ambassador. Rather than simply train anti-Communist leaders for a possible future role, it would offer clandestine support for counterrevolutionary activity. It would complain loudly about the island's decision to expand its airport runway, noting that, while this runway might help attract tourists, it could also be used to assist Soviet and Cuban military planes. Finally, when conditions permitted, the Reagan administration would land the Marines, seize the airport, and offer to finish its construction.

The developmental approach would assign competent diplomats to the region, keep them there, and let them travel freely. It would tone down rhetoric, both positive and harsh. It would encourage the island's leadership to design development projects for external funding, channeled through multilateral agencies. Rather than thunder against the island's decision to extend its airport runway, it would offer assistance to develop the island's tourist industry. But it would also make it clear that if the airport were used to offer military advantage to the Soviet Union or Cuba, the United States and other nations in the region would regard this as a hostile act, against which all necessary multilateral sanctions—including the use of force, if needed—would be employed.

Instead of setting up an anti-Communist training camp, this approach would counsel contacting all Caribbean and Central America participants in the Cuban training program. Figuratively speaking, at least, these persons would be congratulated for having been recognized by the Cubans for leadership potential. They would be urged, should they ever achieve power, to ask Havana what it could offer in terms of access to capital, markets, technology, or jobs for immigrant workers, that is, in response to the nation's major concrete problems. Then they should be urged to approach Washington, to see whether the United States could beat the Cuban offer.

The United States has all the cards for such a competition, if it chooses to play them. All Cuba can offer is élan—and even that is badly tarnished. The United States, if it wishes to do so, can offer concrete responses to the main problems facing the Caribbean and Central America.

The developmental policy would be concerned less with airport runways than with ways of life. It would see beyond military bases to basic human needs, and to the capacity of the United States to help meet them. It would be a policy based not on national insecurity but on national self-confidence.

It is not clear whether the United States, with far-sighted leadership, could sustain a developmental approach toward the Caribbean Basin. But it is time to try.

CHAPTER SEVEN

From Insecurity to *Confianza*

Forging a New U.S. Policy

atin America has been transformed during the past generation. The region is far more populous and urban, its societies better integrated, and its economies more industrialized and productive than they were thirty years ago. The region's class structure has altered; traditional oligarchies have weakened and large middle classes have emerged. Latin America's state bureaucracies have expanded greatly, and technocrats have become influential. The countries of Latin America and the Caribbean have diversified their international relations to a degree that no one anticipated in 1960.

Differences among the countries of Latin America and the Caribbean are greater than they used to be. Brazil has set the pace, outstripping all other nations of the region by rapidly expanding its manufacturing base, nontraditional agricultural production, and export capacity. Argentina, in contrast, has faltered and lost its former prominence. Mexico grew unevenly in the 1960s and 1970s, creating major structural problems for the 1980s. Most islands of the Caribbean have become more integrated with the United States, economically and demographically, while Cuba has substituted a tight alliance with the Soviet Union for its previous dependence on this country. Central America has entered a convulsive round of civil wars in which the United States has become increasingly involved.

Two trends now overshadow all the other changes. Rapid growth throughout most of Latin America from 1960 to 1980 has given way to severe economic crisis. Political instability in the early 1960s and then nearly pervasive authoritarianism in the 1970s have been replaced, however, by a broad regional turn to democratic politics. These two major tendencies—one deeply troubling, the other hopeful—frame the context for U.S.–Latin American relations in the years ahead.

DEMOCRATIC OPENING

Latin America's turn to democratic politics has been gaining momentum. Repressive regimes began to crumble toward the end of the 1970s. In the 1980s, the focus of politics has shifted, especially in South America. The transition from authoritarian rule was the central question in 1980; now the key issue is the consolidation of democracy.

Perhaps the most significant political event in Latin America of the decade has been the end of twenty-one years of military government in Brazil in 1985. The undisputed constitutional succession of Vicepresident José Sarney after the tragic death of President-elect Tancredo Neves advanced the return to democracy in the continent's largest country. Municipal, gubernatorial, and congressional elections have carried forward the process, and direct presidential elections are soon due to take place.

The triumph of democracy in Argentina has been equally striking. Raúl Alfonsín, elected in 1983 in the aftermath of the military government's failed invasion of the Malvinas-Falkland Islands, strengthened his political position by boldly attacking the country's difficult economic problems. Alfonsín has reinforced his mandate by bringing to trial the top military leaders responsible for human rights violations. That senior military officers (including former presidents) could be sentenced to long prison terms without a serious threat to the constitutional order is remarkable.

In Peru, the peaceful transfer of office from Fernando Belaúnde Terry to Alán García Pérez was another feat. Despite economic and political deterioration during his term, Belaúnde became the first elected Peruvian president in forty years to turn the office over to an elected successor. The young and charismatic García has captured his country's imagination. The nation's main problems have proved to be deeply intractable, but civilian democratic rule has been sustained.

The democratic trend in South America has been broad. In Uruguay, after a decade of harsh military rule, Julio María Sanguinetti was inaugurated in 1985, and the country has returned to the civilized political discourse for which it used to be known. No one can be confident that a constitutional regime will last long in Bolivia, where coups have occurred once a year, on the average, for many decades. But, in 1985, power was transferred from the beleaguered Hernán Siles Zuazo to the venerable Victor Paz Estenssoro; this was Bolivia's first transition from one elected civilian to another in twenty-five years. Ecuador's democracy continues to survive despite attempted military coups and bitter recriminations between the president and the civilian opposition.

Of the major South American countries, only Chile and Paraguay still have authoritarian regimes, but clamors for change are heard in both nations. Major steps toward redemocratization have been taken in Chile, where General Augusto Pinochet continues his long-term rule. The National Accord for a Transition to Full Democracy, arranged through the Archbishop of Santiago, established agreement on principles and procedures among eleven parties embracing a broad political spectrum. A coalition of private organizations has established a "civil assembly" that has made it clear how very narrow Pinochet's base of support has become. The Pinochet regime is isolated, within Chile and internationally; it clings to power by force, ironically aided by the Communist party's violent opposition. Alfredo Stroessner, Paraguay's leader since 1954, also faces growing criticism from the Church and other sectors, as well as the democratizing influence of neighboring Argentina and Brazil. The Hemisphere's longest-ruling head of state, Stroessner knows that his regime's days are numbered.

Latin America's turn toward democracy has not been universal. It has not reached Cuba, where Fidel Castro has ruled since 1959. In Haiti, long-time dictator Jean Claude "Baby Doc" Duvalier fled as opposition rose to his family's dynasty, but democracy has yet to be established. The elections in Guyana in 1985 to pick a successor to the late Forbes Burnham took place in an atmosphere of intimidation and fraud. In Panama, President Nicolás Ardito Barletta was pushed aside by the military after less than a year in office.

Internal and external pressures have combined in the 1980s to produce elections in El Salvador, Guatemala, and Honduras, but the significance of each election was strictly limited. Important segments of the population are excluded from political life in El Salvador, where not one of hundreds of political assassinations has led to a trial and conviction. Basic national issues still cannot be discussed in Guatemala; few candidates to the left of center enter the elections. The Honduran electoral procedures were rigged to assure their outcome. In all three countries, the army holds the trumps. In these nations, as in Nicaragua for different reasons, democracy is far from complete.

There have been setbacks and threats to Latin America's democratic trend, even in some of the countries where democratic practices are most enduring. In Colombia, where civilian politics have been uninterrupted for a generation, then-President Belisario Betancur's efforts to negotiate an end to a guerrilla insurgency collapsed in 1985; the country was rocked by the rebels' seizure of the supreme court building and the resulting deaths of scores of hostages, including eleven justices of the court. Even in Venezuela, the most stable democracy in South America, falling standards of living have created antagonisms among former allies and weakened public confidence in the country's political institutions.

Yet notwithstanding limits and setbacks, Latin American democracy has gained important ground in the 1980s. The most optimistic observers never imagined in 1980 that more than 90 percent of South America's population would by now be living under civilian and constitutional regimes. Nor was it expected that the countries of Central America would be holding internationally monitored elections—steps toward democracy, even if not definitive ones. El Salvador and Guatemala are considerably closer today to being functioning democracies than just a few years ago.

Several factors have produced these openings for democracy. Despite drastic economic reverses and declining living standards, there has been little social upheaval and political radicalism in most of South America, certainly far less than might have been expected. Many different groups have come to understand the value of democratic politics. Military officers know how political involvement can damage their institution's coherence and morale. Would-be revolutionaries have learned to appreciate political freedoms and "bourgeois" electoral procedures. Many business and conservative leaders regard participatory politics as a better basis for long-term stability than authoritarian rule. Popular frustrations, in turn, have been constructively invested in the efforts first to end authoritarian military regimes and then to choose, install, and support civilian successors.

ECONOMIC DISTRESS

After a generation of economic growth, Latin America and the Caribbean have experienced prolonged economic crisis in the 1980s. Structural problems arising from inequitable growth, limited domestic markets, excessive reliance on external debt, and overgrown public sectors are underlying causes. But these problems have been aggravated and made critical by external forces: oil price hikes in the mid- and late 1970s; high interest rates; sluggish demand for commodity exports to the industrial countries; increasingly adverse terms of trade for Latin American products; the growing impact of protectionism in OECD markets; and, more recently, the effects on the petroleum-exporting countries of precipitous price cuts and the drying up of commercial bank credit. Latin America's economies have been set back sharply. The region is still suffering through its worst depression since the 1930s.

The statistics on Latin America's distress are stark. Production per capita has fallen nearly 8 percent since 1980, real income per capita by as much as 10 percent if the terms of trade effects are considered.

Individual income has dropped back to 1977 levels; a full decade of growth has been lost. In many countries—including Argentina, Bolivia, Chile, El Salvador, Haiti, Jamaica, Nicaragua, and Peru—per capita income has declined to levels of the early to mid-1960s. Mexico, Venezuela, and Ecuador benefited, as petroleum exporters, from the oil-fueled expansion of the 1970s, but all three countries were then severely affected by the drop in oil prices. Real wages in Mexico have dropped more than 40 percent since 1982. Of the twenty largest countries in the Hemisphere, only Brazil and Colombia avoided economic disaster in the mid-1980s, and both are still vulnerable to new reverses.

Rates of unemployment and underemployment remain high in many countries, upwards of 40 percent in some. Hardships caused by unemployment and low wages have been compounded by deep cuts in public expenditures for health, housing, education, and social security. Malnutrition is worsening in some nations, and infant mortality is on the rise in a few.

Six years of debt management have enabled commercial banks in the United States, Europe, and Japan to reduce their exposures in Latin America and the Caribbean, but Latin American countries have not been able to resume sustainable growth. The apparent recovery that many nations experienced in 1984 was short-lived for most, and no Latin American economy has yet managed conclusively to escape the trap of excessive debt service.

The region's external debt, totalling nearly $400 billion, is truly staggering. The ratio of debt to exports, a standard measure of capacity to repay, deteriorated sharply from 1980 to 1983, and massive Latin American export drives have not succeeded in improving the ratio since then. More than one-third of Latin America's export earnings are now devoted to interest payments.

For the sixth consecutive year, in 1987 the total flow of funds to Latin America from loans and investments was substantially less than interest payments and the profit remittances of foreign companies. During these six years, Latin America transferred approximately $150 billion to the industrialized countries, almost 5 percent of the region's total product for the period; this burden is more than twice the relative size of the punitive German war reparations of the 1920s which helped bring Hitler to power. About one-quarter of Latin America's savings are being drained each year for interest payments, sharply reducing the funds available for investment. Capital flight on a massive scale has further diminished domestic investment and consumption. Investment is down about 25 percent in the 1980s in the region as a whole; some countries—including Argentina, Chile, and Uruguay—have been even harder hit.

Latin America's economies are caught in a vicious circle. Because they are devoting so much of their savings to servicing the debt, the countries of the region are undercutting their ability to invest, grow, and improve their creditworthiness. The region's depressed economies provoke capital flight, further eroding the base for growth. This cycle is intolerable: economically, socially, and politically.

The costs of Latin America's prolonged problems are mounting. Dry statistics about debt, employment, production, investment, income, and trade do not convey the pain Latin Americans are feeling. Translated into human terms, Latin America's crisis of the 1980s means hunger, infant deaths, homeless children, boat people and feet people, street crime—and increasing public impatience.

The exhilarating revival of democratic politics may have assuaged popular discontent earlier in the decade, but now many civilian regimes are encountering sharper dissatisfaction. Throughout the Hemisphere, labor unrest is growing. In countries as diverse as Argentina, Jamaica, Ecuador, Barbados, Peru, Bolivia, and the Dominican Republic, incumbent governments have been defeated or severely weakened since the mid-1980s, largely because of economic conditions. Dissatisfaction with the governments of Brazil and Mexico became extremely evident in the same period. Latin America's democratic leaders cannot continue telling citizens to tighten their belts without providing hope that relief is in sight.

THE AMERICAS AT ODDS

North Americans and Latin Americans approach this juxtaposition of political advance and economic reversal with contrasting perspectives.

In the United States, and especially within the Reagan administration, many assess the Western Hemisphere with satisfaction. Perhaps because it focuses primarily on the commercial banks and the international financial system, the U.S. government repeatedly affirms that Latin America's debt crisis is slowly but surely being overcome. Washington has been heartened by indications that Latin Americans are abandoning statist economic policies and relying instead on the marketplace and on the hope of attracting foreign investment to strengthen their economies. It seems confident that Latin America's largest economies will revive after a necessary period of "structural adjustment"—that is, after a strong dose of austerity and Reaganomics.

The Reagan administration welcomes Latin America's turn to democracy and attributes this trend largely to U.S. policy. It assumes that Latin Americans are grateful to the United States, and expects interAmerican relations to become more cordial as a result. Some within the administration also suggest that the civil wars in Central America are approaching a satisfactory outcome, because the pro-American Duarte government in El Salvador has been gaining ground while the anti-American Sandinista government in Nicaragua has not. Some key administration leaders believe their perseverance in combatting congressional and public opposition to their Central American policy has finally paid off, and they seem bent on expanding U.S. involvement in the isthmus if Congress will allow this.

United States officials are impatient with Latin American criticisms of the U.S. course in Central America and with Latin American attempts to obtain economic concessions on a nonreciprocal basis. But these are minor irritants in what they perceive as a favorable state of inter-American relations.

Many Latin Americans, by contrast, are dissatisfied and apprehensive. They see no end to the region's economic duress, and little evidence that the United States will help much to relieve it. They are concerned about whether Latin America's democracies can endure prolonged austerity. And they fear that Washington's intense focus on combatting Communism in Central America will not only damage that region but also have a polarizing effect in Mexico and much of South America.

Latin Americans who look to the United States for leadership on economic issues have been disappointed. Intermittent indications of U.S. concern have always dissipated. The U.S. government provided emergency assistance in 1982 to Mexico and Brazil, but it then resisted efforts to expand the resources of the World Bank and the International Monetary Fund. In the years after 1982, Washington preferred not to be drawn into the deliberations of the private commercial banks on debt reschedulings; it seemed more interested in discouraging intra–Latin American financial cooperation than in seeking a solution to the credit shortage.

The Baker Plan, designed in 1985 finally to respond to the debt crisis, was greeted with limited enthusiasm by knowledgeable Latin Americans. The Baker proposal called for increased lending to Latin American and other major Third World debtors to a level of $29 billion in three years. This flow of finance would be conditioned on the debtors' adoption of market-oriented programs for economic recovery: trade liberalization, privatization, and measures to attract foreign investment. Latin Americans welcomed Secretary Baker's recognition of the priority of growth, but many regarded the recommended funding levels as inadequate, and saw the structural reform conditions the plan would impose on debtors as too uniform and intrusive. What is more, the plan's most positive aspects—its provisions for additional resource transfers to Latin America—have scarcely been implemented, except for Mexico.

Latin America's democratic leaders are ready to cooperate with the United States, but they have found Washington to be less of an ally and rather more of an obstacle to progressive reform than in the late 1960s. Forced to implement painful austerity programs, many Latin Americans complain that although the United States has talked eloquently about promoting democracy all over the world, this country has done little to alleviate their financial pressures. They perceive that the U.S. government has preached discipline abroad but run up unprecedented domestic budget deficits at home which have contributed to high interest rates. They are quite prepared to cut back bloated public sectors, but they resent homilies from Washington on the virtues of the free market and foreign investment.

Latin America's pragmatic new leaders have had to confront a U.S. administration they regard as disconcertingly ideological. After a generation of profound regional transformations that have made them more self-confident and assertive internationally, top officials in Latin America must cope with a U.S. government that is more unilateral and interventionist than any in memory. Instead of obtaining help from the U.S. government to resolve the Hemisphere's staggering economic problems, they find that officials in Washington are obsessed with Central America. Economic vulnerability makes it hard for Latin Americans to vent their feelings openly, but that inhibition only reinforces their frustration.

The changes that have occurred during the past thirty years, both in Latin America and in this country, increase the likelihood that inter-American tensions will sharpen in the next few years, as conflicts emerge over a number of economic issues. The juxtaposition of U.S. complacency and Latin American apprehension—compounded by the sharp contrast between Latin America's preoccupation with economic problems and the insistent U.S. focus on Central America—could produce intensifying conflict. But many of these same changes, particularly those deriving from Latin America's industrialization and its international emergence and from complementary changes in the U.S. economy, could also provide the basis for expanded inter-American cooperation, if potential mutualities of interest are recognized and acted upon.

During the past generation, the inherent tensions between the United States and Latin America arising from fundamental asymmetries in the Western Hemisphere have been strongly reinforced by major shifts in the Hemisphere's political economy. The larger Latin American nations now export industrial and agricultural products that successfully compete with those from the United States; the declining efficiency of certain sectors of the U.S. economy has fed protectionist pressures in this country. In combination, these factors have exacerbated conflicts over trade. Latin America's massive indebtedness has produced a sharp tension between the region's imperatives to resume growth and improve welfare and the U.S. aim to protect the stability of international finance. Strong pressures in Latin America to reduce imports in order to maintain debt repayment schedules have raised barriers to U.S. exports. Conflicts have emerged, as well, over the increased demand for emigration from Mexico, Central America, and the Caribbean. Friction has also grown over the burgeoning drug traffic entering the United States from the countries of Latin America.

All these sources of conflict in United States–Latin American relations are bound to be aggravated if the region's economic duress is prolonged, and particularly if the perception grows that Washington is insufficiently concerned about Latin America's plight.

If Latin America's massive debt service burden is not reduced, it will be increasingly difficult for the democratic regimes to generate hope that sustainable growth can soon be resumed. Adverse consequences will surely follow. Parties that have refrained from fratricidal competition during the delicate process of democratic transition may succumb to the urge to attack incumbents. If economic and social conditions deteriorate, insurgent movements that until now have had relatively limited backing—M-19 in Colombia and Sendero Luminoso (Shining Path) in Peru are prime examples—may broaden their popular appeal. Narcotics traffickers may take advantage of weakened national governments to expand their control of enclaves within Latin America. Counterinsurgency and anti-narcotics operations, in turn, could contribute to renewed repression and help rekindle the dynamics of instability.

Even more likely, prolonged stagnation or depression in Latin America could push some countries in a national populist direction. If foreign banks and investors appear to prosper while Latin America suffers, demagogues will blame their countries' problems on the banks, foreign corporations, the IMF, and, as the power supposedly behind all of them, the government of the United States. They may push for economic and political nationalism, for closed markets, for expropriation of U.S. firms, and for generally anti–United States positions. Concretely, they could call for extended moratoria or even default on the repayment of external debt. Debt repudiation by any Latin American nation—and particularly by one of the larger countries—could spur similar movements elsewhere. A general Latin American move toward repudiation of the external debt could have serious implications for several major U.S. banks, and perhaps for the entire commercial banking system.

Deteriorating conditions in Mexico, Central America, and the Caribbean islands, in turn, would increase the pressures for emigration, particularly into the United States. A major flow of immigrants into this country might exacerbate exclusionary and racist sentiments already clearly on the rise. Additional support could gather in the United States for measures to "take control of our borders," for going beyond the modest and predictably ineffectual restrictions of the Simpson-Rodino Act. A virtual militarization of the U.S. frontier is not out of the question. And, as the safety valve of emigration is closed in Mexico and elsewhere in the Caribbean Basin, violent reactions could well come to focus on U.S. diplomatic representatives, firms, or expatriates.

Tensions could increase, as well, over drugs, as frustrations rise both in Latin America and in the United States. Some Latin Americans think that massive demand from the United States and dire straits in their own countries justify a less than aggressive campaign against drugs. Intensifying concern about narcotics within the United States is already producing retaliatory threats against Latin American states perceived as uncooperative, increasing calls for a military presence at the U.S. border to prevent drug smuggling, and even the introduction of U.S. troops into South America in pursuit of drug producers. Flaring tensions between Mexico and the United States over narcotics may be a harbinger of more pervasive frictions.

The civil wars in Central America, apart from distracting the attention of Washington from the issues Latin Americans consider urgent, could also lead directly to a deterioration in U.S.–Latin American relations. The Sandinistas in Nicaragua have been hurt by the escalating economic, political, and military pressures the United States has been orchestrating against them, but they show no sign of yielding power. Sentiment rose within the Reagan administration, therefore, to expand U.S. intervention in order to force the Sandinistas to capitulate.

As long as the U.S. aim in Central America is to remove the Sandinistas, the various initiatives to forge a regional peace on the basis of respect for the territorial integrity of all nations have no chance to succeed. Conflict over Central America between the United States and the Contadora nations as well as other Latin American countries is likely to continue, therefore, and would intensify if the United States undertook unilateral military intervention in Nicaragua. By reinforcing already deep tensions over trade, finance, narcotics, and immigration, a U.S. military intervention in Central America, especially if it were prolonged, could help drive Mexico, in particular, into a period of intense friction with the United States. An extended U.S. intervention would fuel the appeal of national populists throughout the Americas.

The "worst-case scenario" for U.S.–Latin American relations would involve the interaction of many different conflicts. If Latin America's economic and social crisis worsens; if unrest and terrorism increase; if some Latin American countries turn back to authoritarianism, this time perhaps with a national populist orientation; if U.S. banks, exporters, and multinational corporations clash with Latin American governments pursuing increasingly autarchic policies; if U.S. protectionism worsens; if tensions over migration and narcotics escalate; if the United States gets even more embroiled in Central America, and especially if U.S. troops ever land there—the cumulative impact on inter-American relations would be profound. An era of deep hostility in United States–Latin American relations would be at hand.

Such intensified hemispheric conflict is by no means inevitable, but it is a plausible and, indeed, a probable course if Latin America's economic crisis is not soon resolved. The security and the stability of the Western Hemisphere, including the United States, are ultimately much more threatened by the economic problems in Mexico and South America than by what is happening in Central America.

THREAT AND OPPORTUNITY

A generation ago, at another time of troubles in Latin America, President John F. Kennedy launched the Alliance for Progress. Latin America in the 1950s had experienced severe economic problems, mounting social pressures, and the growth of revolutionary movements. Fidel Castro's triumph in Cuba demonstrated the appeal these groups could have. The Alliance was designed as a preemptive antidote. The United States would provide financial resources and technical advice, and promote democracy. It would also furnish military training and counterinsurgency assistance to ward off the nascent security threat.

Although it was unilaterally proclaimed, the Alliance for Progress drew substantially on proposals that Latin American leaders had been advancing for years. Although its socioeconomic reforms were sometimes undercut by the emphasis on stability, the Alliance contributed significantly to Latin America's development. Despite the Alliance's flaws and disappointments, many Latin Americans still regard it as the most positive U.S. policy for the Hemisphere to date.

The late 1980s, like the late 1950s, are a time of great ferment in Latin America. The population explosion, massive urbanization, and rapid industrialization have transformed the region. Once entrenched authoritarian regimes have weakened and been replaced. After three decades of rapid but uneven growth, Latin American economies have run into severe problems in the 1980s, and prevailing models have been found wanting. The region's past gains and future prospects are threatened by debt and its consequences.

Washington has been painfully slow to react to Latin America's current economic crisis, but the problems of Mexico and South America finally attracted attention in Washington in the mid-1980s, and led to Secretary Baker's proposals for expanded lending to major Latin American and other Third World debtors. Even if they were fully adopted and implemented, the Baker proposals would not be adequate, either in concept or in magnitude, to resolve the Hemisphere's difficulties. But the possibility that the Baker initiative is only the first step in an inchoate U.S. government response encourages those Latin Americans who believe that the United States is an ally.

Many of today's democratic leaders in the Latin America—Alfonsín, Sarney, de la Madrid, Garcia, Paz Estenssoro, Sanguinetti, Virgilio Barco of Colombia, Guatemala's Vinicio Cerezo, José Napoleon Duarte of El Salvador, Venezuela's Jaime Lusinchi, and others—are, indeed, natural or at least potential friends of the United States. They are the humane, moderate, pragmatic, and reformist leaders who were so hard to find at the time of the Alliance for Progress. They are the region's centrists, trying to build political support against the appeals of ideologues and populists.

Most of them are modern politicians. They are more knowledgeable and realistic about economic issues than either the traditional politicos or the technocrats, civilian or military. Most recognize that public enterprises need to be trimmed and that market mechanisms usually channel resources more efficiently than political decisions, although they also see an important role for the state.

These democratic leaders believe that the overwhelming threats in the Hemisphere are debt, poverty, inequity, and unemployment—not Soviet influence, guerrillas, or terrorists. They have been urging the United States to follow up the Baker Plan with proposals that more adequately address Latin America's economic problems.

Latin American leaders do not want unilaterally imposed U.S. initiatives. They are asking Washington to work with them to help resume and expand growth in the Americas. They know that structural reforms, continued austerity, and financial responsibility will be expected of them, and they are ready to do their part. They are also more able and willing than their authoritarian predecessors to reduce unnecessary military expenditures, fight corruption, and attack the narcotics traffickers. And they want to preempt radical approaches, both from the revolutionary Left and from the national populist Right. What they seek from Washington—apart from attention, sympathy, and respect—is international economic cooperation.

In its own interest, the United States should respond to these appeals with a policy that is as positive as was the Alliance for Progress in 1961. Latin America is far more significant as a potential market for U.S. exports than it was a generation ago. The capacity of Latin American countries to help solve shared problems has greatly increased. The nations of Latin America are more important as international economic associates, if not as military allies.

The United States is no longer able, as it was in the 1960s, to provide billions of dollars in foreign aid to Latin America, but it can help reverse the outflow of funds from the region. The United States no longer exercises overwhelming predominance in the Americas, but it is still by far the Hemisphere's most important actor. Washington certainly cannot solve Latin America's problems, which must be faced primarily by the Latin American nations. But if the United States leaned decisively in the right direction, this could help Latin American nations to confront their difficulties.

The United States must take the initiative if Latin America's crisis of the 1980s is to be turned to opportunity. The time has come for bold U.S. leadership, not intrusive or domineering but respectful and supportive.

The United States should propose measures to help reexpand the flow of funds, goods, and services throughout the Americas; strengthen democracy and protect human rights; curb the deadly traffic in narcotics; and promote hemispheric peace and security, especially in Central America. On all these major issues, the countries of Latin America and the United States share fundamental objectives. On each, despite considerable differences of interest and perspective, great potential exists for enhanced inter-American collaboration. But new policies are needed to convert compatible aims into effective partnership.

Resuming Growth and Expanding Trade

The most important challenge facing Latin America in the late 1980s is to resume economic growth and reduce the massive external debt.

Latin America has the natural and human resources, the physical and institutional infrastructure, the social cohesion and political stability and, increasingly, the pragmatic approaches to policy making which are needed to achieve and sustain growth. The region's strong economic performance during the 1960s and 1970s established its potential and laid a foundation for further development. The devastating combination of external shocks that helped bring Latin America's expansion to a halt—high oil prices, soaring interest rates, and recession in the advanced industrial countries—has largely come to an end. What Latin America mainly needs to resume growth at this stage is renewed flows of foreign capital and improved market access for its exports, together with internal reforms and adjustments. But instead, in the 1980s, the region has had to export capital, sell its products at unfavorable terms of trade, and face protectionist barriers for many of its exports.

The United States has a major stake in Latin America's recovery. Latin America's growth during the 1970s made the region an increasingly important market for the United States, but U.S. exports fell more than 40 percent after 1981, when Latin America had to slash imports to balance its external accounts. This cutback contributes to the burgeoning U.S. trade deficit and to the loss of hundreds of thousands of jobs in this country. Latin America's economic crisis also jeopardizes the profits and even the solvency of several of the largest U.S. banks, still heavily exposed in the region and vulnerable to Latin American defaults or delays in debt repayment.

Renewed growth in Latin America would mean expanded markets for U.S. exports and higher prices for U.S. agricultural commodities; revived Latin American imports could reduce the U.S. trade deficit by as much as 20 percent. Growth in Latin America would contribute to social and political stability in regions of high tension, and thus help ease the pressures for migration to the United States. The Baker proposals represented a belated recognition of the importance to the United States of Latin America's economic recovery.

Most Latin American countries have undertaken programs of economic reform and adjustment consistent with the Baker proposals. To varying degrees, they have expanded their exports, reduced public spending, curbed inflation, and moved toward greater reliance on the private sector. Some countries have made enormous efforts; Mexico, for instance, has closed down or sold off almost half its state-owned enterprises. Argentina and Brazil have implemented sweeping anti-inflation measures and major efforts to stimulate production and expand exports. Countries as diverse as Bolivia, Chile, Ecuador, Uruguay, Guatemala, and (to a lesser extent) Peru have made important growth-oriented changes in their economic policies: devaluing currencies, reducing government subsidies, establishing positive domestic interest rates, and improving tax systems.

Most Latin American nations have strengthened their ability to make productive use of external capital, but they have not had access to that capital. Foreign investment is down in most countries and is unlikely to revive until a recovery is well underway. Latin America desperately needs additional financial flows, but the commercial banks have been reducing their exposures. The Baker Plan called on the commercial banks to increase Third World loans (mainly to Latin America) by a modest 2.5 percent a year, but the banks actually reduced their net new lending to Latin America in 1986. International financial institutions and independent analysts concur in estimating that Latin America as a region would need to obtain an additional $20 billion a year in foreign exchange for several years to resume and sustain growth at acceptable

levels and to meet debt obligations. There is no current prospect, however, that flows of this magnitude will result from free market decisions.

That is the crux of Latin America's problem today. It can only be
solved if the U.S. government makes a political decision to give priority
to facing the hemispheric crisis of debt and trade.

A number of plans have been put forward to confront Latin America's debt crisis. In addition to Secretary Baker's proposals and a coun-
terproposal advanced by Senator Bill Bradley for limited, targeted,
trade-linked debt relief, suggestions have been made by commercial
bankers like Felix Rohatyn, international economists including Harold
Sever and Aldo Ferrer, and others. Despite their differences, these plans
all coincide in emphasizing that there is no escape from the debt trap
without renewed growth in Latin America, and that renewed growth
depends both on improved Latin American economic management and
on expanded external resources for the region. Analysts also agree that
increased capital will not be available to Latin America unless the government of the United States makes this a major goal. Only if Washington recognizes the urgency of promoting hemispheric cooperation as a
political priority can the present vicious cycle by broken.

The United States government should take five specific steps to
promote renewed capital flows to Latin America and the Caribbean.

First, the United States should help strengthen the capacity of international financial institutions to support Latin America's development.
It should participate in general capital increases for the World Bank and
for the Inter-American Development Bank, and should push both institutions to disburse loans more quickly to countries that are ready to use
them well. Washington should also lend its backing to proposals to
modify the World Bank's loan-gearing ratio so as to make more funding
available to developing countries, particularly in Latin America. The
United States should also strongly encourage Japan to invest more of its
trade surpluses in the future of developing countries by providing significantly expanded financial resources to the World Bank and to the various regional banks. Further, the United States should favor the establishment of a new facility in the International Monetary Fund to
compensate for interest rate shocks.

Second, the United States government should try to induce commercial banks to renew lending in Latin America and to reduce their spreads
on loans to countries that are implementing sound economic policies.
Washington was crucial in arranging the 1986 package of commercial
bank loans for Mexico, and similar efforts are called for elsewhere. Part
of what is required is simply jawboning and brokering—helping the
commercial banks recognize that their separate interests and the U.S.
national interest will all suffer if renewed lending does not occur. But

more concrete government actions are also required. Washington should promote changes in U.S. banking regulations to allow banks to capitalize some interest payments without presenting the deferred interest as losses; European banks operate under such regulations and are thus better able to cooperate with Latin American debtors to stretch out their debts. Modified regulations are also needed to allow banks to absorb losses over an extended period on loans they write down. The U.S. government should also consider loan guarantees, directly or through multilateral institutions, to reassure commercial banks that continued lending to Latin American debtors makes sense.

Third, the U.S. government should take the lead in proposing a plan to distribute the cost of some debt relief for Latin American and other Third World debtors. Excessive lending in the 1970s occurred because there were both enthusiastic lenders and eager borrowers, but in the 1980s only the borrowers have been expected to bear the burden of adjustment. Whichever of several different schemes is adopted— capping interest payments, selling existing loans at a discount to an international agency that would write down and stretch out current debts, providing interest rate subsidies, or reducing interest rates— international agreement is needed to share the cost of writing down a significant proportion of Latin America's debt. Commercial banks should be willing to absorb some of these costs in exchange for the advantages of predictability and for having some of the costs absorbed by the U.S. Treasury. The ultimate benefits for the United States of economic progress and political stability in Latin America would fully justify this unusual investment.

Fourth, the U.S. government should redouble its efforts to reduce this country's fiscal deficit and to reduce real interest rates. Lowered interest rates are vital for Latin America; a 1 percent decrease in Latin America's debt service burden would provide close to 25 percent of the external capital needed to fuel growth at desirable levels. By helping to stimulate renewed growth in the United States as well, lowered interest rates would also contribute to expanded markets for Latin American exports. This is not the place for an extended discussion of the U.S. budget, but it is clear that mutual and balanced reduction of military expenditures must become a major aim of U.S. policy toward the Soviet Union if the federal deficit is to be brought down. Increased taxes will surely also be required.

Finally, the United States should forcefully and consistently promote the trade policies needed to expand global commerce. Washington must muster the political will necessary to resist increasing domestic pressures for protectionism, and to cooperate with Latin America in the "Uruguay Round" of trade negotiations. A sound basis exists for inter-

American collaboration in the new trade deliberations, for both parts of the Hemisphere share a strong interest in reducing agricultural subsidies and protectionism in Europe and in pushing Japan and western European nations to expand their imports. These important common aims should not be obscured by frictions over other commercial conflicts.

Strengthening Democracy

Latin America's turn toward democracy in the 1980s provides exceptional opportunities for inter-American cooperation beyond the economic realm. The United States and the other democratic nations of the Americas share an interest in fostering open, constitutional, and participatory politics throughout the Hemisphere. A region of consolidated democracies will be more humane and peaceful than one where authoritarian regimes predominate. The rule of law, tolerance for diversity, and respect for fundamental human rights will be better protected. A democratic Hemisphere should also be more stable, for effective democracy is the best insurance against guerrilla movements, terrorism, and anomic violence—and against extremism from the Left or the Right. The pragmatic economic reforms needed in Latin America are more likely to occur in a democratic context.

Neither the United States nor any other nation can impose democracy on another. Democracy is not an export commodity; it cannot simply by shipped from one setting to another.

Yet the United States and the other democracies of the hemisphere can do much together to nurture the trend toward democracy. The few remaining authoritarian regimes are isolated and thus more vulnerable to international pressure. The turn of so many countries toward democracy facilitates expanded international support. A democratic network is growing throughout the Hemisphere, involving parties, trade unions, professional associations, women's groups, religious organizations, and students. Because of the Carter administration's human rights policy and the Reagan administration's receptivity to the democratic trend, the United States government is now regarded by many in Latin America as supportive of democratization. The conditions for multilateral cooperation on behalf of democracy in the Americas have never been better.

The nations of the Hemisphere can work together to strengthen democracy in several ways:

First, they can emphasize a consistent concern with the protection of fundamental human rights. Human rights and democracy go together; democracy cannot be sustained where human rights are jeopardized. The countries of the Hemisphere should fully support the work of the Inter-American Commission on Human Rights, the Inter-American

Court on Human Rights, and the Inter-American Institute on Human Rights, and they should also assist the various nongovernmental organizations that monitor human rights violations without partisan or ideological favor.

Through diplomacy that is discreet, tempered, and professional—but not so quiet as to go unheard—the democracies of the Hemisphere should repudiate regimes that grossly and systematically violate human rights. These regimes should be denied military and economic assistance, and they should not be treated as friends or allies. The specter of international isolation may help turn former supporters of an authoritarian regime into influential opponents at a delicate moment in the transition process. Conversely, the Hemisphere's democratic leaders should express solidarity with one another, strengthening political and diplomatic relations through state visits, telephone contacts, and the like.

Second, the countries of the Hemisphere can fortify the social underpinnings of democracy by confronting the gross inequities in Latin America that breed revolution and repression. Bilateral and multilateral programs are needed to alleviate poverty, encourage family planning, improve basic education and primary health care, and support small-scale agriculture. Democratic politics both facilitates and requires that Latin America face the fundamental issue of income distribution.

Third, the nations of the Americas can cooperate to strengthen the institutions and practices that are the very fabric of democracy. Inter-American programs can provide technical assistance to legislatures on such matters as budget, oversight, and civilian control of the military in order to enable congresses to play larger and more constructive roles in democratic governance. Regional programs can improve the training and reinforce the commitment of judicial and law enforcement officials. Inter-American efforts should be institutionalized to provide an impartial and professional capacity for monitoring elections to assure that they are free and fair. Latin American political parties, professional associations, trade unions, and other nongovernmental organizations can be helped internationally with training, funding, and advice. External support, material and moral, can also be provided to protect the freedom of the press and to enhance the contribution of journalism to democratic politics.

In all such efforts, multilateral programs are far more likely to be effective than bilateral ones, and nongovernmental mechanisms are more acceptable than official ones. The recently established nongovernmental National Endowment for Democracy and the affiliated Democratic and Republican party institutes (all three set up as private organizations but with public funding) can be helpful, but they, too, should keep their involvement responsive and restrained. Any attempt to impose a Washington-conceived "Democracy Agenda" on Latin America is bound to backfire.

As the Hemisphere's largest and most influential democracy, the United States has a special role. Washington could contribute significantly, for example, by mobilizing its influence on Latin America's armed forces to reinforce their commitment to constitutional procedures. Whether or not Latin America's current democratic openings take hold will depend in important measure on the region's military leaders, who have been responsive historically to U.S. influence. Through the advice of its military missions, the content of its training programs, and the broader influence of consistent political signals, the United States could help keep Latin America's armed forces in the barracks and out of politics. Latin American business leaders, too, are likely to be affected by unambiguous indications from the United States government that democratic politics should be maintained.

The most important contribution the United States could make to strengthen Latin American democracy, however, is indirect: helping to remove the major obstacle to its consolidation. Latin America's democracies are beset by fierce economic and social pressures, exacerbated by the oppressive burden of debt. United States leadership to alleviate these pressures through positive actions to resolve the debt crisis would provide Latin America's democracies the breathing space they need to meet popular needs and expectations, and would thus reinforce the appeal of democratic politics.

Curbing the Drug Trade

A deadly traffic in illegal narcotics has existed in the Western Hemisphere for decades, but major expansion of the drug trade since the late 1970s has made this a newly salient issue in inter-American relations. As the drug traffic has grown to unprecedented proportions, both Latin Americans and North Americans have become increasingly concerned. Growing tensions have emerged in the Hemisphere over differences of perception, method, and emphasis; conflicts about narcotics have become an important part of the agenda in U.S. relations with several Latin American countries.

The United States is the world's largest market for illicit drugs. Although statistics about such an illegal enterprise are inexact, experts concur in estimating that scores of billions of dollars are involved, and that the use of drugs in this country is increasing. One estimate suggests that twenty million people in the United States use marijuana and that four million use cocaine each month. Consumption of "crack," a less expensive and more dangerous variant of cocaine, may be reaching epidemic proportions.

A major share of urban crime in the United States is drug related, and narcotics finance many other activities run by organized crime syndicates. Drug scandals have affected police departments in several cities. Major U.S. banks have been implicated in the "laundering" of illegal drug revenues. Most tragically, an increasing proportion of this country's youth have become hooked, with devastating effects on their health, productivity, attitudes, and behavior. Public concern has grown to the point that in 1986 the president and the Congress competed with each other to devise comprehensive anti-drug programs before the mid-term elections. By October, the Congress approved and President Reagan signed a comprehensive 1.7-billion-dollar package of measures to fight drugs, including steps to improve anti-narcotics education and vigorously to expand law enforcement.

At least a dozen Latin American countries are involved in the chain of drug production and distribution. Peru, Bolivia, Colombia, Ecuador, and Mexico are all major producers; together they supply an estimated two-thirds of the U.S. market. In these countries, the drug trade not only endangers public health and safety directly; it also threatens social and political stability. In several nations, drug corruption has deeply penetrated police forces, military establishments, judicial systems, and the executive and legislative branches. In some Andean countries, narcotics traffickers challenge governments for control of extensive enclaves.

The drug traffic is big business in the United States; it looms even larger, in relative terms, in some Latin American economies. Cocaine earnings in Bolivia are estimated to be three times the value of all the country's other exports. Repatriated drug profits are said to account for about 20 percent of Peru's export earnings. A similar share of Colombia's foreign exchange is earned from the drug trade, and drug income has also become a major source of dollars for Mexico. During the 1980s, when debt service obligations have been rising and the prices of Latin America's legal exports have been falling, drugs have been the only significant regional export increasing in value.

The massive drug trade has strained relations between the United States and Latin American drug-producing nations. Recent U.S. administrations have asked Latin American governments to eradicate illegal drug crops, close down drug-processing plants, and seize drug shipments. The United States has offered limited funding, technical assistance, and personnel for anti-drug efforts. But Washington has not simply requested action and offered assistance; it has pushed Latin American nations to accept U.S. help for such programs. The United States has employed diplomatic pressures, public rebuke, and even threats to cut off economic assistance and market access to force Latin American acceptance of U.S. personnel and programs.

Latin Americans, although concerned about drugs, resent U.S. importunings, especially because they regard the vast demand for drugs in the United States as the main source of the problem. Whereas many in the United States blame the curse of narcotics on the Latin American countries where the drugs are grown and processed, Latin Americans think the drug culture of the United States is responsible. Latin American reluctance to move vigorously against the drug trade has been reinforced by the economic crisis. It is hard to deprive those growing the crops of their livelihood when local economies are in critical shape, unemployment is high, and no relief from debt and depression seems near.

The potential for greater tensions between the United States and Latin America over drugs has been illustrated in the case of Mexico. Mexican law officers have mistreated U.S. anti-drug agents, U.S. officials have publicly accused Mexican officials of corruption, and U.S. customs agents have threatened to violate Mexican sovereignty by flying into Mexico in pursuit of suspected drug traffickers. But the Mexican case is not isolated; tensions have also emerged with Bolivia, Peru, and other countries.

Although the potential for conflict is high, there are also new prospects for inter-American cooperation against drugs. Latin Americans increasingly recognize that narcotics are a domestic problem, too. In part, this change of attitude reflects the widening of drug abuse within Latin America. More important, the new democratic regimes of Latin America recognize that they must combat the drug trade and fight corruption to retain domestic legitimacy. Several Latin American nations—Peru, Colombia, Bolivia, and Mexico in particular—have become increasingly committed to the campaign against narcotics.

Curbing the Hemisphere's drug traffic will require effective cooperation between the United States and Latin America, for neither can succeed in stopping the narcotics trade without the other. Much more emphasis is needed within the United States on drug education programs to cut demand. Until the passage of the 1986 legislation, the United States had actually reduced federal expenditures for drug education by 40 percent during the first five years of the Reagan administration. The decision in 1986 to reverse course by nearly doubling federal appropriations for drug education and by launching a national "crusade" against the use of illegal drugs was a step in the right direction, but the amount appropriated for education was still only 1 percent of the sum devoted to fighting narcotics, and the Reagan administration's budget request for 1988 reduced this amount. The Hemisphere's campaign against drugs depends for its success on a sustained reduction in U.S. demand; major efforts are needed to persuade the youth of the United States of the dreadful effects of addictive drugs.

A second important aspect of a hemispheric strategy should be multilateral efforts to eradicate and seize illegal drugs. Increased U.S. financial assistance to a regionally administered anti-narcotics fund would provide necessary external resources for crop destruction and interdiction programs without raising difficult questions of intervention and national sovereignty, at least in their most sensitive form. The recently created Inter-American Commission on Narcotics, established within the framework of the Organization of American States, could provide a needed multilateral mechanism for attacking this major regional problem. Latin American nations and the United States should cooperate closely with the new commission.

Eradication and interdiction programs would be much more likely to be carried out if there were other sources of income for the peasants now growing drug crops. Alternative crops alone are not an adequate answer, for they are far less profitable. In the long run, sustained economic development in Latin America is needed to provide the environment for weaning drug-producing regions from that activity. The link back to the debt crisis is obvious; sustained development in Latin America cannot occur as long as massive debt service obligations deprive the region of the capital it needs for investment, social services, and growth. A U.S. initiative to relieve Latin America's debt, coupled with multilateral programs to fight drugs, could elicit Latin American cooperation, which up to now has been hesitant and sporadic.

Promoting Peace and Security

The prospects for cooperation in the Western Hemisphere are diminished as long as Washington is prosecuting a war in Central America. The intense U.S. focus on Nicaragua distracts attention and resources away from the rest of Latin America. It undermines the possibility of forging a major effort to respond to the region's economic crisis by fracturing the potential domestic coalition in the United States which might support such an effort. Equally important, expanding U.S. intervention in Nicaragua makes it difficult for some key countries in the Hemisphere to collaborate closely with the United States. Direct U.S. military action in Nicaragua, were it to occur, would provoke deep resentments throughout Latin America. Prolonged U.S. intervention in Central America would preclude effective inter-American partnership.

After several years of an escalating U.S. campaign against Nicaragua, it will not be easy to resolve the conflict or to return Central American issues to their proper perspective. There is, moreover, a real problem to be faced in Central America. Nicaragua's government today maintains close ties with Cuba and the Soviet Union. The Sandinista leaders are committed revolutionaries, most are hostile to the United

States, and many are Marxist-Leninists. Whatever debate there may be
about nuance and degree, Nicaragua's regime has been authoritarian
and repressive of political freedom.

Apart from its ideology and its internal politics, Nicaragua under the
Sandinistas could harm the security of the Hemisphere. It has supported
revolutionary movements elsewhere and it could even conceivably provide the Soviet Union with the opportunity to install threatening bases,
weapons, or strategic facilities. These security threats must be dealt
with. The question is not whether Nicaragua represents a challenge but
how best to respond to it.

Despite strong public and congressional opposition, the Reagan administration has supported a counterrevolutionary insurgency (the *contras*) which is trying to unseat the Sandinistas. This policy has unques-
tionably hurt the Sandinistas, but it has not solved the Central American
problem. Aid to the *contras* is not sufficient to overthrow the Sandinistas
or to coerce them, and they are unlikely to be induced to change their
objectionable policies by an approach that is all stick and no carrot. By
all accounts, the Sandinistas are solidly entrenched.

The *contra* policy has reinforced Nicaragua's dependence on Cuba
and the Soviet Union and strengthened the influence of the most intran-
sigent members of the Sandinista coalition. The Sandinistas have used
external attack and economic duress to excuse failure and justify repressive control. Aid to the *contras* has fueled a regional arms race and
polarized the politics of Nicaragua's neighbors. Virtually all Latin American nations, as well as most countries in Europe and elsewhere, oppose
U.S. policy. What is worse, the current course may eventually leave the
United States with a cruel choice between outright intervention and
painful humiliation. The *contra* policy is increasingly embroiling the
United States in a destructive war, with an ever growing likelihood of
direct military involvement.

The core security concerns of the Hemisphere in Central America are
to prevent the establishment of a Soviet-Cuban base and to curb Sandinista support for revolutionary movements elsewhere. These could be
better protected by a verifiable and enforceable peace settlement with
Nicaragua than by continuing to poke at the Sandinistas. Such a settlement would also serve the interests of the other Central American nations, which fear Nicaraguan encroachments but are also concerned
about a widening war. Many other countries in the Hemisphere—
particularly the Contadora nations rimming Central America—want to
preempt a U.S. intervention.

Despite its limits and disappointments, the Contadora diplomatic initiative to resolve the Central American conflicts provided real hope for
regional peace. It illustrated the increased potential for effective cooper-

ation in the Americas, although the Reagan administration has never regarded it this way. Washington paid lip service to Contadora but often obstructed its work. And the same has been true more recently of the U.S. response to the Central American peace initiative launched by President Arias; the United States has not been fully supportive. The time has come to change course.

The draft treaties tabled by the Contadora foreign ministers in June 1986 offer concrete provisions that should be included and made more precise in a regional peace agreement: on weapons reductions and limits; troop strengths; maneuvers and training exercises; and foreign military advisers. The proposed treaties would ban external support to insurgent movements as well as prohibit strategic bases and advanced weapons systems. Further details concerning verification, monitoring, and enforcement remain to be worked out, and concrete commitments are still needed from the Contadora nations and others in the Hemisphere to participate directly in implementing any agreement. But the elements of a viable security arrangement exist in the Contadora proposals. If the United States decides to concentrate on achieving its main security aims in Central America, it will find a promising basis for doing so in the Contadora drafts.

Focusing sharply on core security issues in Central America, and relying on multilateral diplomacy rather than on unilateral force to resolve them, will not turn Nicaragua into a democratic nation. Nor can we expect the Central American peace talks to lead to a quick and full democratic opening in Nicaragua. The aim of protecting regional security in Central America should not be held hostage, however, to the promotion of internal political change in Managua. The democratic nations of the Hemisphere should be deeply concerned about human rights and democracy in Nicaragua. But they should confine their efforts to peaceful pressures. These are the most acceptable and effective means of influencing internal affairs in an enduring way—in Nicaragua, in Chile, or anywhere else. Democracy cannot be imposed by force.

Some argue that a U.S. decision to make peace with the Sandinistas would undermine the credibility of the United States. To the extent that this country is perceived as having linked its own prestige to the fate of the *contras,* this concern may be justified. But the credibility of the United States is being eroded by a military approach to Nicaragua that is imprudent, disproportionate, and ineffective. The stature of the United States will continue to decline as long as Washington persists with a policy that divides the American people and Congress, that must be conducted covertly and even illegally, that has to be defended with hyperbole and disinformation, that commands little international support, that fosters repression and destruction within Nicaragua, and that provokes instability in neighboring countries.

The United States would be better off committing itself to a negotiated settlement with Nicaragua. The security of the United States and of the rest of the Hemisphere could be protected by enforceable arrangements to contain Sandinista Nicaragua, coupled with strong support for economic and social development in the rest of Central America and the Caribbean. Then the countries of the Americas together could turn their attention to the urgent problems of economic stagnation, poverty, and inequity in the whole Hemisphere, to the historic chance to strengthen democracy, and to other opportunities to solve shared hemispheric problems.

Looking beyond the difficult case of Nicaragua, the Contadora process reflects the increasing assertiveness of major Latin American nations which could foster enhanced inter-American cooperation on security issues. No longer do major Latin American governments consider hemispheric security Washington's concern alone. Latin American nations are willing to commit themselves, diplomatically and perhaps practically as well, to keep Soviet and Cuban strategic facilities and combat forces out of the region. They may well be willing to play a direct role in keeping extra-hemispheric power from being projected into the Americas in exchange for an end to unilateral interventionism by the United States. If the United States drops its cavalier attitude toward Latin American security initiatives, favorable conditions may now exist for fashioning a new set of hemispheric security accords and for creating effective inter-American institutional mechanisms to carry them out.

IMPLEMENTING A NEW POLICY

One U.S. administration after another has promised to improve U.S.–Latin American relations. Whether the revised stance is dubbed a Good Neighbor Policy, an Alliance for Progress, a Mature Partnership, a New Dialogue, or a Caribbean Basin Initiative, the pattern has been similar. A policy is unveiled with some fanfare, but the announced approach usually turns out to be ineffective. More often than not, the new U.S. initiative is quietly abandoned.

An administration eager to build cooperation in the Western Hemisphere should begin by analyzing why so many previous efforts to improve inter-American relations have failed.

Attempts to alter U.S. relations with Latin America have sometimes been undermined because U.S. government actions that adversely affect the region are undertaken in other policy arenas. "Latin American policy" is overwhelmed by decisions made in spite of their impact in the

Hemisphere or simply without regard to their regional effect. Domestic U.S. choices about fiscal and monetary policy, trade and tax reforms, agricultural subsidies, energy and immigration have major consequences for Latin America. To the extent that these choices conflict with important Latin American needs, attempts to improve inter-American relations cannot amount to more than damage control.

Further, nongovernmental forces beyond the scope of any U.S. administration shape much of U.S.–Latin American relations. Latin American and Caribbean countries are greatly influenced by banks, corporations, trade unions, religious groups, tourists, and the media. Such actors may have more impact than the U.S. government on major issues in the Hemisphere, including access to capital, markets, and technology.

The fragmented process of U.S. policy making often frustrates new approaches to Latin America. United States policy emerges from a struggle within the executive branch among those (especially in the White House) who make general declarations, career foreign service officers who focus on a particular region, and functional bureaucrats who concentrate on substantive issues such as trade, finance, or security. Rarely, if ever, are these three sources equally involved in fashioning an approach. Typically it is the new recruits, ideologically and politically aligned with the president, who enunciate a new policy; often they fail to take sufficient account of the views of career regional and functional specialists. But the permanent bureaucracy has a considerable capacity to restrain such initiatives, particularly in the process of implementation. Except when a president sustains strong personal interest in an issue, there is a built-in tendency for new programs to erode, and for the previous course to reassert itself.

Private interests, too, may block a proposed shift in U.S. policy. Although a suggested change may promise to benefit U.S. society as a whole, a group that thinks it will be adversely affected can prevent the measure's adoption. Because the processes of policy making and implementation are so complex and permeable, with so many points of access in the executive branch and Congress, those with a strong stake in a particular measure usually prevail, especially in the absence of an overarching national interest.

United States decisions affecting Latin America in the last generation have rarely, if ever, derived from a coherent strategic vision that became the touchstone of policy. The closest step in this direction was the Alliance for Progress, but the Alliance included contradictory elements that vitiated its effectiveness. Ronald Reagan's approach to Latin America has been consistently anti-Communist but it has included no broad positive appeal. The Reagan administration has communicated clearly what it is trying to prevent in the Western Hemisphere, but not what it wants to achieve.

This lack of any positive organizing concept for Latin American policy has been compounded by discontinuities of personnel; the average tenure in office of the assistant secretary of state for inter-American affairs since 1960 has been 18 months, less than that in any comparable foreign policy post. Individuals in that position have varied greatly in their capacity to manage the complex inter-agency processes of policy making, but none has sustained a preeminent role long enough to lend coherence to the Latin American policy of the United States.

Finally, every U.S. approach toward Latin America in the last generation has foundered in part because it failed to take account of how much Latin America has changed, and particularly how substantially the Hemisphere's political economy has been altered. The Carter administration took rhetorical notice of Latin America's transformation but did not alter U.S. economic policies enough to accommodate the region's new potential and needs. The Reagan approach has largely disregarded Latin America's evolution and sought to reimpose U.S. predominance.

If a U.S. commitment to enhanced cooperation in the Americas is to be implemented, all these recurrent problems need to be faced.

First, a Western Hemisphere policy must be linked to a program for the economic recovery of the United States. No proposals for relieving Latin America's debt burden or for opening U.S. markets to Latin America's exports will be adopted—nor would they be sustainable—unless they are part of a strategy for restoring dynamism to the economies of the United States and other advanced industrial nations. No special policy of trade and tariff preferences for Latin America would affect the region's development as much as expanded growth by the advanced industrial countries, growth that could bring higher prices for Latin America's export commodities and larger markets for the region's products. Perhaps no U.S. measure to support Latin America's development directly would be as significant as reducing the fiscal deficit of the United States and thus relieving the pressure on interest rates.

Second, a U.S. commitment to Western Hemisphere cooperation must enlist the support of domestic groups. United States banks and exporters have a strong self-interest in the economic recovery of Latin America. Although U.S. trade unions feel threatened by Latin American exports, organized labor can gain from economic development in the countries of Latin America and the Caribbean; rising wage rates and living standards in these countries could help protect the gains of many U.S. workers, who could also benefit from the expansion of Latin American markets for U.S. exports. United States agricultural and industrial employers who need unskilled workers, as well as U.S. workers who need job protection, could benefit from a regulated program for temporary labor immigration. Latino communities, increasingly visible in U.S. politics and significant in electoral terms, might take a strong positive interest in a program of cooperation with their countries of origin. Religious and human rights groups would ardently support a program of consistent U.S. backing for democratic consolidation. The entire nation would gain from effective inter-American programs to control the flow of drugs. Public opinion polls have repeatedly shown that a considerable majority of the American public would favor an approach to Central America that both protects the core security interests of the United States and reduces the likelihood of U.S. military intervention.

The elements exist for a national coalition in support of hemispheric cooperation, but they need to be nurtured. Different constituencies can be mobilized in support of an approach that emphasizes economic expansion, democratic consolidation, and cooperative problem solving instead of focusing on security conceived narrowly in military terms. Building such a coalition is preeminently a task for farsighted political leadership.

Opposition to the recommended approach would predictably come from firms and trade unions that fear competition from Latin America's exporters. Although the familiar myths (based on earlier realities) suggest that it is "big business" in the United States that traditionally opposes the policies Latin Americans seek, in the 1980s it is often small business and some segments of organized labor that stand to be hurt by a U.S. program that supports Latin American development.

The United States, consequently, can only adopt and sustain trade policies that facilitate Latin American growth if it simultaneously undertakes programs to ease the transition from marginal sectors in its own economy. Among the needed measures are retraining programs for workers and coordinated business adjustment assistance, including incentives for modernization. The Reagan administration's moves to reduce or eliminate such programs for budgetary reasons have been false economies. Comprehensive efforts are needed to improve the competitiveness of U.S. industry by moving up the technological scale; investments for this purpose will pay rich dividends.

Opposition will also come from those who fervently believe that Nicaragua is part of a worldwide Communist challenge to the United States, and that this test should be the focal point of U.S. policy in the Hemisphere. Concern about Communist gains in the Caribbean Basin existed among some sectors of the U.S. public even before the Reagan years, and it has been reinforced by his administration's obsession with Nicaragua. But repeated presidential efforts to expand popular support for confrontation with the Sandinistas have been unsuccessful. An administration that explains to the American public why U.S. interests are actually much more threatened by the debt crisis and its consequences than by the Sandinistas may well find that only a small minority will cling to the current misplaced emphasis.

Finally, the prospects that a program for Western Hemisphere cooperation will be carried out could be significantly improved by sustained intragovernmental coordination. A president who wants to launch a policy of hemispheric cooperation should name a person of stature who enjoys his personal confidence to manage inter-American affairs. This official should be charged by the president to work closely with people at the State Department and all other relevant agencies—Treasury, Defense, the Central Intelligence Agency, Agriculture, Commerce, the Immigration and Naturalization Service, the Customs Service, the Drug Enforcement Administration, the Office of the Special Trade Representative, the U.S. International Trade Commission, and others—to achieve a coherent approach. A presidential mandate to give priority to improving Western Hemisphere cooperation will not automatically produce results, but the designation of a senior official with this responsibility should help, as should sustained presidential interest in his or her work. Latin America has periodically enjoyed rhetorical prominence in Washington; showing the president's concern by naming a major figure to oversee Western Hemispheric relations would be more impressive and effective than additional speeches and good-will visits.

FROM INSECURITY TO *CONFIANZA*

In recent years, U.S. policies toward Latin American have been interventionist politically, often protectionist in economic terms, increasingly restrictive of immigration, patronizing in style, and unilateral in implementation. These policies have been grounded in insecurity and ultimately aimed at preserving dominance.

The time has come to adopt a different stance—one that is built on confidence and trust, on what Latin Americans call *confianza*. The United States should recognize and accept Latin America's many changes instead of ignoring or resisting them. It should regard Latin America's nations neither as automatic allies nor as mere counters in a global contest, but rather as potential partners for confronting shared problems.

The United States should take the first steps toward improved inter-American relations by negotiating a secure peace with Nicaragua and by concentrating more attention on how to restore economic growth and

strengthen democracy throughout the Americas. These steps, if vigorously pursued and sustained, could help open a new and positive period
in the Western Hemisphere. Such a U.S. initiative may not produce
instant inter-American partnership, given the legacy of imposition and
mutual distrust. But the chances that Latin American nations will themselves adopt the policies needed for Western Hemisphere cooperation
surely depend in large part on whether the United States genuinely
seeks their help.

The United States today needs the cooperation of Latin America
more than ever before. Latin American nations are also increasingly
aware of the benefits of accord with the United States. Washington can
no longer presume, command, or coerce the cooperation of Latin America, but it can help to build Hemispheric collaboration in the mutual
interest of all in the Americas. If Washington can abandon the habits of
dominance, the United States and Latin America can turn from conflict
toward partnership.

Guide to Sources

This book is based on extensive research, numerous personal interviews, and many discussions over the past several years. I have checked and double-checked factual statements, and have incorporated into the analysis what I learned from knowledgeable colleagues who commented on drafts.

Basic social and economic data are taken primarily from standard official sources. I have relied principally on the annual *Statistical Abstract of Latin America*, published by the University of California at Los Angeles (UCLA); the *Statistical Yearbook for Latin America*, published by the United National Economic Commission for Latin America and the Caribbean (ECLAC); and the *Statistical Abstract of the United States*, as well as various publications of the Treasury, Commerce, and State departments and the Central Intelligence Agency of the United States government. I have also drawn on publications of the World Bank (especially on its annual *World Development Reports*), the Inter-American Development Bank, the International Monetary Fund, ECLAC, the Population Reference Bureau, and the Latin American Demographic Center (CELADE).

Economic figures for 1986 are mostly from ECLAC's "Panorama Económico de America Latina, 1986" (released in September 1986) and from the "Balance Preliminar para el año 1986" (released in mid-December 1986).

The following pages acknowledge the readers who commented on individual chapters of the manuscript and provide a guide for major sources which I recommend to those interested in further reading. For the most part, I have listed each item only once, even though it may be relevant for more than one theme. The guide is organized by chapters, and by topics within chapters.

CHAPTER ONE
Latin America's Transformation

I appreciate the comments on a draft of this chapter made by Alan Angell, Peter D. Bell, Natalio Botana, Rodrigo Botero, Julio Cotler, Susan

Eckstein, Jonathan Hartlyn, Pedro-Pablo Kuczynski, Gabriel Murillo, Alejandro Portes, Carlos Quijano, Francisco Weffort, Alexander Wilde, and Gary Wynia.

LOOKING BACKWARD: LATIN AMERICA'S PROSPECTS IN THE EARLY 1960S

Mildred Adams, ed. *Latin America: Evolution or Explosion?* New York: Dodd, Mead, 1963.

Richard N. Adams et al. *Social Change in Latin America Today: Its Implications for United States Policy.* New York: Random House, 1960.

The American Assembly. *The United States and Latin America.* New York: American Assembly, Columbia University, 1959.

Susanne Jonas Bodenheimer. *The Ideology of Developmentalism: The American Political Science's Paradigm-Surrogate for Latin American Studies.* Sage Professional Papers in Comparative Politics, no. 15. Beverly Hills, Calif.: Sage Publications, 1970.

Regis Debray. *Revolution in the Revolution? Armed Struggle and Political Struggle in Latin America.* New York: Grove Press, 1967.

Albert O. Hirschman. *Journeys toward Progress: Studies of Economic Policy-Making in Latin America.* New York: W. W. Norton, 1963.

John J. Johnson. *Political Change in Latin America: The Emergence of the Middle Sectors.* Stanford, Calif.: Stanford University Press, 1958.

Robert R. Kaufman and Arpad J. von Lazar, eds. *Reform and Revolution: Readings in Latin American Politics.* Boston: Allyn and Bacon, 1969.

Seymour Martin Lipset. "Some Social Requisites of Democracy: Economic Development and Political Legitimacy." *American Political Science Review* 53, no. 1 (1959).

Martin C. Needler. *Political Development in Latin America: Instability, Violence, and Evolutionary Change.* New York: Random House, 1968.

James Petras and Maurice Zeitlen, eds. *Latin America: Reform or Revolution?* Greenwich, Conn.: Fawcett, 1968.

Charles O. Porter and Robert J. Alexander. *Struggle for Democracy in Latin America.* New York: Macmillan, 1961.

Raúl Prebisch. *The Economic Development of Latin America and Its Principal Problems.* New York: United Nations Economic Commission for Latin America, 1950.

Walt W. Rostow. *The Stages of Economic Growth: A Non-Communist Manifesto.* New York: Cambridge University Press, 1960.

Karl M. Schmitt and David Burks. *Evolution or Chaos? Dynamics of Latin American Politics.* New York: Praeger, 1963.

Tad Szulc. *Twilight of the Tyrants.* New York: Holt, 1959.

Claudio Veliz, ed. *Obstacles to Change in Latin America.* Oxford: Oxford University Press, 1969.

DEMOGRAPHY

Douglas Butterworth and John K. Chance. *Latin American Urbanization.* Cambridge: Cambridge University Press, 1981.

Sergio Diaz-Briquets. *International Migration within Latin America and the Caribbean: An Overview.* New York: Center for Migration Studies, 1983.

Robert Fox. *Urban Population Growth Trends in Latin America.* Oxford: Oxford University Press, 1975.

Jorge E. Hardoy, ed. *Urbanization in Latin America: Approaches and Issues.* New York: Doubleday, 1975.

Thomas W. Merrick. "Population Pressures in Latin America." Population Reference Bureau, *Population Bulletin* 41, no. 3 (1986).

ECONOMY

Werner Baer. "The Economics of Prebisch and ECLA." *Economic Development and Cultural Change* 10, no. 2 (1962).

Fernando H. Cardoso and Enzo Faletto. *Dependency and Development in Latin America.* Berkeley and Los Angeles: University of California Press, 1979.

William R. Cline. *International Debt and the Stability of the World Economy.* Washington, D.C.: Institute for International Economics, 1983.

William R. Cline and Sidney Weintraub, eds. *Economic Stabilization and the Developing Countries.* Washington, D.C.: Brookings Institution, 1981.

Esperanza Durán, ed. *Latin America and the World Recession.* Cambridge: Cambridge University Press, 1985.

Thomas O. Enders and Richard P. Mattione. *Latin America: The Crisis of Debt and Growth.* Washington, D.C.: Brookings Institution, 1984.

Fernando Fajnzylber. *La industrialización trunca de América Latina.* México, D.F.: Editorial Nueva Imagen, 1983.

David Felix. "On Financial Blowups and Authoritarian Regimes in Latin America." In *Latin American Political Economy: Financial Crisis and Political Change,* edited by Jonathan Hartlyn and Samuel A. Morley. Boulder, Colo.: Westview Press, 1986.

Albert Fishlow. "Coping with the Creeping Crisis of Debt." Working Paper no. 181, Department of Economics, University of California, Berkeley, 1984.

———. "Latin American Adjustment to the Oil Shocks of 1973 and 1979." In *Latin American Political Economy: Financial Crisis and Political Change,* edited by Jonathan Hartlyn and Samuel A. Morley. Boulder, Colo.: Westview Press, 1986.

———. "Latin American External Debt: A Case of Uncertain Development." In *Trade, Stability, Technology, and Equity in Latin America,* edited by M. Syrquin and S. Teitel. New York: Academic Press, 1982.

———. "A Tale of Two Presidents: The Political Economy of the Brazilian Adjustment to the Oil Shocks." Working Paper, Department of Economics, University of California, Berkeley, 1986.

Carlos Fortín. "The Failure of Repressive Monetarism: Chile, 1973–1983." *Third World Quarterly* 6 (April 1984).

Alejandro Foxley. *Latin American Experiments in Neo-Conservative Economics.* Berkeley and Los Angeles: University of California Press, 1983.

David Goodman and Michael Redclift. *From Peasant to Proletarian: Capitalist Development and Agrarian Transitions.* Oxford: Basil Blackwell, 1981.

Jonathan Hartlyn and Samuel A. Morley, eds. *Latin American Political Economy: Financial Crisis and Political Change.* Boulder, Colo.: Westview Press, 1986.

Albert O. Hirschman. *A Bias For Hope: Essays on Development in Latin America.* New Haven: Yale University Press, 1971.

———. "The Political Economy of Import Substitution Industrialization." *Quarterly Journal of Economics* 82 (February 1968).

———. "The Political Economy of Latin American Development: Seven Exercises in Retrospection." Paper prepared for the 13th Congress of the Latin American Studies Association, Boston, October 1986.

Inter-American Development Bank. "External Debt: Crisis and Adjustment." In *Economic and Social Progress in Latin America.* Washington, D.C.: IDB, 1985.

———. *External Debt and Economic Adjustment in Latin America.* Washington, D.C.: IDB, 1986.

———. *External Debt and Economic Development in Latin America: Background and Prospects.* Washington, D.C.: IDB, 1984.

Alain de Janvry. *The Agrarian Question and Reformism in Latin America.* Baltimore: Johns Hopkins University Press, 1981.

Pedro-Pablo Kuczynski. "Latin American Debt." *Foreign Affairs* 61, no. 2 (1982–83).

———. "Latin American Debt: Act Two." *Foreign Affairs* 62, no. 1 (1983).

Steven Sanderson. *The Transformation of Mexican Agriculture: International Structure and Politics of Rural Change.* Princeton, N.J.: Princeton University Press, 1986.

John Sheahan. "Market-Oriented Economic Policies and Political Repression in Latin America." *Economic Development and Cultural Change* 28 (January 1980).

Rosemary Thorp and Laurence Whitehead, eds. *Inflation and Stabilization in Latin America.* London: Macmillan, 1979.

United Nations Economic Commission on Latin America and the Caribbean. *External Debt in Latin America: Adjustment Policies and Renegotiation.* Boulder, Colo.: L. Reiner, 1984.

Victor Urquidi and Rosemary Thorp, eds. *Latin America in the International Economy.* London: Macmillan, 1973.

Miguel Urrutia. *Winners and Losers in Colombia's Economic Growth of the 1970s.* Oxford: Oxford University Press, 1985.

Arturo Valenzuela and Samuel Valenzuela. "Modernization and Dependence: Alternative Perspectives in the Study of Latin American Underdevelopment." *Comparative Politics* 10, no. 4 (1978).

Richard Webb. *Government Policy and the Distribution of Income in Peru, 1963–1973.* Cambridge: Harvard University Press, 1977.

Eduardo Wiesner. "Domestic and External Causes of the Latin American Debt Crisis." *Finance and Development* 22, no. 1 (1985).

John Williamson. *IMF Conditionality.* Washington, D.C.: Institute for International Economics, 1983.

Miguel Wionczek, ed. *Politics and Economics of External Debt Crisis: The Latin American Experience.* Boulder, Colo.: Westview Press, 1985.

SOCIETY

Oscar Altimir. "Poverty in Latin America: A Review of Concepts and Data." *CEPAL Review,* no. 13 (April 1981).

William Ascher. *Scheming for the Poor: The Politics of Redistribution in Latin America.* Cambridge: Harvard University Press, 1984.

Ray Bromley, ed. *The Urban Informal Sector: Critical Perspectives on Unemployment and Housing.* Oxford: Pergamon, 1979.

Manuel Castells. "Squatters and Politics in Latin America: A Comparative Analysis of Urban Social Movements in Chile, Peru, and Mexico." In *Towards a Political Economy of Urbanization in Third World Countries,* edited by Helen I. Safa. Delhi: Oxford University Press, 1982.

David Felix. "Income Distribution and the Quality of Life in Latin America: Patterns, Trends, and Policy Implications." *Latin American Research Review* 18, no. 2 (1983).

Alan Gilbert and Peter Ward. "Community Action by the Urban Poor: Democratic Involvement, Community Self-Help, or a Means of Social Control?" *World Development* 12, no. 8 (1984).

Larissa A. Lomnitz. *Networks and Marginality: Life in a Mexican Shantytown.* New York: Academic Press, 1977.

Carmelo Mesa-Lago. "Social Security and Extreme Poverty in Latin America." *Journal of Development Economics* 12 (1983).

June Nash and Helen I. Safa. *Sex and Class in Latin America.* New York: Praeger, 1976.

———. eds. *Women and Change in Latin America: New Directions in Sex and Class.* South Hadley, Mass.: Bergen and Garvey, 1986.

Joan M. Nelson. *Access to Power: Politics and the Urban Poor in Developing Nations.* Princeton, N.J.: Princeton University Press, 1979.

Andrew Pearse. *The Latin American Peasant.* London: Frank Cass, 1975.

Janice Perlman. *The Myth of Marginality: Urban Poverty and Politics in Rio de Janeiro.* Berkeley and Los Angeles: University of California Press, 1976.

Alejandro Portes. "Latin American Class Structures: Their Composition and Change during the Last Decades." *Latin American Research Review* 20, no. 3 (1985).

Alejandro Portes and John Walton. *Urban Latin America: The Political Condition from Above and Below.* Austin: University of Texas Press, 1976.

Bryan Roberts. *Cities of Peasants: The Political Economy of Urbanization in the Third World.* London: Edward Arnold, 1978.

Paulo Souza and Victor Tokman. "The Informal Urban Sector in Latin America." *International Labor Review* 114, no. 3 (1976).

Victor Tokman. "Growth, Underemployment, and Income Distribution." In

Trade, Stability, Technology, and Equity in Latin America, edited by M. Syrquin and S. Teitel. New York: Academic Press, 1982.
————. "Wages and Employment in International Recessions: Recent Latin American Experiences." *CEPAL Review* 20 (August 1983).

POLITICS

Thomas C. Bruneau. *The Church in Brazil: The Politics of Religion.* Austin: University of Texas Press, 1982.

David Collier, ed. *The New Authoritarianism in Latin America.* Princeton, N.J.: Princeton University Press, 1979.

Richard R. Fagen. "Studying Latin American Politics: Some Implications of a *Dependencia* Approach." *Latin American Research Review* 12, no. 2 (1977).

Alejandro Foxley. *Para una democracia estable: Económica y política.* Santiago: Editorial Aconaqua, 1985.

Howard Handelman and Thomas Sanders. *Military Government and the Movement towards Democracy in South America.* Bloomington: Indiana University Press, 1981.

Penny Lernoux. *Cry of the People: The Struggle for Human Rights in Latin America—The Catholic Church in Conflict with U.S. Policy.* Middlesex: Penguin, 1982.

Daniel Levine, ed. *Church and Politics in Latin America.* Beverly Hills, Calif.: Sage Publications, 1980.

Juan Linz and Alfred Stepan, eds. *The Breakdown of Democratic Regimes: Latin America.* Baltimore: Johns Hopkins University Press, 1978.

Guillermo O'Donnell. *Modernization and Bureaucratic Authoritarianism: Studies in South American Politics.* Berkeley: Institute of International Studies, University of California, 1973.

————. "Reflections on the Patterns of Change in the Bureaucratic-Authoritarian State." *Latin American Research Review* 12, no. 1 (1978).

Guillermo O'Donnell, Phillippe Schmitter, and Laurence Whitehead, eds. *Transitions from Authoritarian Rule: Prospects for Democracy.* Baltimore: Johns Hopkins University Press, 1986.

Karen Remmer. "Redemocratization and the Impact of Authoritarian Rule in Latin America." *Comparative Politics* 17, no. 3 (1985).

Karen Remmer and Gilbert Merkx. "Bureaucratic Authoritarianism Revisited." *Latin American Research Review* 17, no. 2 (1982).

Brian H. Smith. *The Church and Politics in Chile: Challenges to Modern Catholicism.* Princeton, N.J.: Princeton University Press, 1982.

INTERNATIONAL RELATIONS

Cole Blasier. *The Giant's Rival: The USSR and Latin America.* Pittsburgh, Pa.: University of Pittsburgh Press, 1983.

Robert D. Bond, ed. *Contemporary Venezuela and Its Role in International Affairs.* New York: New York University Press, 1977.

Jack Child. *Geopolitics and Conflicts in South America: Quarrels among Neighbors.* New York: Praeger, 1985.

Jorge I. Dominguez. "The Foreign Policies of Latin American States in the 1980s: Retreat or Refocus?" In *Global Dilemmas,* edited by Samuel P. Huntington and Joseph S. Nye, Jr. Cambridge: Center for International Affairs, Harvard University, 1985.

————. ed. *Cuba: Internal and International Affairs.* Beverly Hills, Calif.: Sage, 1982.

Edward Gonzalez. "A Comparison of Soviet and Cuban Approaches to Latin America." *Studies in Communism* 5, no. 1 (1972).

Leon Gouré and Morris Rothenberg. *Soviet Penetration of Latin America.* Washington, D.C. Center for Advanced International Studies, University of Miami, 1975.

Wolf Grabendorff and Riordan Roett, eds. *Latin America, Western Europe, and the United States: Reevaluating the Atlantic Triangle.* New York: Praeger, 1984.

Jerry F. Hough. *The Struggle for the Third World: Soviet Debates and American Options.* Washington, D.C.: Brookings Institution, 1986.

Stephen D. Krasner. *Structural Conflict: The Third World against Global Liberalism.* Berkeley and Los Angeles: University of California Press, 1985.

Robert S. Leiken. *Soviet Strategy in Latin America.* The Washington Papers, vol. 10, no. 93. New York: Praeger, 1982.

Jennie K. Lincoln and Elizabeth Ferris, eds. *The Dynamics of Latin American Foreign Policies: Challenges for the Eighties.* Boulder, Colo.: Westview Press, 1984.

Gabriel Marcella and Daniel Papp. "The Soviet-Cuban Relationship: Symbiotic or Parasitic?" In *The Soviet Union in the Third World: Successes and Failures,* edited by Robert H. Donaldson. Boulder, Colo.: Westview Press, 1981.

Heraldo Muñoz, ed. *Las políticas exteriores latinoamericana frente a la crisis.* Buenos Aires: Grupo Editor Latinoamericano, 1985.

Heraldo Muñoz and Joseph S. Tulchin, eds. *Latin American Nations in World Politics.* Boulder, Colo.: Westview Press, 1984.

Elizabeth Kridl Valkenier, "New Trends in Soviet Economic Relations with the Third World." *World Politics* 22, no. 3 (1970).

COUNTRY STUDIES (OTHER THAN FOR MEXICO, BRAZIL, AND THE CARIBBEAN BASIN COUNTRIES, NOTED IN CHAPTERS 4, 5, AND 6).

ARGENTINA

Marcelo Cavarozzi. *Autoritarismo y Democracia, 1955–1983.* Buenos Aires: Centro Editor, 1983.

Guillermo O'Donnell. *El estado burocrático-autoritario, 1966–1973.* Buenos Aires: Editorial de Belgrano, 1982.

Gary Wynia. *Argentina in the Postwar Era: Politics and Economic Policy Making in a Divided Society.* Albuquerque: University of New Mexico Press, 1978.

CHILE

Sergio Bitar. *Transición, socialismo y democracia: la experiencia chilena.* México, D.F.: Siglo Veintiuno Editores, 1979.

Manuel A. Garretón. *El proceso político chileno.* Santiago: FLACSO, 1983.

Paul E. Sigmund. *The Overthrow of Allende and the Politics of Chile, 1964–1976.* Pittsburgh, Pa.: University of Pittsburgh Press, 1977.

Barbara Stallings. *Class Conflict and Economic Development in Chile. 1958–1973.* Stanford, Calif.: Stanford University Press, 1978.

Arturo Valenzuela. *The Breakdown of Democratic Regimes: Chile.* Baltimore: Johns Hopkins University Press, 1978.

Arturo Valenzuela and Samuel Valenzuela, eds. *Military Rule in Chile: Dictatorship and Oppositions.* Baltimore: Johns Hopkins University Press, 1986.

COLOMBIA

Albert Berry, Ronald G. Hellman, and Mauricio Solaún. *Politics of Compromise: Coalition Government in Colombia.* New Brunswick, N.J.: Transaction Books, 1980.

Jonathan Hartlyn. *The Politics of Coalition Rule: The Colombian National Front and Its Aftermaths.* Forthcoming. Cambridge: Cambridge University Press, 1987.

Alexander Wilde. *Conversaciones de caballeros: la quiebra de la democracia en Colombia.* Bogota: Ediciones Tercer Mundo, 1982.

PERU

David Collier, *Squatters and Oligarchs: Authoritarian Rule and Policy Change in Peru.* Baltimore: Johns Hopkins University Press, 1976.

Abraham F. Lowenthal, ed. *The Peruvian Experiment: Continuity and Change under Military Rule.* Princeton, N.J.: Princeton University Press, 1976.

Cynthia McClintock and Abraham F. Lowenthal, eds. *The Peruvian Experiment Reconsidered.* Princeton, N.J.: Princeton University Press, 1983.

Alfred Stepan. *State and Society: Peru in Comparative Perspective.* Princeton, N.J.: Princeton University Press, 1978.

URUGUAY

Edy Kaufman. *Uruguay in Transition.* New Brunswick, N.J.: Transaction Books, 1978.

Martin Weinstein. *Uruguay: The Politics of Failure.* Westport, Conn.: Greenwood Press, 1975.

VENEZUELA

Terry Karl. "Petroleum and Political Pacts: The Transition to Democracy in Venezuela." Washington, D.C.: Woodrow Wilson International Center for Scholars, 1982.

Daniel H. Levine. *Conflicts and Political Change in Venezuela.* Princeton, N.J.: Princeton University Press, 1973.

John D. Martz and David J. Myers, eds. *Venezuela: The Democratic Experience.* 2d ed. New York: Praeger, 1986.

Franklin Tugwell. *The Politics of Oil in Venezuela.* Stanford, Calif.: Stanford University Press, 1975.

PROSPECTS FOR DEMOCRACY

Douglas A. Chalmers and Craig H. Robinson. "Why Power Contenders Choose Liberalization." *International Studies Quarterly* 26 (March 1982).

Larry Diamond and Seymour Martin Lipset. "Developing and Sustaining Democratic Government in the Third World." Paper prepared for the Annual Meeting of the American Political Science Association, Washington, D.C., August 28–31, 1986.

Paul Drake and Eduardo Silva, eds. *Elections and Democratización in Latin America, 1980–85.* San Diego: University of California, 1986.

Manuel A. Garretón. *Dictaduras y democratizacion.* Santiago: FLASCO, 1984.

Charles Gillespie. "'Democradura' or 'Reforma Pactado': Comparative Perspectives on Democratic Restoration in Uruguay." Paper presented at the World Congress of the International Political Science Association, Paris, July 15–20, 1985.

Albert O. Hirschman. "Notes on the Consolidation of Democracy." *Rival Views of Market Societies and Other Recent Essays.* New York: Viking, 1986.

Samuel P. Huntington. "Will More Countries Become Democratic?" *Political Science Quarterly* 99 (Summer 1984).

Jane S. Jaquette. "Women's Political Participation, Feminism, and the Transition to Democracy in Latin America." In *Latin America and Caribbean Contemporary Record,* vol. 5 (1985–86), edited by Abraham F. Lowenthal. New York: Holmes and Meier, 1987.

Scott Mainwaring. "The Consolidation of Democracy: A Rapporteur's Report." Working Paper no. 73, Helen Kellogg Institute for International Studies, University of Notre Dame, Notre Dame, Ind., 1986.

Candido Mendes, Marcilio Marques Moreira et al. "From Authoritarian to Representative Government in Brazil and Argentina." *Government and Opposition* 19, no. 2 (1984).

Guillermo O'Donnell. "Notes for the Study of Democratic Consolidation in Contemporary Latin America." Paper presented for discussion by the working group on "Opportunities and Dilemmas of the Consolidation of Democracy in Latin America," São Paulo, December 16–17, 1985.

John A. Peeler. *Latin American Democracies: Colombia, Costa Rica, Vene-zuela.* Chapel Hill: University of North Carolina Press, 1985.

Alan Rouquie et al. *Como renascen os democracias.* Rio de Janeiro: Brasiliense, 1984.

Eduardo Viola and Scott Mainwaring. "Transitions to Democracy: Brazil and Argentina in the 1980s." *Journal of International Affairs* 38, no. 2 (1985).

CHAPTER TWO

The United States and Latin America Since 1960: Hegemony in Decline

Cole Blasier, Walter LaFeber, Heraldo Muñoz, Paul Sigmund, and Thomas Skidmore made helpful comments on a draft of this chapter.

U.S.–LATIN AMERICAN RELATIONS: GENERAL BACKGROUND

Philip Agee. *Inside the Company: CIA Diary.* New York: Stonehill, 1975.

Cole Blasier. *The Hovering Giant: U.S. Responses to Revolutionary Change in Latin America,* rev. ed. Pittsburgh, Pa.: University of Pittsburgh Press, 1985.

John Child. *Unequal Alliance: The Inter-American Military System, 1938–1979.* Boulder, Colo.: Westview Press, 1980.

Gordon Connell-Smith. *The Inter-American System.* New York: Oxford University Press, 1966.

George J. Eder. *Inflation and Development in Latin America: A Case History of Inflation and Stabliziation in Bolivia.* Ann Arbor: Program in International Business, Graduate School in Business Administration, University of Michigan, 1968.

Clarence H. Haring. *South America Looks at the United States.* New York: Macmillan, 1929.

Richard H. Immerman. *The CIA in Guatemala: The Foreign Policy of Intervention.* Austin: University of Texas Press, 1982.

F. Parkinson. *Latin America, the Cold War, and the World Powers, 1945–1973: A Study in Diplomatic History.* Beverly Hills, Calif.: Sage Publications, 1974.

David Atlee Phillips. *The Night Watch: Twenty-five Years of Peculiar Service.* New York: Atheneum, 1977.

Robert A. Pollard. *Economic Security and the Origins of the Cold War, 1945–50.* New York: Columbia University Press, 1985.

Carlos Rangel. *The Latin Americans: Their Love-Hate Relationship with the United States.* New York: Harcourt Brace Jovanovich, 1977.

Stephen Schlesinger and Stephen Kinzer. *Bitter Fruit: The Untold Story of the American Coup in Guatemala.* Garden City, N.Y.: Doubleday, 1981.

Jerome Slater. *The OAS and United States Foreign Policy.* Columbus: Ohio State University Press, 1967.

Arthur P. Whitaker. *The Western Hemisphere Idea: Its Rise and Decline.* Ithaca, N.Y.: Cornell University Press, 1984.

DECLINE OF HEGEMONY

Sergio Bitar. "Economics and Security: Contradictions in U.S.–Latin American Relations." In *The United States and Latin America in the 1980s*, edited by Kevin J. Middlebrook and Carlos Rico. Pittsburgh, Pa.: University of Pittsburgh Press, 1986.

———. "United States–Latin America Relations: Shift in Economic Power and Implications for the Future." *Journal of Inter-American Studies and World Affairs* 26, no. 1 (1984).

Morris J. Blachman, William M. LeoGrande, and Kenneth E. Sharpe, eds. *Confronting Revolution: Security through Diplomacy in Central America.* New York: Pantheon Books, 1986.

Cole Blasier. *The Giant's Rival: The USSR and Latin America.* Pittsburgh, Pa.: University of Pittsburgh Press, 1983.

Robert Bond. "Regionalism in Latin America: Prospects for the Latin American Economic System (SELA)." *International Organization* 32, no. 2 (1978).

Jessica Pernitz Einhorn. *Expropriation Politics.* Lexington, Mass.: Lexington Books, 1974.

Charles T. Goodsell. *American Corporations and Peruvian Politics.* Cambridge: Harvard University Press, 1974.

Wolf Grabendorff. "The United States and Western Europe: Competition or Cooperation on Latin America?" *International Affairs* 58, no. 4. (1984).

Frank Hong. "Is Size a Disadvantage in Dealing with the Transnational Corporations?" *Inter-American Economic Affairs* 33, no. 4 (1980).

Hiroshi Iton. "Japan: Japanese–Latin American Economic Relations." *Asian Thought and Society: An International Review* 5, no. 15 (1980).

James R. Kurth. "The United States, Latin America, and the World: The Changing International Context of U.S.–Latin American Relations." In *The United States and Latin America in the 1980s*, edited by Kevin J. Middlebrook and Carlos Rico. Pittsburgh, Pa.: University of Pittsburgh Press, 1986.

Robert S. Leiken. *Soviet Strategy in Latin America.* The Washington Papers, vol. 10, no. 93. New York: Praeger, 1982.

Jacques Levesque. *The USSR and the Cuban Revolution.* New York: Praeger, 1978.

William H. Luers. "The Soviets and Latin America: A Three Decade U.S. Policy Triangle." *Washington Quarterly* 7, no. 1 (1984).

Nikki Miller and Laurence Whitehead. "The Soviet Interest in Latin America: An Economic Perspective." In *The Soviet Union and the Third World*, edited by Robert Cassen. London: Chatham House, 1985.

Theodore Moran. *Multinational Corporations and the Politics of Dependence: Copper in Chile.* Princeton, N.J.: Princeton University Press, 1974.

Paul E. Sigmund. *Multinationals in Latin America: The Politics of Nationalization* Madison: University of Wisconsin Press, 1980.

Laurence Whitehead. "Debt, Diversification, and Dependency: Latin America's International Political Relations." In *The United States and Latin America in the 1980s,* edited by Kevin J. Middlebrook and Carlos Rico. Pittsburgh, Pa.: University of Pittsburgh Press, 1986.

THE UNITED STATES AND LATIN AMERICA IN THE 1960S: THE ALLIANCE FOR PROGRESS AND BEYOND

General

Milton Eisenhower. *The Wine is Bitter: The United States and Latin America.* Garden City, N.Y.: Doubleday, 1963.

Eduardo Frei. "The Alliance That Lost Its Way." *Foreign Affairs* 45, no. 3 (1967).

Simon G. Hansen. *Five Years of the Alliance for Progress: An Appraisal.* Washington, D.C.: Inter-American Affairs Press, 1967.

Jerome Levinson and Juan de Onis. *The Alliance That Lost Its Way.* Chicago: Quadrangle Books, 1970.

Abraham F. Lowenthal. " 'Liberal,' 'Radical,' and 'Bureaucratic Perspectives' on U.S.–Latin American Policy: The Alliance for Progress in Retrospect." In *Latin America and the United States: The Changing Political Realities,* edited by Julio Cotler and Richard Fagen. Stanford, Calif.: Stanford University Press, 1974.

Nelson Rockefeller. *The Rockefeller Report on the Americas.* Chicago: Quadrangle Books, 1969.

William D. Rogers. *The Twilight Struggle: The Alliance for Progress and the Politics of Development in Latin America.* New York: Random House, 1967.

Howard J. Wiarda. "Did the Alliance 'Lose Its Way?' " Paper presented at the Conference on "The Alliance for Progress: Twenty-Five Years Later," Center for Advanced Studies of the Americas, Washington D.C., March 14–16, 1986.

Cases

BRAZIL

Phyllis R. Parker. *Brazil and the Quiet Intervention, 1964.* Austin: University of Texas Press, 1979.

CUBA

Carla Anne Robbins. *The Cuban Threat.* New York: McGraw-Hill, 1983.

Richard E. Welch, Jr. *Response to Revolution: The U.S. and the Cuban Revolution, 1959–1961.* Chapel Hill: University of North Carolina Press, 1985.

Peter Wyden. *The Bay of Pigs: The Untold Story.* New York: Simon and Schuster, 1979.

DOMINICAN REPUBLIC

Piero Gleijeses. *The Dominican Crisis: The 1965 Constitutionalist Revolt and American Intervention.* Baltimore: Johns Hopkins University Press, 1978.

Abraham F. Lowenthal. *The Dominican Intervention.* Cambridge: Harvard University Press, 1972.

GUYANA

Ashton Chase. *A History of Trade Unionism in Guyana*. Ruimveldt, De-merara: New Guyana, 1967.

Gordon K. Lewis. *The Growth of the Modern West Indies*. New York: Monthly Review Press, 1968.

Stanley Meiser. "Dubious Role of AFL-CIO Meddling in Latin America." *Nation*, February 10, 1984.

THE UNITED STATES AND LATIN AMERICA IN THE 1970S

Commission on United States–Latin American Relations (The Linowitz Commission). *The Americas in a Changing World*. New York: Quadrangle Books, 1975.

————. *The United States and Latin America: Next Steps*. New York: Center for Inter-American Relations, 1976.

Nathaniel Davis. *The Last Two Years of Salvador Allende*. Ithaca, N.Y.: Cornell University Press, 1985.

Luigi Einaudi. "Latin American Development and the United States." In *Beyond Cuba: Latin America Takes Charge of Its Future*, edited by Luigi Einaudi. New York: Crane, Russak, 1974.

Mark Falcoff. *Small Countries, Large Issues: Studies in U.S.–Latin American Asymmetries*. Washington, D.C.: American Enterprise Institute for Public Policy Research, 1984.

George D. Moffett III. *The Ratification of the Panama Canal Treaties*. Ithaca, N.Y.: Cornell University Press, 1985.

John Odell. "Growing Trade and Growing Conflict between Latin America and the United States." In *The United States and Latin America in the 1980s*, edited by Kevin J. Middlebrook and Carlos Rico. Pittsburgh, Pa.: University of Pittsburgh Press, 1986.

Lars Schoultz. *Human Rights and the United States Policy toward Latin America*. Princeton, N.J.: Princeton University Press, 1981.

U.S. Congress. Senate. Select Committee on Intelligence Activities. *Covert Action in Chile, 1963–1973*. Staff Report, 94th Cong., 1st sess. Washington, D.C.: U.S. Government Printing Office, 1975.

Cyrus Vance. *Hard Choices*. New York: Simon and Schuster, 1983.

THE UNITED STATES AND LATIN AMERICA IN THE 1980S

Raymond Bonner. *Weakness and Deceit: U.S. Policy and El Salvador*. New York: Times Books, 1984.

Shirley Christian. *Nicaragua: Revolution in the Family*. New York: Random House, 1985.

The Committee of Santa Fe. "A New Inter-American Policy for the Eighties." Washington, D.C., 1980.

Roger Fontaine, Cleto D. Giovanni, and Alexander Kruger. "Castro's Specter." *Washington Quarterly* 3, no. 4 (1980).

Alexander Haig, Jr. *Caveat: Realism, Reagan, and Foreign Policy*. New York: Macmillan, 1984.

Eldon Kenworthy. "Grenada as Theater." *World Policy Journal* 1, no. 3 (1984).

Jeane Kirkpatrick. "Dictatorships and Double Standards." *Commentary,* November 1979.

Joseph Kraft. *The Mexican Rescue.* New York: Group of Thirty, 1984.

Luis Maira, ed. *Una nueva era de hegemonía norteamericana?* Buenos Aires: Grupo Editor Latinoamericano, 1986.

Robert Pastor. "Does the United States Push Revolutions to Cuba? The Case of Grenada." *Journal of Inter-American Studies and World Affairs* 28, no. 1 (1986).

————. *Condemned to Repetition: The United States and Nicaragua.* Princeton, N.J.: Princeton University Press, 1987.

Susan Kaufman Purcell. "Demystifying Contadora." *Foreign Affairs* 64, no. 1 (1985).

The Report of the National Bipartisan Commission on Central America. Washington, D.C.: U.S. Government Printing Office, January 1984.

Nestor Sanchez. "The Communist Threat." *Foreign Policy* 52 (Fall 1983).

Pedro Sanjuan. "Why We Don't Have a Latin American Policy." *Washington Quarterly* 3, no. 4 (1980).

Paul E. Sigmund. "Latin America: Change or Continuity?" *Foreign Affairs* 60, no. 3 (1981).

Sistema Económico Latinoamericano. *Latin American–U.S. Relations, 1982–1983.* Boulder, Colo.: Westview Press, 1984.

Robert Wesson and Heraldo Muñoz, eds. *Latin American Views of U.S. Policy.* New York: Praeger, 1986.

CHAPTER THREE

Rethinking U.S. Interests in the Western Hemisphere

I am grateful to Sergio Bitar, Roger Hansen, Viron P. Vaky, Ronald Steel, and Gregory F. Treverton, all of whom commented on a draft of this chapter.

U.S. INTERESTS: TRADITIONAL DISCUSSIONS

Security

Ethel B. Dietrich. "Inter-American Cooperation." In *The Economic Defense of the Western Hemisphere: A Study of Conflict.* A symposium of the Latin American Economic Institute. Washington, D.C.: American Council on Public Affairs, 1941.

Laurence Duggan. *The Americas: The Search for Hemispheric Security.* New York: Holt, 1949.

Alton Frye. *Nazi Germany and the American Hemisphere, 1933–1941.* New Haven: Yale University Press, 1967.

David Green. *The Containment of Latin America: A History of the Myths and Realities of the Good Neighbor Policy.* Chicago: Quadrangle Books, 1971.

R. Bruce McColm. "The Cuban and Soviet Dimension." In *Crisis and Op-*

portunity: U.S. Policy in Central America and the Caribbean, edited by Mark Falcoff and Robert Royal. Washington, D.C.: Ethics and Public Policy Center, 1984.

J. Lloyd Mecham. *The United States and Inter-American Security, 1889–1960.* Austin: University of Texas Press, 1961.

Dana G. Munro. *Intervention and Dollar Diplomacy in the Caribbean, 1900–1921.* Princeton, N.J.: Princeton University Press, 1964.

———. *The United States and the Caribbean Republics, 1921–1933.* Princeton, N.J.: Princeton University Press, 1974.

David Ronfeldt. *Geopolitics, Security, and U.S. Strategy in the Caribbean Basin.* Santa Monica, Calif.: Rand Corporation, 1983.

Politics

Samuel F. Bemis. *The Latin American Policy of the United States: An Historical Interpretation.* New York: Harcourt, Brace, 1943.

John M. Cabot. *Toward Our Common American Destiny.* Medford, Mass.: Fletcher School of Law and Diplomacy, 1955.

R. Harrison Wagner. *U.S. Policy toward Latin America: A Study in Domestic and International Politics.* Stanford, Calif.: Stanford University Press, 1970.

Economics

Marvin Bernstein, ed. *Foreign Investment in Latin America: Cases and Attitudes.* New York: Knopf, 1966.

Richard J. Bloomfield. "Who Makes Foreign Policy? Some Latin American Case Studies." Paper presented at the Center for International Affairs, Harvard University, Cambridge, March 1972.

Jorge I. Dominguez. *Economic Issues and Political Conflict: U.S.–Latin American Relations.* Boston: Butterworth, 1982.

Stephen Krasner. *Defending the National Interest: Raw Materials and U.S. Foreign Policy.* Princeton, N.J: Princeton University Press, 1978.

Robert B. Williamson, William P. Glade, Jr., and Karl M. Schmitt, eds. *Latin American–U.S. Economic Interactions: Conflict, Accommodation, and Policies for the Future.* Washington, D.C.: American Enterprise Institute for Public Policy Research, 1974.

CHANGING CONCEPTS OF U.S. INTERESTS

Security

Jorge I. Dominguez. "The United States and Its Regional Security Interests: The Caribbean, Central, and South America." *Daedalus,* Fall 1980.

———. *U.S. Interests and Policies in the Caribbean and Central America.* Washington, D.C.: American Enterprise Institute for Public Policy Research, 1982.

Thomas Enders. "A Comprehensive Strategy for the Caribbean Basin." *Caribbean Review,* Spring 1982.

Richard E. Feinberg. *The Intemperate Zone: The Third World Challenge to U.S. Foreign Policy.* New York: W. W. Norton, 1983.

Margaret Daly Hayes. *Latin America and the U.S. National Interest: A Basis for U.S. Foreign Policy.* Boulder, Colo.: Westview Press, 1984.

————. "Security to the South: U.S. Interests in Latin America." *International Security* 5, no. 1 (1980).

Jeane Kirkpatrick, "U.S. Security and Latin America." *Commentary,* January 1981.

Donald E. Nuechterlein. *National Interests and Presidential Leadership.* Boulder, Colo.: Westview Press, 1978.

Lars Schoultz. *National Security and United States Policy toward Latin America.* Princeton, N.J. Princeton University Press, 1987.

U.S. Congress. House. Defense Intelligence Agency. Subcommittee on Foreign Affairs. *Hearings on Impact of Cuban-Soviet Ties in the Western Hemisphere.* 96th Cong., 2d sess. Washington, D.C.: U.S. Government Printing Office, 1980.

U.S. Congress. Senate. Committee on Foreign Relations. *Hearings on Panama Canal Treaties.* 95th Cong., 1st sess. Washington, D.C.: U.S. Government Printing Office, 1977.

Politics

P. T. Bauer and Basil Yaney. "Against the New Economic Order." *Commentary,* April 1977.

John C. Dreier. "Old Wine in New Bottles: The Changing Inter-American System." *International Organization* 22, no. 2 (1968).

Jeffrey A. Hart. *The New International Economic Order: Conflict and Cooperation in North-South Economic Relations, 1974–77.* New York: St. Martin's Press, 1983.

Stephen Krasner. "North-South Economic Relations." In *Eagle Entangled: U.S. Foreign Policy in a Complex World,* edited by Kenneth Oye. New York: Longman, 1979.

————. *Structural Conflict: The Third World against Global Liberalism.* Berkeley and Los Angeles: University of California Press, 1985.

Karl P. Savant and Hajo Hasenpflug, eds. *The New International Economic Order: Confrontation or Cooperation Between North and South?* Boulder Colo.: Westview Press, 1977.

Economics

Bela Balassa, Gerardo M. Bueno, Pedro-Pablo Kuczynski, and Mario Henrique Simonsen. *Toward Renewed Economic Growth in Latin America.* Washington, D.C.: Institute for International Economics, 1986.

William R. Cline. "External Debt, System Vulnerability, and Development." *Columbia Journal of Business,* Spring 1982.

Albert Fishlow. "Making Liberal Trade Policies Work in the 1980s." In *U.S. Foreign Policy and the Third World: Agenda 1982,* edited by Roger Hansen et al. Washington, D.C.: Overseas Development Council, 1982.

Albert Fishlow, Jean Carriere, and Sueo Sekiguchi. *Trade in Manufactured Products with Developing Countries: Reinforcing North-South Partnership.* Report of the Trilateral Task Force on North-South Trade of the Trilateral Commission, Triangle Papers no. 21. New York, 1981.

Overseas Development Council. U.S. Third World Policy Perspective Series. (Current volumes include *Adjustment Crisis in the Third World* [1984] and *Uncertain Future: Commercial Banks in the Third World* [1985]).

Riordan Roett. "Democracy and Debt in South America: A Continent's Dilemma." *Foreign Affairs* 62, no. 3 (1983).

———. "The Foreign Debt Crisis and the Process of Redemocratization in Latin America." Testimony before the Subcommittee on Western Hemisphere Affairs of the Committee on Foreign Affairs, House of Representatives, 98th Cong., 2d sess. Washington, D.C.: U.S. Government Printing Office, 1984.

G. Edward Schuh. *The U.S. and the Developing Countries: An Economic Perspective.* Washington, D.C.: National Planning Association, 1986.

Demography and Migration

Peter G. Brown and Henry Shue, eds. *The Border That Joins: Mexican Migrants and U.S. Responsibility.* Totowa, N.J.: Rowman and Littlefield, 1983.

Wayne Cornelius. "Mexican Migration to the United States." In *Mexico-U.S. Relations,* edited by Susan K. Purcell. New York: Academy of Political Science, 1981.

Sergio Diaz-Briquets. *Conflict in Central America: The Demograpic Dimension.* Washington, D.C.: Population Reference Bureau, 1986.

James Fallows. "Immigration: How It's Affecting Us." *Atlantic Monthly,* November 1983.

Kevin J. McCarthy and R. Burciaga Valdez. *Current and Future Effects of Mexican Immigration in California.* Santa Monica, Calif.: Rand Corporation, 1986.

Robert Pastor, ed. *Migration and Development in the Caribbean: The Unexplored Connection.* Boulder, Colo.: Westview Press, 1985.

Alejandro Portes. *Latin Journey: Cuban and Mexican Immigrants in the United States.* Berkeley and Los Angeles: University of California Press, 1985.

John Saunders, ed. *Population Growth in Latin America and U.S. National Security.* Winchester, Mass.: Allen and Unwin, 1986.

Michael S. Teitelbaum. "Migration and U.S.–Latin American Relations in the 1980s." In *The United States and Latin America in the 1980s,* edited by Kevin J. Middlebrook and Carlos Rico. Pittsburgh, Pa.: University of Pittsburgh Press, 1986.

———. *Latin Migration North: The Problem for U.S. Foreign Policy.* New York: Council on Foreign Relations, 1984.

Narcotics

Ethan A. Nadelmann. "International Drug Trafficking and U.S. Foreign Policy." *Washington Quarterly* 8, no. 4 (1985).

U. S. Congress. House. Select Committee on Narcotics Abuse and Control. *Latin American Study Missions Concerning International Narcotics Prob-*

lems. 99th Cong., 2d sess. Washington, D.C.: U.S. Government Printing Office, 1986.

William Walker III. *Drug Control in the Americas.* Albuquerque: University of New Mexico Press, 1981.

Fundamental Values, Human Rights, and Democracy

Peter D. Bell. "Democracy and Double Standards: The View from Chile." *World Policy Journal* 2, no. 4 (1985).

Margaret E. Crahan. "Human Rights and U.S. Foreign Policy: Realism versus Stereotypes." In *The United States and Latin America in the 1980s,* edited by Kevin J. Middlebrook and Carlos Rico. Pittsburgh, Pa.: University of Pittsburgh Press, 1986.

John Samuel Fitch. "A Human Rights Policy for Latin America in the 1980s." Discussion Paper no. 3, Center for Public Policy Research, University of Colorado, Boulder, June 15, 1982.

Joshua Muravchik. *The Uncertain Crusade: Jimmy Carter and the Dilemmas of Human Rights Policy.* Lanham, Md.: Hamilton Press, 1986.

Guillermo O'Donnell. "The United States, Latin America, Democracy: Variations on a Very Old Theme." In *The United States and Latin America in the 1980s,* edited by Kevin J. Middlebrook and Carlos Rico. Pittsburgh, Pa.: University of Pittsburgh Press, 1986.

Lars Schoultz. "The Carter Administration and Human Rights." In *Human Rights and Basic Needs in the Americas,* edited by Margaret E. Crahan. Washington, D.C.: Georgetown University Press, 1982.

Cyrus Vance. "The Human Rights Imperative." *Foreign Policy* 63 (Summer 1986).

Sandy Vogelgesang. *American Dream, Global Nightmare: The Dilemma of U.S. Human Rights Policy.* New York: Norton, 1980.

Howard J. Wiarda. "Can Democracy Be Exported? The Quest for Democracy in U.S.–Latin American Policy." In *The United States and Latin America in the 1980s,* edited by Kevin J. Middlebrook and Carlos Rico. Pittsburgh, Pa.: University of Pittsburgh Press, 1986.

———, ed. *Human Rights and U.S. Human Rights Policy: Theoretical Approaches and Some Perspectives on Latin America.* Washington, D.C.: American Enterprise Institute for Public Policy Research, 1982.

CHAPTER FOUR

The United States and Mexico: Uneasy Neighbors

I have gained immensely from criticisms of drafts of this chapter made by the following: Adolfo Aguilar, Gerardo Bueno, Jorge Castañeda, Wayne Cornelius, Ann Craig, Manuel García y Griego, Nathan Gardels, Brian Latell, Lorenzo Meyer, Mario Ojeda Gómez, Clark Reynolds, Carlos Rico, Alan Riding, David Ronfeldt, Luis Rubio, Peter H. Smith, Gabriel Székely, Cathryn Thorup, Sidney Weintraub, and Donald Wyman.

SOCIETY AND POLITICS

Frank Brandenburg. *The Making of Modern Mexico.* Englewood Cliffs, N.J.: Prentice-Hall, 1964.

Manuel Buendía. "En resumen: Una revolución vendida." In "Simposio: La crisis de Mexico." *Nexos* 68 (August 1986).

Wayne Cornelius. "Political Liberalization in the 1985 Election in Mexico." In *Elections and Democratization in Latin America, 1980–1985,* edited by Paul W. Drake and Eduardo Silva. San Diego: Center for Iberian and Latin American Studies, Center for U.S.-Mexican Studies, and Institute of the Americas, University of California, 1986.

Susan Eckstein. *The Poverty of Revolution: The State and the Urban Poor in Mexico.* Princeton, N.J.: Princeton University Press, 1977.

Nora Hamilton. *The Limits of State Autonomy: Post-Revolutionary Mexico.* Princeton, N.J.: Princeton University Press, 1982.

Roger D. Hansen. *The Politics of Mexican Development.* Baltimore: Johns Hopkins University Press, 1971.

Daniel Levy and Gabriel Székely. *Mexico: Paradoxes of Stability and Change.* Boulder, Colo.: Westview Press, 1983.

Kevin J. Middlebrook. "Political Liberalization in an Authoritarian Regime: The Case of Mexico." In *Elections and Democratization in Latin America, 1980–1985,* edited by Paul W. Drake and Eduardo Silva. San Diego: Center for Iberian and Latin American Studies, Center for U.S.-Mexican Studies, and Institute of the Americas, University of California, 1986.

Juan Molinár Horcasitas. "The Mexican Electoral System: Continuity by Change." In *Elections and Democratization in Latin America, 1980–1985,* edited by Paul W. Drake and Eduardo Silva. San Diego: Center for Iberian and Latin American Studies, Center for U.S.-Mexican Studies, and Institute of the Americas, University of California, 1986.

Octavio Paz. *The Labyrinth of Solitude.* New York: Grove Press, 1961.

———. *Tiempos Nublados.* Barcelona: Ed. Seix Barral, 1983.

Susan Kaufman Purcell. *The Mexican Profit-Sharing Decision: Politics in an Authoritarian Regime.* Berkeley and Los Angeles: University of California Press, 1975.

Susan Kaufman Purcell and John F. H. Purcell. "State and Society in Mexico: Must a Stable Polity Be Institutionalized?" *World Politics* 32, no. 2 (1980).

Jose Luis Reyna and Richard Weinert, eds. *Authoritarianism in Mexico.* Philadelphia: Institute for the Study of Human Issues, 1977.

Alan Riding. *Distant Neighbors: A Portrait of the Mexicans.* New York: Knopf, 1984.

David F. Ronfeldt, ed. *The Modern Mexican Military: A Reassessment.* Monograph Series, no. 15. San Diego: Center for U.S.-Mexican Studies, University of California, 1984.

Peter H. Smith. *Labyrinths of Power: Political Recruitment in Twentieth-Century Mexico.* Princeton, N.J.: Princeton University Press, 1979.

Dale Story. *Industry, the State, and Public Policy in Mexico.* Monograph no. 66. Austin: Institute of Latin American Studies, University of Texas, 1986.

Laurence Whitehead. "Por qué México es casi ingobernable." *Revista Mexicana de Sociología* 42 (January–March 1980).

ECONOMIC DEVELOPMENT

Sven W. Arndt, Donald R. Lessard, and Clark W. Reynolds, with the collaboration of Raúl Hinojosa. "Growth and Debt: Mexico and the United States in the Medium Term." Working Paper no. 5, Competing in a Changing World Economy Project. Washington, D.C.: American Enterprise Institute for Public Policy Research, September 1986.

José Ayala and Clemente Ruiz Durán. "Development and Crisis in Mexico: A Structuralist Approach." In *Latin American Political Economy: Financial Crisis and Political Change,* edited by Jonathan Hartlyn and Samuel A. Morley. Boulder, Colo.: Westview Press, 1986.

Bela Balassa. "Trade Policy in Mexico." *World Development* 11, no. 9 (1983).

Rolando Cordera and Carlos Tello. *México: La disputa por la nación.* México, D.F.: Siglo Veintiuno Editores, 1981.

Wayne Cornelius. "The Political Economy of Mexico under de la Madrid: Austerity, Routinized Crisis, and Nascent Recovery." *Mexican Studies* 1, no. 1 (1985).

———. "The Political Economy of Mexico under de la Madrid: The Crisis Deepens, 1985–1986." In *Latin America and Caribbean Contemporary Record,* vol. 5 (1985–86), edited by Abraham F. Lowenthal. New York: Holmes and Meier, 1987.

E.V.K. FitzGerald. "Stabilisation Policy in Mexico: The Fiscal Deficit and Macroeconomic Equilibrium, 1960–77." In *Inflation and Stabilisation in Latin America,* edited by Rosemary Thorp and Laurence Whitehead. New York: Holmes and Meier, 1979.

David R. Mares. "Explaining Choice of Development Strategies: Suggestions from Mexico, 1970–1982." *International Organization* 39, no. 4 (1985).

Roberto Newell G. and Luis Rubio F. *Mexico's Dilemma: The Political Origins of Economic Crisis.* Boulder, Colo.: Westview Press, 1984.

Clark W. Reynolds. *The Mexican Economy.* New Haven: Yale University Press, 1970.

———. "Why Mexico's 'Stabilizing Development' Was Actually Destabilizing (With Some Implications for the Future)." *World Development* 6, no. 7/8 (1978).

Clark W. Reynolds and Jaime Corredor. "The Effects of the Financial System on the Distribution of Income and Wealth in Mexico." *Food Research Institute Studies* 15, no. 1 (1976).

Leopoldo Solís. *Economic Policy Reform in Mexico: A Case Study for Developing Countries.* New York: Pergamon Press, 1981.

Dale Story. "Trade Politics in the Third World: A Case Study of the Mexican GATT Decision." *International Organization* 36, no. 4 (1982).

Gabriel Székely. *La economía política del petroleo en México, 1976–1982.* México, D.F.: El Colegio de México, 1983.

Carlos Tello. *La política económica en México, 1970–1976.* México, D.F.: Siglo Veintiuno Editores, 1979.

Raymond Vernon. *The Dilemma of Mexico's Development.* Cambridge: Harvard University Press, 1963.

René Villarreal. *La contrarevolución monetarista.* México, D.F.: Océano, 1984.

————. *El desequilíbrio externo en la industrialización de México, 1929–1975.* México, D.F.: Fondo de Cultura Económico, 1976.

————. "The Policy of Import Substitution Industrialization, 1929–1975." In *Authoritarianism in Mexico,* edited by Jose Luis Reyna and Richard Weinert. Philadelphia: Institute for the Study of Human Issues, 1977.

Laurence Whitehead. "Mexico from Bust to Boom: A Political Evaluation of the 1976–79 Stabilisation Programme." *World Development* 8, no. 11 (1980).

Donald L. Wyman, ed. *Mexico's Economic Crisis: Challenges and Opportunities.* Monograph Series, no. 12. San Diego: Center for U.S.-Mexico Studies, University of California, 1983.

U.S.-MEXICO RELATIONS

General

Jorge Castañeda. "Special Problems and a Not-So-Special Relationship: Mexican Foreign Policy and the United States." In *Mexico Today,* edited by Tommie Sue Montgomery. Philadelphia: Institute for the Study of Human Issues, 1982.

Howard F. Cline. *The United States and Mexico.* New York: Atheneum, 1971.

Guy F. Erb and Cathryn Thorup. *U.S.-Mexican Relations: The Issues Ahead.* Paper no. 35. Washington, D.C.: Overseas Development Council, November 1984.

George W. Grayson. *The United States and Mexico: Patterns of Influences.* New York: Praeger Special Studies, 1984.

Robert H. McBride, ed. *Mexico and the United States: Energy, Trade, Investment, Immigration, Tourism.* Englewood Cliffs, N.J.: Prentice-Hall, 1981.

Richard A. Nuccio. "The Redefinition of U.S.-Mexican Relations, 1977–1980." Paper presented for the CIDE seminar, Mexico City, July 1980.

Octavio Paz. "Mexico and the United States." *New Yorker,* September 17, 1979.

Susan Kaufman Purcell, ed. *Mexico–United States Relations.* New York: Academy of Political Science, 1981.

————. "Mexico-U.S. Relations: Big Initiatives Can Cause Big Problems." *Foreign Affairs* 60, no. 2 (1981–82).

Clark W. Reynolds and Carlos Tello, eds. *U.S.-Mexico Relations: Economic and Social Aspects.* Stanford, Calif.: Stanford University Press, 1983.

U.S. Congress. House. Committee on Foreign Affairs. *Twenty-Fourth Mexico-U.S. Interparliamentary Conference, Washington, D.C., May 1984. Background Materials for U.S. Delegation Use.* 98 Cong., 2d sess.

————. *Twenty-Fifth Mexico-U.S. Interparliamentary Conference, Washington, D.C., May 1985. Background Materials for U.S. Delegation Use.* 99th Cong., 1st sess.

Carlos Vásquez and Manuel García y Griego, eds. *Mexico-U.S. Relations: Conflict and Convergence.* Berkeley and Los Angeles: University of California Press, 1983.

Laurence Whitehead. "Mexico and the United States: Deterioro Sin Fin?" In *Latin America and Caribbean Contemporary Record,* vol. 5 (1985–86), edited by Abraham F. Lowenthal. New York: Holmes and Meier, 1987.

Josefina Zorada Vazquez and Lorenzo Meyer. *The United States and Mexico.* Chicago: University of Chicago Press, 1985.

Issues

THE BORDER REGION

Jorge Bustamante. "Migración interna e internacional y distribución del ingreso: La frontera norte de México." *Comercio Exterior* 34 (1984).

Lay James Gibson and Alfonso Corona Rentería, eds. *The U.S. and Mexico: Borderland Development and the National Economies.* Boulder, Colo.: Westview Press, 1985.

Stanley A. Ross, ed. *Views Across the Border: The United States and Mexico.* Albuquerque: University of New Mexico Press, 1978.

TRADE, INVESTMENT, AND FINANCE

Manuel Armendáriz E. and Eric Alvarez G. *A Mexican View of U.S. Protectionism.* Monograph no. 13. U.S.-Mexico Project. Washington, D.C.: Overseas Development Council, August 1982.

Douglas C. Bennett and Kenneth E. Sharpe. *Transnational Corporations versus the State: The Political Economy of the Mexican Auto Industry.* Princeton, N.J.: Princeton University Press, 1985.

Guy F. Erb. *An American View of Mexican Trade Policy.* Monograph no. 2. U.S.-Mexico Project. Washington, D.C.: Overseas Development Council, April 1982.

Rosario Green. "México: Crisis financiera y deuda externa." *Comercio Exterior* 33 (1983).

Joseph Kraft. *The Mexican Rescue.* New York: Group of Thirty, 1984.

Peggy B. Musgrave, ed. *Mexico and the United States: Studies in Economic Interaction.* Boulder, Colo.: Westview Press, 1985.

Andrew James Samet and Gary Clyde Hufbauer, *"Unfair" Trade Practices: A Mexican-American Drama.* Monograph no. 1. U.S.-Mexico Project. Washington, D.C.: Overseas Development Council, April 1982.

René Villarreal. "Proteccionismo industrial, fomento a las exportaciones y el nuevo GATT de los 80s." *Economista Mexicana* 14 (January–February 1980).

Sidney Weintraub. *Free Trade between Mexico and the United States.* Washington, D.C.: Brookings Institution, 1984.

ENERGY

Heberto Castillo. *Pemex sí, peusa no.* México, D.F.: CISA, 1981.

Richard R. Fagen and Henry R. Nau. "Mexican Gas: The Northern Connection." In *Capitalism and the State in U.S.-Latin American Relations,* edited by Richard Fagen. Stanford, Calif.: Stanford University Press, 1979.

George Grayson. *The Politics of Mexican Oil.* Pittsburgh, Pa.: University of Pittsburgh Press, 1980.

Lorenzo Meyer. *México y los Estados Unidos en el conflicto petrolero, 1917–1942.* México, D.F.: El Colegio de México, 1972.

Kevin J. Middlebrook. "Energy Security in U.S.-Mexican Relations." In *Energy and Security,* edited by David A. Deese and Joseph S. Nye. Cambridge, Mass.: Ballinger Publishing, 1980.

David Ronfeldt, Richard Nehring, and Arturo Gandara. *Mexico's Petroleum and U.S. Policy: Implications for the 1980s.* Santa Monica, Calif.: Rand Corporation, June 1980.

Edward Williams. *The Rebirth of the Mexican Petroleum Industry.* Boston: Lexington Books, 1979.

IMMIGRATION AND EMPLOYMENT

Jorge Bustamante. *U.S. Immigration Policy: A Mexican Perspective on President Reagan's Proposal.* Washington, D.C.: Overseas Development Council, 1982.

Wayne Cornelius. *Mexican Migration to the United States: Causes, Consequences, and U.S. Responses.* Boston: Center for International Studies, Massachusetts Institute of Technology, July 1978.

Ann Craig. *Mexican Immigration: Changing Terms of the Debate in the United States and Mexico.* Research Report no. 4. San Diego: Center for U.S.-Mexican Studies, University of California, 1981.

Mary M. Kritz, Charles B. Keely, and Silvano Tomasi, eds. *Global Trends in Migration: Theory and Research on International Population Movements.* New York: Center for Migration Studies, 1981.

Clark W. Reynolds. "The United States-Mexican Labor Market of the Future." *Food Research Institute Studies* 18, no. 3 (1982).

Mitchell A. Seligson and Edward Williams. *Maquiladoras and Migration: Workers in the Mexico-United States Border Industrialization Program.* Austin: Mexico-United States Border Research Program, University of Texas, 1981.

Michael S. Teitelbaum. *Latin Migration North: The Problem for U.S. Foreign Policy.* New York: Council on Foreign Relations, 1985.

U.S. Congress. House. Select Commission on Immigration and Refugee Policy. *U.S. Immigration Policy and the National Interest.* Reprinted by

House and Senate, Committees on the Judiciary, Joint Committee Print. 97th Cong., 1st sess. August 1981.

NARCOTICS

Richard B. Craig. "Illicit Drug Traffic and U.S.-Latin American Relations." *Washington Quarterly* 8, no. 4 (1985).

Rensselaer W. Lee III. "The Latin American Drug Connection." *Foreign Policy* 61 (Winter 1985–86).

Ethan A. Nadelmann. "International Drug Trafficking and U.S. Foreign Policy." *Washington Quarterly* 8, no. 4 (1985).

INTERNATIONAL RELATIONS AND FOREIGN POLICY

Jorge Castañeda. "Revolution and Foreign Policy: Mexico's Experience." *Political Science Quarterly* 78, no. 3 (1963).

Jorge G. Castañeda. "Don't Corner Mexico." *Foreign Policy* 60 (Fall 1985).

Jorge I. Dominguez, ed. *Mexico's Political Economy: Challenges at Home and Abroad*. Beverly Hills, Calif.: Sage Publications, 1982.

Richard R. Fagen and Olga Pellicer, eds. *The Future of Central America: Policy Choices for the U.S. and Mexico*. Stanford, Calif.: Stanford University Press, 1983.

René Herrera Zuniga and Mario Ojeda Gómez. "Mexican Foreign Policy and Central America." In *Central America: International Dimensions of the Crisis,* edited by Richard E. Feinberg. New York: Holmes and Meier, 1982.

Mario Ojeda Gómez. *Alcances y límites de la política exterior de México*. México, D.F.: El Colegio de México, 1976.

Olga Pellicer, ed. *La política exterior de México: Desafios en los ochenta*. México, D.F.: Centro de investigación y docencia económicas, 1983.

PROSPECTS FOR THE FUTURE

Roderic A. Camp, ed. *Mexican Trends: The Next Five Years*. Washington, D.C.: Department of State, 1985.

Jorge G. Castañeda. "Mexico at the Brink." *Foreign Affairs* 64, no. 2 (1985–86).

———. "Mexico's Coming Challenges." *Foreign Policy* 64 (Fall 1986).

Brian Latell. *Mexico at the Crossroads: The Many Crises of the Political System*. Stanford, Calif.: Hoover Institute, June 1986.

Jimmy W. Wheeler et al. *The Future of Mexico*. New York: Hudson Institute, 1981.

GENERAL SOURCES

For current developments in Mexico and U.S.-Mexico relations, see the periodic publications of the Center for U.S.-Mexico Studies at the University of California, San Diego, and of the U.S.-Mexico Project at the Overseas Development Council. Mexican perspectives are available in the annual volumes on *México–Estados Unidos,* published since 1982 by El Colegio de México. Mexican political currents are most easily followed in *Proceso* and *Razones,* two weekly news magazines. For economic matters, the best source is *Comercio Exterior.*

CHAPTER FIVE
The United States and Brazil: Managing Conflict

A previous version of chapter 5 of this volume appeared in *Headline Series* 279, entitled *Brazil and the United States* (1986), written by Dr. Abraham F. Lowenthal and copyrighted and published by the Foreign Policy Association (FPA), 729 Seventh Avenue, New York, N.Y. 10019. This material appears with the permission of the FPA.

I gratefully acknowledge Diego Asencio, Sergio Correa da Costa, John Crimmins, Stephen Dachi, David Fleischer, Jeff Frieden, Elio Gaspari, Margaret Daly Hayes, Mónica Hirst, Helio Jaguaribe, Peter Knight, Celso Lafer, Bolivar Lamounier, Marcilio Marques Moreira, Paulo Sérgio Pinheiro, Rubens Ricupero, Ronaldo Sardenberg, Sally Shelton-Colby, Alexander Watson, and Robert Wesson, all of whom provided helpful criticisms of drafts of this chapter.

SOCIETY AND POLITICS

Luiz Bresser Pereira. *Pactos políticos: Do populismo a redemocratizacão.* São Paulo: Editora Brasiliense, 1985.

E. Bradford Burns. *A History of Brazil.* New York: Columbia University Press, 1970.

———. *Nationalism in Brazil: An Historical Survey.* New York: Praeger, 1968.

Aspásia Camargo and Walder de Góes. *O drama da sucessão e a crise do regime.* Rio de Janeiro: Editora Nova Fronteira, 1984.

Fernando H. Cardoso. "O papel dos empresários no processo de transicão: O caso Brasileiro." *Dados* 26 (1983).

Joan R. Dassin. "The Brazilian Press and the Politics of Abertura." *Journal of Inter-American Studies and World Affairs* 26, no. 3 (1984).

Albert Fishlow. "A Tale of Two Presidents: The Political Economy of the Brazilian Adjustment to the Oil Shocks." Working Paper, Department of Economics, University of California, Berkeley, 1986.

David Fleischer. "Brazil at the Crossroads: The Elections of 1982 and 1985." In *Elections and Democratization in Latin America, 1980–1985,* edited by Paul W. Drake and Eduardo Silva. San Diego: Center for Iberian and Latin American Studies, Center for U.S.-Mexican Studies, and Institute of the Americas, University of California, 1986.

———. "Constitutional and Electoral Engineering in Brazil: A Double-Edged Sword, 1964–1982." *Inter-American Economic Affairs* 37, no. 4 (1984).

Peter Flynn. "Brazil: The Politics of the Cruzado Plan." *Third World Quarterly* 8, no. 4 (1986).

Barbara Freitag et al. *Nova república: Um balance.* São Paulo: L and PM Editores, 1986.

Sylvia Anne Hewlett. *The Cruel Dilemmas of Development: Twentieth-Century Brazil.* New York: Basic Books, 1980.

Helio Jaguaribe et al. *Brasil: Sociedade democrática.* Rio de Janeiro: José Olympio Editora, 1985.

————. *Sociedad y política en la actualidad brasileña.* Buenos Aires: Editor Latinoamericano, 1985.

Bolívar Lamounier and José Eduardo Faria, eds. *O futuro da abertura: Um debate.* São Paulo: Cortez Editora, 1981.

Scott Mainwaring. *The Catholic Church and Politics in Brazil, 1916–1985.* Stanford, Calif.: Stanford University Press, 1986.

————. "The Transition to Democracy in Brazil." Working Paper no. 66, Helen Kellog Institute for International Studies, University of Notre Dame, Notre Dame, Ind., 1986.

Peter McDonough. *Power and Ideology in Brazil.* Princeton, N.J.: Princeton University Press, 1981.

Política e estratégia 2, no. 3 (1984).

Riordan Roett. *Brazil: Politics in a Patrimonial Society.* 4th ed. New York: Praeger, 1984.

————, ed. *Brazil in the Seventies.* Washington, D.C.: American Enterprise Institute for Public Policy Research, 1976.

————, ed. *Brazil in the Sixties.* Nashville, Tenn.: Vanderbilt University, 1972.

Emir Sader, ed. *E agora, PT? Caráter e identidade.* São Paulo: Editora Brasiliense, 1986.

José Sarney. "Brazil: A President's Story." *Foreign Affairs* 65, no. 1 (1986).

Ronald M. Schneider. *The Political System of Brazil: Emergence of a "Modernizing Authoritarian Regime."* New York: Columbia University Press, 1971.

Simon Schwartzman. *Bases do autoritarismo brasileiro.* 2d ed. Rio de Janeiro: Editora Campus, 1982.

Thomas E. Skidmore. *Politics in Brazil, 1930–1964.* New York: Oxford University Press, 1967.

Glaucio Ary Dillon Soares. "Elections and the Redemocratization of Brazil." In *Elections and Democratization in Latin America, 1980–1985,* edited by Paul W. Drake and Eduardo Silva. San Diego: Center for Iberian and Latin American Studies, Center for U.S.-Mexican Studies, and Institute of the Americas, University of California, 1986.

Bernard Sorj and Maria Hermínia T. de Almeida, eds. *Sociedade e política no Brasil pós-64.* São Paulo: Editora Brasiliense, 1983.

Alfred Stepan. *The Military in Politics: Changing Patterns in Brazil.* Princeton, N.J.: Princeton University Press, 1971.

————, ed. *Authoritarian Brazil: Origins, Policy, and Future.* New Haven: Yale University Press, 1973.

Michael Wallerstein. "The Collapse of Democracy in Brazil: Its Economic Determinants." *Latin American Research Review* 15, no. 3 (1980).

Francisco Weffort. *Por que democracia?* São Paulo: Editora Brasiliense, 1984.

Robert Wesson and David V. Fleischer. *Brazil in Transition.* New York: Praeger, 1983.

ECONOMICS

Persio Arida et al. *Inflacão zero: Brasil, Argentina, Israel.* Rio de Janeiro: Editora Paz e Terra, 1986.

Persió Arida, ed. *Dívida externa, recessão e ajuste estrutural: O Brasil diante da crise.* Rio de Janeiro: Editora Paz e Terra, 1982.

Edmar Bacha. "Choques externos e perspectivas de crescimento: O caso do Brasil, 1973–89." *Pesquisa e Planejamento Economico* 14, no. 3. (1984).

Werner Baer. *The Brazilian Economy: Growth and Development.* New York: Praeger, 1983.

Joel Bergsman. *Brazil: Industrialization and Trade Policies.* London: Oxford University Press, 1970.

Thomas C. Bruneau and Philippe Faucher, eds. *Authoritarian Capitalism: Brazil's Contemporary Economic and Political Development.* Boulder, Colo.: Westview Press, 1981.

Maria da Conceicão Tavares and Mauricio Dias David, eds. *A economia política da crise: Problemas e impasses da política economica Brasileira.* Rio de Janeiro: Co-Edicão, 1982.

José Roberto Mendonca de Barros and Douglas H. Graham. "The Brazilian Economic Miracle Revisited: Private and Public Sector Initiative in a Market Economy." *Latin American Research Review* 13, no. 2 (1978).

Peter Evans. *Dependent Development: The Alliance of Multinational, State, and Local Capital in Brazil.* Princeton, N.J.: Princeton University Press, 1979.

Albert Fishlow. "Brazilian Development in Long-Term Perspective." *American Economic Review* 70, no. 2 (1980).

———. "Origins and Consequences of Import Substitution in Brazil." In *International Economics and Development,* edited by Luis Eugenio Di Marco. New York: Academic Press, 1972.

Jeff Freiden. "The Brazilian Borrowing Experience: From Miracle to Debacle and Back." *Latin American Research Review* 22, no. 1 (1987).

Celso Furtado. *Analise do modelo Brasileiro.* Rio de Janeiro: Editora Civilizacão Brasileira, 1972.

———. *A Fantasia Organizada.* Rio de Janeiro: Editora Paz e Terra, 1985.

———. *No to Recession and Unemployment: An Examination of the Brazilian Economic Crisis.* London: Foundation for Social and Economic Research, 1984.

———. "Rescuing Brazil, Reversing Recession." *Third World Quarterly* 6, no. 3 (1984).

Peter Knight. "Brazilian Socioeconomic Development: Issues for the Eighties." *World Development* 9, no. 11/12 (1981).

Carlos Geraldo Langoni. *A crise do desenvolvimento: Uma estratágia para o futuro.* Rio de Janeiro: José Olympio Editora, 1985.

Pedro J. Malán and Regis Bonelli. "The Brazilian Economy in the Seventies: Old and New Developments." *World Development* 5, no. 1/2 (1977).

Marcilio Marques Moreira. *The Brazilian Quandary.* New York: Priority Press, 1986.

Samuel Morley and Gordon W. Smith. "The Choice of Technology: Multinational Firms in Brazil." *Economic Development and Cultural Change* 25, no. 2 (1977).

Richard S. Newfarmer. "TNC Takeovers in Brazil: The Uneven Distribution of Benefits in the Market for Firms." *World Development* 7, no. 1 (1979).

Paulo Nogueira Baptista, Jr. *Mito e realidade na dívida externa brasileira.* Rio de Janeiro: Editora Paz e Terra, 1983.

Jorge Salazar-Carillo and Roberto Fendt, Jr. *The Brazilian Economy in the Eighties.* New York: Pergamon Press, 1985.

Thomas J. Trebat. *Brazil's State-Owned Enterprises: A Case Study of the State as Entrepreneur.* New York: Cambridge University Press, 1983.

Carlos von Doellinger and Leonardo C. Cavalcanti. *Empresas multinacionais na industria Brasileira.* Rio de Janeiro: IPEA/INPES, Colecão Relatorios de Pesquisa, no. 29, 1975.

John D. Wirth. *The Politics of Brazilian Development.* Stanford, Calif.: Stanford University Press, 1970.

BRAZILIAN FOREIGN POLICY

Encontro do política externa: Brasílla, 28 e 29 de novembro de 1984. Brasílla: Câmara dos Deputados, Coordenacão de Publicacões, 1985.

Norman Gall. "Atoms for Brazil, Dangers for All." *Foreign Policy* 23 (Summer 1976).

Celso Lafer. *O Brasil e a crise mundial.* São Paulo: Editora Perspectiva, 1984.

Política e estratégia. 3, no. 2 (1985).

Janio Quadros. "Brazil's New Foreign Policy." *Foreign Affairs* 40, no. 1 (1961).

Riordan Roett. "Brazil and the Inter-American System." In *The Future of the Inter-American System,* edited by Tom J. Farer. New York: Praeger, 1979.

Ronald M. Schneider. *Brazil: Foreign Policy of a Future World Power.* Boulder, Colo.: Westview Press, 1976.

Wayne A. Selcher. *Brazil in the Global Power Systems.* Occasional Paper Series. Washington, D.C.: Center of Brazilian Studies, School of Advanced International Studies, Johns Hopkins University, 1980.

———. *Brazil's Multilateral Relations: Between First and Third Worlds.* Boulder, Colo.: Westview Press, 1978.

———, *Brazil in the International System: The Rise of a Middle Power.* Boulder, Colo.: Westview Press, 1981.

U.S.-BRAZIL RELATIONS

Moniz Bandeira. *Presenca dos Estados Unidos no Brasil.* Rio de Janeiro: Editora Civilizacão Brasileira, 1973.

C. Fred Bergsten. "Brazil and the United States in the World Economy: A New Mode of Relations." *Vital Speeches of the Day,* February 15, 1978.

Jan K. Black. *United States Penetration of Brazil.* Philadelphia: University of Pennsylvania Press, 1977.

Robert J. Branco. *The United States and Brazil: Opening a New Dialogue.* Washington, D.C.: National Defense University Press, 1984.

Center for Brazilian Studies, Johns Hopkins University. *Report of the Commission on United States–Brazilian Relations.* Washington, D.C., 1980.

Economic Commission for Latin American and the Caribbean. *Trade Relations between Brazil and the United States.* Brasilia, 1985.

Albert Fishlow. "Flying Down to Rio." *Foreign Affairs* 57, no. 2 (1978–79).

———. "The United States and Brazil: The Case of the Missing Relationship." *Foreign Affairs* 60, no. 4 (1982).

Roger Fontaine. *Brazil and the United States: Toward a Maturing Relationship.* Washington, D.C.: American Enterprise Institute for Public Policy Research, 1974.

———. "The End of a Beautiful Relationship." *Foreign Policy* 28 (Fall 1977).

Stanley E. Hilton. *Brazil and the Great Powers, 1930–1939.* Austin: University of Texas Press, 1975.

———. "The United States, Brazil, and the Cold War." *Journal of American History* 68, no. 3 (1981).

Monica Hirst, ed. *Brasil–Estados Unidos na transição democratica.* Rio de Janeiro: Editora Paz e Terra, 1985.

Carlos Estevam Martins. "Brazil and the United States from the 1960s to the 1970s." In *Latin America and the United States: The Changing Political Realities,* edited by Julio Cotler and Richard R. Fagen. Stanford, Calif.: Stanford University Press, 1974.

Frank D. McCann, Jr. *The Brazilian-American Alliance, 1937–1945.* Princeton, N.J.: Princeton University Press, 1973.

Phyllis R. Parker. *Brazil and the Quiet Intervention, 1964.* Austin: University of Texas Press, 1979.

Riordan Roett. *The Politics of Foreign Aid in the Brazilian Northeast.* Nashville, Tenn.: Vanderbilt University, 1972.

Robert Wesson. *The United States and Brazil: Limits of Influence.* New York: Praeger, 1981.

GENERAL SOURCES

A handy way to keep up on Brazil is through *InfoBrazil,* the monthly newsletter published by the Center for Brazilian Studies, Johns Hopkins School of Advanced International Studies, Washington, D.C. Major Brazilian sources include *Veja* (a weekly news magazine); *Exame* (a monthly business-oriented magazine); the studies on economic matters put out by the Getulio Vargas Foundation; the social and political studies issued by such research centers as CEBRAP, IUPERJ, IDESP, and CEDEC. The Instituto Brasileiro de Geografia e Estatística (IBGE) issues excellent reports summarizing Brazilian socioeconomic data.

CHAPTER SIX

The United States and the Caribbean Basin: The Politics of National Insecurity

I gratefully acknowledge Richard Newfarmer and Edelberto Torres-Rivas, who provided criticisms on a draft of this chapter.

THE CARIBBEAN

Society and Politics

Cole Blasier and Carmelo Mesa-Lago, eds. *Cuba in the World,* Pittsburgh, Pa.: University of Pittsburgh Press, 1979.

Juan Manuel Garcia Passalacqua. *Puerto Rico: Equality and Freedom at Issue.* New York: Praeger, 1984.

Edward Gonzalez and David Ronfeldt. *Castro, Cuba, and the World.* Santa Monica, Calif.: Rand Corporation, 1986.

————. *Post-Revolutionary Cuba in a Changing World.* Santa Monica, Calif.: Rand Corporation, 1975.

Franklin W. Knight. *The Caribbean: The Genesis of a Fragmented Nationalism.* New York: Oxford University Press, 1978.

Barry Levine, ed. *The New Cuban Presence in the Caribbean.* Boulder, Colo.: Westview Press, 1983.

Gordon K. Lewis. *The Growth of the Modern West Indies.* New York: Monthly Review Press, 1968.

David Lowenthal. *West Indian Societies.* London: Oxford University Press, 1972.

Sidney W. Mintz. *Caribbean Transformations.* Hawthorne, N.Y.: Aldine Publishing, 1974.

Sidney W. Mintz and Sally Price, eds. *Focus: Caribbean.* Pamphlet Series. Washington, D.C.: Woodrow Wilson International Center for Scholars, 1984.

Arturo Morales Carrión. *Puerto Rico: A Political and Cultural History.* New York: W. W. Norton, 1983.

Vidiadhar Surajrased Naipaul. *The Middle Passage: Impressions of Five Societies: British, French, and Dutch in the West Indies and South America.* New York: Macmillan, 1963.

Kenneth E. Sharpe. *Peasant Politics: Struggle in a Dominican Village.* Baltimore: Johns Hopkins University Press, 1977.

Archibald W. Singham. *The Hero and the Crowd in a Colonial Polity.* New Haven: Yale University Press, 1968.

M. G. Smith. *The Plural Society in the British West Indies.* Berkeley and Los Angeles: University of California Press, 1965.

Carl Stone. *Democracy and Clientelism in Jamaica.* New Brunswick, N.J.: Transaction Books, 1980.

Eric Williams. *From Columbus to Castro: The History of the Caribbean, 1492–1969.* London: André Deutsch, 1970.

Economics

George L. Beckford. *Persistent Poverty: Underdevelopment in Plantation Regions of the Third World.* New York: Oxford University Press, 1972.

William G. Demas. *The Economics of Development in Small Countries.* Montreal: McGill University Press, 1965.

Carmelo Mesa-Lago. *The Economy of Socialist Cuba.* Pittsburgh, Pa.: University of Pittsburgh Press, 1982.

Ransford W. Palmer. *Problems of Development in Beautiful Countries: Perspectives on the Caribbean.* Lanham, Md.: North-South Publishing, 1984.

Robert Pastor, ed. *Migration and Development in the Caribbean: The Unexplored Connection.* Boulder, Colo.: Westview Press, 1985.

U.S.-Caribbean Relations

HISTORY

Bruce Calder. *The Impact of Intervention: The Dominican Republic During the U.S. Occupation of 1916–1924.* Austin: University of Texas Press, 1984.

Gordon Connell-Smith. "The Grenada Invasion in a Historical Perspective: From Monroe to Reagan," *Third World Quarterly* 6, no. 2 (1984).

Jorge I. Dominguez. *Cuba: Order and Revolution.* Cambridge: Harvard University Press, 1978.

Virginia R. Dominguez. *From Neighbor to Stranger: The Dilemma of Caribbean Peoples in the United States.* New Haven: Antilles Research Program at Yale, 1975.

Piero Gleijeses. *The Dominican Crisis: The 1965 Constitutionalist Revolt and American Intervention.* Baltimore: Johns Hopkins University Press, 1978.

Lester D. Langley. *The United States and the Caribbean, 1900–1970.* Athens: University of Georgia Press, 1980.

Abraham F. Lowenthal. *The Dominican Intervention.* Cambridge: Harvard University Press, 1972.

Dana G. Munro. *Intervention and Dollar Diplomacy in the Caribbean, 1900–1921.* Princeton, N.J.: Princeton University Press, 1964.

———. *The United States and the Caribbean Republics, 1921–1933.* Princeton, N.J.: Princeton University Press, 1974.

Whitney T. Perkins. *Constraint of Empire: The United States and Caribbean Inverventions.* Westport, Conn.: Greenwood Press, 1981.

Richard E. Welch, Jr. *Response to Revolution: The U.S. and the Cuban Revolution, 1959–1961.* Chapel Hill: University of North Carolina Press, 1985.

Sumner Welles. *Naboth's Vineyard: The Dominican Republic, 1844–1924.* New York: Payson and Clarke, 1928.

CURRENT ISSUES AND POLICY

Michael R. Adams. "Coast Guarding the Caribbean." U.S. Naval Institute, *Proceedings,* August 1982.

Robert Bach, "Caribbean Migration: Causes and Consequences" *Migration Today* 10, no. 5 (1982).

Roy S. Bryce-Laporte and Dolores M. Mortimer, eds. *Caribbean Immigration to the United States*. Washington, D.C.: Research Institute on Immigration and Ethnic Studies, Smithsonian Institution, 1983.

Jorge I. Dominguez and Virginia R. Dominiguez. *The Caribbean: Its Implications for the United States*. Headline Series no. 253. New York: Foreign Policy Association, 1981.

H. Michael Erisman, ed. *The Caribbean Challenge: U.S. Policy in a Volatile Region*. Boulder, Colo.: Westview Press, 1984.

Mark Falcoff. "How to Think about Cuba." *Washington Quarterly* 6, no. 2 (1983).

Edward Gonzalez. *A Strategy for Dealing with Cuba in the 1980s*. Santa Monica, Calif.: Rand Corporation, 1982.

James R. Greene and Brent Scowcroft, eds. *Western Interests and U.S. Policy Options in the Caribbean Basin: Report of the Atlantic Council's Working Group on the Caribbean Basin*. Boston: Oelgeschlager, Gunn and Hain, 1984.

R. Bruce McColm. "Central America and the Caribbean: The Larger Scenario." *Strategic Review*, Summer 1983.

John B. Martin, *U.S. Policy in the Caribbean*. Boulder, Colo.: Westview Press, 1978.

Reid Reading and Alan Adelman, eds. *Confrontation in the Caribbean Basin: International Perspectives on Security, Sovereignty, and Survival*. Pittsburgh, Pa.: Center for Latin American Studies, University Center for International Studies, University of Pittsburgh, 1984.

David F. Ronfeldt. *Geopolitics, Security, and U.S. Strategy in the Caribbean Basin*. Santa Monica, Calif.: Rand Corporation, 1983.

Jiri Valenta. *Soviet Strategy in the Caribbean Basin: The Grenada Case Study*. Washington, D.C.: Kennan Institute for Advanced Russian Studies, The Wilson Center, 1984.

———. "The USSR, Cuba, and the Crisis in Central America." *Orbis* 25, no. 3 (1981).

Jiri Valenta and Virginia Valenta. "Leninism in Grenada." *Problems of Communism* 33 (July–August 1984).

CENTRAL AMERICA

Society and Politics

Enrique Baloyra, *El Salvador in Transition*. Chapel Hill: University of North Carolina Press, 1982.

John Booth. *The End and the Beginning: The Nicaraguan Revolution*. Boulder, Colo.: Westview Press, 1982.

William H. Durham. *Scarcity and Survival in Central America: Ecological Origins of the Soccer War*. Stanford, Calif.: Stanford University Press, 1979.

Wolf Grabendorff et al. *Political Change in Central America: Internal and External Dimensions*. Boulder, Colo.: Westview Press, 1984.

William LeoGrande and Carla Anne Robbins. "Oligarchs and Officers: The Crisis in El Salvador." *Foreign Affairs* 58, no. 5 (1980).

Richard Millett. *Guardians of the Dynasty: A History of the U.S. Created Guardia Nacional de Nicaragua and the Somoza Family.* Maryknoll, N.Y.: Orbis Books, 1977.

David Nolan. *FSLN: The Ideology of the Sandinistas and the Nicaraguan Revolution.* Miami: University of Miami Press, 1985.

Steve C. Ropp and James A. Morris, eds. *Central America: Crisis and Adaption.* Albuquerque: University of New Mexico Press, 1984.

Edelberto Torres-Rivas. *Crisis del poder en Centroamerica.* San José, Costa Rica: EDUCA, 1981.

Howard J. Wiarda, ed. *Politics and Social Change in Latin America: The Distinct Tradition.* Amherst: University of Massachusetts Press, 1982.

Ralph Lee Woodward, Jr. *Central America: A Nation Divided,* 2d ed. New York: Oxford University Press, 1985.

Economics

William R. Cline and Enrique Delgado, eds. *Economic Integration in Central America.* Washington, D.C.: Brookings Institution, 1978.

Juan M. del Aguila. "The Limits of Reform Development in Contemporary Costa Rica." *Journal of Inter-American Studies and World Affairs* 24, no. 3 (1982).

Roger D. Hansen. *Central America: Regional Integration and Economic Development.* Washington, D.C.: National Planning Association, 1967.

U.S.-Central American Relations

HISTORY

Richard E. Feinberg, ed. *Central America: International Dimensions of the Crisis.* New York: Holmes and Meier, 1982.

Walter LaFeber. *Inevitable Revolutions: The United States in Central America.* New York: W. W. Norton, 1983.

Henry L. Stimson. *American Policy in Nicaragua.* New York: Charles Scribner's Sons, 1927.

CURRENT ISSUES AND POLICY

Morris J. Blachman, William M. LeoGrande, and Kenneth E. Sharpe, eds. *Confronting Revolution: Security through Diplomacy in Central America.* New York: Pantheon Books, 1986.

Raymond Bonner. *Weakness and Deceit: U.S. Policy and El Salvador.* New York: Times Books, 1984.

James Chace. *Endless War: How We Got Involved in Central America and What Can Be Done.* New York: Vintage Books, 1984.

Shirley Christian. *Nicaragua: Revolution in the Family.* New York: Random House, 1985.

Kenneth M. Coleman and George C. Herring, eds. *The Central American Crisis and the Failure of U.S. Policy.* Wilmington, Del.: Scholarly Resources, 1985.

Christopher Dickey. *With the Contras: A Reporter in the Wilds of Nicaragua.* New York: Simon and Schuster, 1985.

Richard R. Fagen and Olga Pellicer, eds. *The Future of Central America:*

Policy Choices for the U.S. and Mexico. Stanford, Calif.: Stanford University Press, 1983.

Doug Hellinger. *Supporting Central American and Caribbean Development: A Critique of the Caribbean Basin Initiative and an Alternative Regional Assistance Plan.* Washington, D.C.: The Development Group for Alternative Policies, August 1983.

Robert S. Leiken, ed. *Central America: Anatomy of Conflict.* New York: Pergamon Press, 1984.

William M. LeoGrande. "Through the Looking Glass: The Report of the National Bipartisan Commission on Central America." *World Policy Journal* 1, no. 2 (1984).

Thomas H. Moorer and Georges A. Fauriol. *Caribbean Basin Security.* Washington, D.C.: The Washington Papers/104, CSIS, 1984.

Report of the National Bipartisan Commission on Central America. Washington, D.C.: U.S. Government Printing Office, January 1984.

Laurence Whitehead. "Explaining Washington's Central American Policies." *Journal of Latin American Studies* 15 (November 1983).

Howard J. Wiarda, ed. *Rift and Revolution: The Central American Imbroglio.* Washington, D.C.: American Enterprise Institute for Public Policy Research, 1984.

GENERAL SOURCES

The following serial publications are helpful for keeping up with current developments in the Caribbean and Central America.

Caribbean Contact (monthly).

Caribbean Review (quarterly from Florida International University).

Caribbean Studies (quarterly from the University of Puerto Rico).

Cuban Studies/Estudios Cubanos (quarterly from the University of Pittsburgh).

Social and Economic Studies (quarterly from the University of the West Indies).

Latin American Monitor: Central America (monthly).

Update Latin America (bi-monthly).

Pensamiento Propio (Nicaraguan monthly published by the Instituto de Investigaciones Económicas y Sociales, Managua).

CHAPTER SEVEN

From Insecurity to *Confianza:* Forging a New U.S. Policy

In preparing this chapter, I have drawn not only on the sources previously noted and on those listed below, but also on a number of unpublished papers and memoranda prepared for the Inter-American Dialogue; the project on "The Future of Collective Security in the Americas" organized by the World Peace Foundation; the conference on "The Future of Inter-American Relations" held at the Institute of the Americas on November 19–20, 1984; and the consultation on "Reinforcing Democracy in the Americas" held at the Carter Center of Emory University on November 17–18, 1986.

David R. Ayón and Ricardo Anzaldua Montoya. "Latinos and U.S. Policy toward Latin America." In *Latin America and Caribbean Contemporary Record,* vol. 5 (1985–86), edited by Abraham F. Lowenthal. New York: Holmes and Meier, 1987.

Bela Balassa, Gerardo M. Bueno, Pedro-Pablo Kuczynski, and Mario Henrique Simonsen. *Toward Renewed Economic Growth in Latin America.* Washington, D.C.: Institute for International Economics, 1986.

I. M. Destler. *American Trade Politics: System under Stress.* Washington, D.C. and New York: Institute for International Economics and the Twentieth Century Fund, 1986.

Richard E. Feinberg and contributors. *Between Two Worlds: The World Bank's Next Decade.* Washington, D.C.: Overseas Development Council, 1986.

Inter-American Dialogue. *Rebuilding Cooperation in the Americas.* Washington, D.C.: Aspen Institute, 1986.

Jane S. Jaquette. *The Future of Inter-American Relations: A Conference Report.* La Jolla, Calif.: Institute of the Americas, 1985.

James R. Kurth. "The United States, Latin America, and the World: The Changing International Context of U.S.–Latin American Relations." In *The United States and Latin America in the 1980s,* edited by Kevin J. Middlebrook and Carlos Rico. Pittsburgh, Pa.: University of Pittsburgh Press, 1986.

Abraham F. Lowenthal et al. *The Conduct of Routine Relations: The United States and Latin America.* Appendix 1, Report of the Commission on the Organization of the Government for the Conduct of Foreign Policy. Washington, D.C.: U.S. Government Printing Office, 1975.

Andrew Maguire and Janet Welsh Brown, eds. *Bordering on Trouble: Resources and Politics in Latin America.* Bethesda, Md.: Adler and Adler, 1986.

Harold Molineu. *U.S. Policy toward Latin America: From Regionalism to Globalism.* Boulder, Colo.: Westview Press, 1986.

Richard S. Newfarmer, ed. *From Gunboats to Diplomacy: New U.S. Policies for Latin America.* Baltimore: Johns Hopkins University Press, 1984.

Robert B. Reich. *The Next American Frontier.* New York: Times Books, 1983.

David F. Ronfeldt. *Rethinking the Monroe Doctrine.* Santa Monica, Calif.: Rand Corporation, 1985.

Viron P. Vaky. "Political Changes in Latin America: A Foreign Policy Dilemma for the United States." *Journal of Inter-American Studies and World Affairs* 28, no. 2 (1986).

Alfred T. Watkins. *Till Debt Do Us Part.* Lanham, Md.: University Press of America with the Roosevelt Center for American Policy Studies, 1986.

Howard J. Wiarda. *In Search of Policy: The United States and Latin America.* Washington, D.C.: American Enterprise Institute for Public Policy Research, 1984.

Index

ABRAHAM F. LOWENTHAL is professor of international relations at the University of Southern California and executive director of the Inter-American Dialogue. He was the founding director of the Latin American Program at the Woodrow Wilson International Center for Scholars and director of studies at the Council on Foreign Relations. Lowenthal is the author of *The Dominican Intervention* and the editor of four books. He writes often for the *Washington Post*, the *New York Times*, the *Los Angeles Times*, the *Miami Herald*, and other newspapers.